The Twitter Machine

For Ivan and Amahl

*who have brought me more joy
than I had thought possible*

THE TWITTER MACHINE:

Reflections on Language

N. V. Smith

Basil Blackwell

Copyright © N. V. Smith 1989
First published 1989
Basil Blackwell Ltd
108 Cowley Road, Oxford, OX4 1JF, UK
Basil Blackwell Inc.
432 Park Avenue South, Suite 1503
New York, NY 10016 USA

British Library Cataloging in Publication Data
A CIP catalogue record for this book is
available from the British Library.

Library of Congress Cataloging in Publication Data
Smith, N. V. (Neilson Voyne)
The twitter machine : reflections on language / by N.V. Smith.
p.   cm.
Bibliography: p.
Includes index.
ISBN 0–631–16925–3 — ISBN 0–631–16926–1 (pbk.)
1. Linguistics.   2. Language and languages.   I. Title
II. Title: Reflections on language
P121.S577   1989
410—dc19

Typeset in 11 on 13pt Baskerville
by Columns of Reading
Printed in Great Britain by
T.J. Press (Padstow) Ltd.

Contents

Preface

> But what if language were really the goal towards which everything in existence tends?
>
> Calvino, *Mr Palomar*

This collection of essays has grown out of a desire to make the excitement and fun of modern linguistics accessible to a wider audience. I have been motivated by three considerations.

First, there is a perception in the discipline that 'generative linguistics has been sparsely and inadequately popularized'. This remark in *The Generative Enterprise* was greeted by Chomsky with the response that 'As far as the general public is concerned . . . there's essentially nothing' and that 'somebody ought to be thinking about it' (Chomsky, 1982: p. 55). I have been thinking about it, and even if no less inadequate, the popularization is no longer quite so sparse.

Second, there are examples in other fields which are so successful that it seems a pity not to try to emulate them. In particular, I have been inspired by the essays of Stephen Jay Gould on Natural History, to think something similar could be done for Language and Linguistics. For Gould, 'the world has been different ever since Darwin' (Gould, 1980: p. 13); for me, the world has been different ever since Chomsky, and I would like to show why. There are of course differences, most notably that Chomsky is still alive, but I think the two figures are comparable in intellectual stature and importance, and in their ability to make us rethink human nature and our position in the world.

Third, nobody else seems to be doing it, and after twenty-five years as a professional linguist, I think I am beginning to have sufficient grasp of the field to try. Besides, it seems a pity to throw away the lectures I have intermittently prepared for various audiences, especially when it is clear just from reading the newspapers that there is an avid and unassuaged interest in language among the members of the general public.

It is a pleasure to acknowledge the help and influence of my colleagues and friends. My first and greatest intellectual debt is to Noam Chomsky, whose work over the past thirty-five years has re-defined the field of linguistics. His radical insights have largely created the discipline to which I have devoted my professional life. I shall always be indebted. My second debt is to Deirdre Wilson, who has given me constant theoretical guidance over the years, and whose work on Relevance Theory with Dan Sperber has brought the same innovation and insight to our use of language as Chomsky's work on grammar has to our knowledge of language. My third debt is to Jerry Fodor, whose devastating wit and deep insights on the Language of Thought have provided a framework in which the rest can make sense.

None of the above has seen any part of this book, and can accordingly be absolved of all responsibility for errors and idiocies. Three people, however, have read and commented on every word. Annabel Cormack of the University of Reading has given me the benefit of her unmatched knowledge of syntax and semantics, and has repeatedly made me aware of over-simplifications, missed generalizations and invalid arguments. My elder son, Amahl Smith, currently at the City University of New York, has acted as my philosophical mentor, psycholinguistic critic and general devil's advocate. My younger son, Ivan Smith, has acted as guinea-pig and quality controller. He has repeatedly saved me from unclarities, where I had taken for granted positions I needed to argue for; he has been an endless source of scientific analogies and happy turns of phrase; and he has eliminated more misprints than I thought I could perpetrate. Despite this close involvement in the development of these essays, none of the above is to be blamed for the remaining defects either. I didn't always take the advice they offered (an omission I shall doubtless regret), so their only responsibility lies in having encouraged me to continue by saying it was worthwhile. My thanks are also due to my wife, Saras, for keeping (us) sane while the rest of the family immersed itself in twittering.

None of the essays presented here has been published before, but many of them take up issues I have discussed elsewhere in books or articles, or are reformulations of lectures I have given over the past ten years at conferences or on tours in various countries. I am grateful to all those who helped in any way by comment, conversation or criticism.

Each of the essays is supposed to be self-contained, but to give them a coherent background I have written a general introduction outlining some of the main claims of modern linguistics. In addition (although there are no footnote numbers in the text) I have given notes at the end of each essay containing references to the literature, acknowledgements of examples I have filched from colleagues, occasional explanations of more esoteric points, and cross-references to other essays dealing with the same or a related topic. It should be possible to ignore the notes if you feel so inclined. On the other hand, they should enable you to get to grips with the subject treated if your appetite is whetted.

Except for the final essay, which is rather *sui generis*, the earlier essays are generally easier than the later ones and tend to introduce ideas which are built on later. Where this strategy fails, recourse can be had to the Appendix which explains the formalisms used, or to the Glossary which provides a definition of all the technical terms used in the book. Ideally, the book will thus serve as an idiosyncratic and informal introduction to linguistics for the student as well as providing intellectual entertainment for the general reader.

1

Introduction

According to a recent review,

Linguistics . . . is or are the scientific study of language – never, perhaps
a tremendously useful discipline at the best of times, but reduced by
Chomsky and his disciples to a postively mind-boggling level of stupidity
and insignificance. If ever Mrs Thatcher wants an excuse to close down
a university, she has only to look at its department of linguistics.

As a linguist my own prejudices run in a slightly different direction.
Linguistics is complex, intellectually exciting and even useful. Like
chemistry, it has developed its own technical vocabulary to capture
concepts and nuances not current in everyday language: 'speech is
as complex as metabolism', and needs for its description as
complex a jargon. Like physics, it displays no unanimity among its
practitioners (it would be hard to think of a more radical difference
than that between Bohr and Einstein on the interpretation of
quantum physics), but there is still a huge domain of 'issues on
which linguists can agree', whatever their disagreements. Though
utility is no prerequisite to intellectual profundity, linguistics – like
biology and psychology, of which it ultimately forms a part – is also
useful. The speech therapist training a child whose speech is
delayed or a stroke victim whose language has decayed, relies
crucially on linguistics. The information scientist designing auto-
mated question-answering data bases, needs an understanding of
all aspects of language structure. The teacher of English as either a
first or second language, exploits the analyses and findings of
linguists. The stylistician, the psychologist, the philosopher . . . the
list of those who reflect on as well as use language is almost endless
. . . all benefit, and benefit from, work in linguistics.

These essays are designed to give a taste of the range and excitement of the subject to the interested outsider and the beginning insider. Most should be accessible without any prior knowledge, but to make them easier to follow I introduce here some of the core concepts and components of contemporary theory. A brief summary of the standard formalization for syntax and phonology is provided in the Appendix.

Knowledge and Modularity

Linguistics is about what we know as speakers (and hearers) of a language, about how to formalize that knowledge explicitly, and about explaining how we acquire and use that knowledge. Which language we are speakers of doesn't matter. In their overall structure and complexity all languages are, as far as we know, equal: English and Xhosa, Arabic and Zulu are on a par, and my choice of predominantly English examples is simply a matter of mutual convenience.

Our knowledge of language is only one part of our cognitive system. In the terminology of Fodor, it is one *module*, comparable to our visual and auditory systems, each of which serves as an 'input system' to our central thought processes. Input systems are special-purpose devices which operate autonomously to provide grist for the cognitive mill. They are special-purpose (or 'domain-specific') in that they are sensitive to only a subset of the impinging stimuli: auditory *or* visual, but not both, for instance. Their working is autonomous (or 'informationally encapsulated') in that it is unaffected by some aspects of the knowledge available to the mind as a whole: optical illusions such as the Müller–Lyer illusion (in which a line with inward pointing arrow-heads is seen as longer than a line of the same length with outward pointing arrow-heads) are still seen as illusions even when one knows the facts, and both meanings of ambiguous words like 'pen' are accessed even when the context makes one relevant and the other irrelevant. Input systems characteristically operate 'fast' and 'mandatorily': you can no more fail to understand a sentence in your native language than you can fail to see a horse in front of you – always assuming that you have your eyes and your ears unblocked. They are subject to idiosyncratic pathological breakdown: you can lose your vision while retaining audition or the language faculty; and they are typically subserved by specific neural architecture: particular bits of the brain are dedicated to vision, and other bits to language.

The central system of thought is different from the input systems in all these respects, and is also functionally distinct. The core function of the central system is the 'fixation of belief' (deciding what is true about the outside world), a process that may involve all the input systems and ratiocinative processes peculiar to the central system itself. Our knowledge of the input systems, especially language, is vastly greater than our knowledge of thought processes more generally, but it seems clear that the complexity and idiosyncrasy of the workings of the input systems make it implausible that they be analysed as simply special cases of central processes. That is, the categories required in the analysis of language and vision seem to be largely disjoint both from each other and from those used in the analysis of thought. An initial theory of the central system is provided by Relevance Theory, introduced briefly below.

To view the language faculty as one of a number of modules which jointly constitute our mind is incidentally to ascribe *psychological reality* to the constructs of that module. Chomsky has always insisted that the linguistic principles he discusses are mentally represented and that linguistics itself is a sub-part of psychology. The implication of this is that linguistic arguments can be evaluated in terms not merely of their logical elegance but in terms of their adequacy in accounting for the details of language use, of language change over time, and most importantly of language acquisition by the child. Such evidence will not always be available, but even in its absence, the 'best' currently developed grammar will always be adjudged psychologically real. This does not mean that the linguist is laying claim to an expertise which belongs to the psychologist, but rather that the hypothesized elements of the language module are claimed to be 'real' in the sense of being causally involved in explaining both our knowledge and our use of language. Moreover, the suggestion that our grammar is psychologically real should not be interpreted as meaning that experimental evidence of the kind adduced by psychologists is accorded some kind of intrinsic priority in the evaluation of theories. Such evidence is important, just as fossil evidence is important in evolution, but in neither discipline should one kind of evidence be ascribed a status superior to that of other kinds.

Creativity and Rules

What is immediately most striking about our knowledge of English is its open-endedness. Despite the fact that at any one moment our vocabulary is finite, we can go on creating and understanding utterances we have never heard before. The examples in (1) all show in different ways that we can produce and process any of an indefinitely large number of sentences:

la The surface area of Mars is roughly 143,000,000 square kilometers.
lb It's a long, long, long, long . . . way to Tipperary.
lc The witness tried to persuade the judge that the defendant had attempted to incite the rioters to attack the building which he believed the terrorists had booby-trapped.

Example (1a), with its astronomically large number, seems unremarkable, but shows that, just as there is an infinite number of numbers, there is an infinite number of sentences: a conclusion borne out by the other two examples in (1) without any recourse to arithmetic. There is no limit (except boredom and longevity) to the number of times you can repeat 'long', or the convolutions you can introduce into the description of a trial, so each example confirms the point that there is in principle no longest sentence, and hence that the number of sentences at our command is not finite. The implication of this simple observation, combined with the obvious fact that we *are* finite, is that such sentences must be produced 'creatively' by reference to some set of *rules* that we know, rather than being fished out of a large stock of sentences stored in memory: no memory is infinitely large.

The objection that no-one has produced or could produce an infinitely long sentence, and that therefore one doesn't need to postulate that we use rules, is unconvincing. If you have a knitting pattern for a scarf, it is unlikely to tell you how long to knit it When you stop has nothing to do with knitting theory and everything to do with your patience, how much wool you have, and the size of your customer. Similarly, you can utter as long a sentence as you and your audience can stand. When you stop has nothing to do with linguistic theory and everything to do with your patience, how much breath you have and the tolerance of your interlocutor. This suggests a crucial difference between our *competence*, our linguistic knowledge, and our *performance*, how we use that knowledge to produce and understand utterances on particular occasions.

There is further evidence both that our linguistic behaviour is rule-governed, and that it is necessary to distinguish our competence and our performance. Consider the examples in (2):

2a I speak very well English.
2b The French is a beautiful language.

Each of these sentences contains a mistake. The mistakes are not sufficient to impair comprehension but they are immediately recognizable as wrong by native speakers, and would be corrected if the social situation didn't make such action impolite. The possibility of making mistakes entails the existence of rules or norms by reference to which mistakes are judged to be such. Even when produced deliberately, for instance for sarcastic or rhetorical effect, mistakes are still recognizable and have the same implication: even if we are unable to formulate the rules in question, because we are not conscious of them, we all have knowledge of the rules of our native language and recognize violations of them.

Evidence of this rule-government is even shown by little children who invent their own rules: rules which are usually free of the exceptions characteristic of the adult language. For instance, in (3):

3a This teddy is *his* – It's *his* teddy.
3b This teddy is *mine* – It's *mine* teddy.

recorded from a typical 2-year-old, the child has generalized the adult pattern in (3a) to the 'incorrect' but more regular form in (3b). He couldn't have imitated this from his parents, but must have induced the rule for himself.

Grammar

If our knowledge of language is correctly viewed as being in the form of rules, a core part of linguistics will be to specify the types and properties of these rules. As a minimum we need to distinguish *lexical*, *syntactic*, *semantic*, *phonological* and *morphological* information, each of which is said to constitute a *component* or (sub-module) of the grammar. That is, just as language is one module of the mind, syntax is one module of the grammar, and within syntax there are further modules, each characterized by particular principles and properties.

The *lexicon*, representing our knowledge of the vocabulary of our language, contains information relating to each of the four other components about every word in the individual's language. For instance, *bumblebee* is a noun (syntactic information), is stressed on the first syllable (phonological information), means a kind of insect (semantic information), and is composed of two sub-parts, *bumble* and *bee*, (morphological information). The lexicon also serves as a means of access to our non-linguistic knowledge, containing information of an *encyclopaedic* kind: for example, that bumblebees are hairy, buzz, sting when offended, fall into two main genera, *Bombus* and *Psythirus*, and are spelt 'b-u-m-b-l-e-b-e-e'. Whereas the linguistic knowledge we have is likely to be essentially invariant from speaker to speaker, our encyclopaedic knowledge is much more idiosyncratic: I am very fond of bumblebees and associate them with heather and holidays; someone with a bee sting allergy is likely to have a different view.

Syntax deals with our knowledge of sentence structure, most obviously the phenomena of word order illustrated in (4) and (5):

4a   The hurricane demolished the greenhouse.
4b   *Demolished the greenhouse the hurricane.

5a   I have never seen such a gale.
5b   Never have I seen such a gale.
5c   *Never I have seen such a gale.

where the asterisk (*) prefixed to the examples in (4b) and (5c) indicates that they are ungrammatical and not possible sentences of English despite the fact that they consist exclusively of English words. (This notation is used throughout the book.) Also traditionally handled by the syntax are the 'agreement' (as singular or plural) of the verb with the subject in (6):

6a   More than one tile *is* missing.
6b   Fewer than two tiles *are* missing.

and the different grammatical relations exhibited by the contrast between the examples in (7):

7a   I asked her what to eat.
7b   I told her what to eat.

where the subject of 'eat' (the person who ends up doing the eating) is me in (7a) and her in (7b). A comparable example of the different relations holding between pairs of words in a sentence is provided by (8):

8   Ingres enjoyed painting his models nude.

in which either Ingres or his models could be unclothed.

Ambiguity is one of the major concerns of *semantics*, the study of meaning, which also covers relations of 'contradiction' as in (9) and 'entailment' in (10):

6   The storm frightened me and the storm didn't frighten me.
10   'The president of Burkina Faso has been murdered' entails 'Someone is dead'.

All these semantic phenomena have standardly been treated in terms of the philosopher's notion of *truth*. A contradiction is a statement that is necessarily false: in this case because it asserts and denies the same proposition simultaneously. Entailment is a relation which guarantees the truth of one proposition given the truth of another: in (10), the murder of an individual guarantees that someone is dead. Ambiguous sentences are those which can be true in situations which are potentially mutually incompatible, so that one could, without contradiction, deny that Ingres enjoyed being nude while he painted his models, while affirming that he liked his models to be nude when he painted them. For some semanticists the analysis of the meaning of a sentence is then reducible to an analysis of the conditions under which that sentence would be true, its *truth conditions*. The majority of linguists working within generative grammar, however, ignore problems of truth and restrict their semantic analysis to the treatment of syntactically definable problems of the kind raised by the interaction of quantification and negation, as illustrated in the multiply ambiguous (11):

11   Four examiners didn't mark all the scripts.

A great deal of attention has been paid in linguistics to ambiguity because duality of meaning is often reflected by duality of syntactic structure: that is, if a sentence is ambiguous it frequently (though not always) happens that it also needs two different syntactic analyses. Typical examples are provided by (7) and (8) above.

Phonology deals with our knowledge of the sound system and pronunciation of our language. In English, for instance, words can differ from each other by beginning with a 't' rather than a 'd', and 's' rather than a 'th', and so on. Accordingly we have four different words *tick*, *Dick*, *sick* and *thick*. In French, there is a contrast between 't' and 'd' (though they are by no means identical to their English look-alikes), but no contrast between 's' and 'th', so native speakers of French have considerable difficulty in coping with our 'th'. In Hindi, there is a contrast not only between 't' and 'd', but also between each of these and 'aspirated' and 'retroflex' equivalents, so they have eight possibilities where we only have two. In Malayalam, there is a further contrast still, resulting in a system which has twelve possibilities compared to our two. The difficulty for the English-speaking learner of Hindi or Malayalam can be imagined. A theory of phonology must make possible adequate descriptions of all such sounds and systems.

Characterizing the inventory of sounds that a language disposes of is probably the easiest task for the phonology. In addition to specifying such things as whether a word begins with a 'p' or a 'b', it must also give an explicit account of phenomena involving differences of stress and intonation of the kind illustrated in (12) and (13) respectively:

12a   Ivan is twelve and Esme is thir*teen*.
12b   Ivan is fifteen and Esme is *thir*teen.

13a   Mrs Thatcher is a heroine!
13b   Mrs Thatcher is a heroine?

Just as there is a significant correlation between (some aspects of) the syntax and the semantics, so is there also a correlation between the syntax and the phonology, with the intonation being dependent on whether a statement, a question or an exclamation is being uttered.

As syntax deals with the structure of sentences, *morphology* deals with our knowledge of the internal structure of words: that 'heroine' consists of the elements (called 'morphemes') 'hero' and '–ine'; that 'rich' and 'enrich', 'dark' and 'darken' are all possible but that 'richen' and 'endark' are impossible; that 'take, took, taken' form a series like 'speak, spoke, spoken' and not like 'bake, book, bacon', and so on.

Pragmatics

The various components of our linguistic knowledge, described formally by means of a 'generative grammar', jointly define our competence, but account for only a sub-part of our ability to communicate. To understand not only what is said but also why it is said, one has first to decode the linguistic content of the utterance concerned, and then use that decoded form as a basis for inferring what your interlocutor intended to communicate. This inferential process of utterance interpretation is the domain of pragmatics. That the decoding is only a necessary (and totally automatic) preliminary is clear from the inscrutability of an utterance like that in (14):

14   He's taken the collection.

Our grammar tells us that some male person has done something involving a collection, but whether the 'he' refers to the church-warden you were just chatting to, or an unknown burglar; whether 'take' is synonymous with 'solicit', or 'steal'; and whether the 'collection' is the money solicited, or the Meissen absconded with, are all left to our central cognitive system to work out. That is, we need to fix a referent for the pronoun 'he', and we need to disambiguate the words 'take' and 'collection'. How we do this depends crucially on the relative *relevance* of the alternatives. By uttering a sentence, a speaker guarantees that what he or she is saying is worth your attention. If you have just entered a ransacked room with someone who then says (14) to you, you will interpret it as a comment on a theft rather than as a quotation from the vicar, simply because that is the only construal worth your attention – the only reading that is relevant in that context.

The last three words are crucial. Utterances are interpreted in a context, and achieve their relevance by combining with that context to yield 'contextual effects': that is, to allow the deduction of conclusions which would follow neither from the utterance alone nor from the context alone. These effects can be of three kinds: they can yield new information, they can contradict some previously held belief, or they can strengthen some tenuously held belief. Suppose I confide in you that (15) is the case:

15   Peter is a Freemason.

This may give you new information about Peter which will enable you to deduce any of a number of propositions about him: that he is the kind of person who belongs to secret societies, he is unlikely to be a Roman Catholic, he probably enjoys dressing up, and so on; any or all of which may be of further relevance to you. Alternatively, you may have suspected that Peter was an atheist, and the information in (15), in conjunction with your encyclopaedic knowledge that Freemasons have to believe in a 'Supreme Being', will contradict this assumption, leading to a revision in your set of beliefs. Lastly, depending on how much you trust me, (15) may simply strengthen or weaken your half-formulated feeling that Peter is a strange man.

The possibilities are endless, limited only by our ingenuity in devising new contexts in which to interpret the utterance concerned. However, the heart of the pragmatic theory assumed here, Relevance Theory, is a 'Principle of Relevance' which, in guaranteeing that an utterance is worth your attention, also guarantees that the cost of processing that utterance will always be more than offset by the contextual effects gained.

With the advent of an explicit theory of pragmatics, we are now in a position to confront all aspects of the study of language: the study both of our grammatical knowledge (our competence) and of how that knowledge is put to use in utterance production and interpretation.

The Central Problem

In the earliest work on generative grammar, *The Logical Structure of Linguistic Theory*, Chomsky presented the 'three fundamental problems' of linguistics as being those in (16):

16a   'Constructing grammars for particular languages';
16b   'Giving a general theory for linguistic structure of which each of these grammars is an exemplification'; and
16c   'Justifying and validating the results of [the] inquiries'.

and elsewhere in the same work he characterized the 'primary question' for linguistic theory as 'how can speakers produce and understand new sentences?' To a certain extent these issues are still relevant, but there are two radical reorientations in more recent work that bear scrutiny. First, constructing grammars for particular languages is no longer seen as the crucial enterprise it once was: largely because the purely descriptive problems involved in such an enterprise have to a considerable extent been solved, and the more significant problem is how to provide explanatory principles accounting for why grammars have the form they do. Second, it is striking that there is no mention at this stage of the problem of language acquisition, a problem which, for the past twenty years has been paramount.

These two concerns – developing explanations of a depth analogous to that found in the hard sciences, and accounting for the ability of a child to acquire knowledge of language – both typify the field and account for its attractiveness to philosophers, psychologists, anthropologists, and indeed to anyone who shares Chomsky's view that 'the study of language is part of a more general enterprise: to map out in detail the structure of mind'.

Notes

p. 1   The opening quotation is from Waugh, 1988. It is not uncommon for linguistics to get a bad press: Hampton (1970: p. 33) has one of his characters describe it as 'a yet more complicated method of over-simplification'; Lodge (1984: p. 23) writes 'I never could remember which came first, the morphemes or the phonemes. And one look at a tree-diagram makes my mind go blank', and proceeds (p. 24) with 'Theory . . . That word brings out the Goering in me'. Examples could be multiplied.

p. 1   The analogy to metabolism is from Burgess (1986: p. 187).

p. 1   The 'issues on which linguists can agree' are documented in Hudson, 1981.

p. 1   The claim that linguistics is part of psychology, ultimately biology, is made frequently: for instance in the opening sentence of Chomsky, 1987b; in Chomsky (1987c: p. 27), and so on.

p. 2   On modularity, see Fodor (1983). The best overview of input systems and their relation to the central system is Carston, 1988.

p. 3   For a discussion of 'psychological reality', see Chomsky (1980a), and Smith (1987b). For a somewhat different view of what constitutes psychological reality, cf. Bresnan (1982). There is an interesting critique of realism, mentalism, and other core ideas of Chomsky's work in D'Agostino, 1986.

p. 3 On the priority of particular kinds of evidence, cf. Chomsky (1980b) and, in the context of evolution, Morgan (1984).

p. 4 By 'creativity' is meant novelty, rather than 'poetic' creativity. For discussion, see D'Agostino (1986).

p. 5 The competence/performance distinction originates in Chomsky (1965). For detailed discussion, see Smith and Wilson (1979).

p. 5 The examples in (3) were from my younger son, Ivan, at 2 years 2 weeks. He wishes it to be known that he is *not* typical.

p. 6 The best introduction to generative syntax is Radford (1988).

p. 7 Semanticists concentrating on truth-conditional analyses include Montague and his followers. For discussion, cf. Ladusaw (1988). A typical example of those who ignore problems of truth-conditionality is provided by May (1985).

p. 7 The example in (11) is modified from Kempson and Cormack (1979).

p. 7 For the term 'generative' and its implications, see the Appendix.

p. 9 The pragmatic theory discussed is the Relevance Theory of Sperber and Wilson: cf. their 1986a. It should perhaps be pointed out that pragmatics is in an even greater state of flux than the rest of the discipline. For a general overview, including discussion of non-Relevance-based approaches, cf. Horn (1988).

p. 10 Chomsky's *Logical Structure* is his 1955. It was published with a long historical introduction as his 1975a. The 'problems' in (16) are from p. 1. The 'primary question' is from p. 6, quoting the original p. 293.

p. 11 The problem of first language acquisition was first raised in Lees (1957). In his 1975a, Chomsky writes that 'to raise this issue seemed to me, at the time, too audacious' (p. 35).

p. 11 On the transition from 'description' to 'explanation', see Chomsky (1987b).

p. 11 The final quotation is from Chomsky (1975b: p. 86).

p. 11 The most accessible of Chomsky's own (linguistic) writings are his 1972, 1975c, 1980a, 1986, 1987c and 1988a. The current definitive overview of his ideas in linguistics is his 1986, which is somewhat technical in parts. The best summary of his philosophical work is D'Agostino (1986). An earlier overview is provided by Smith and Wilson (1979). An indispensable debate is Piattelli-Palmarini (1980).

2

Why Theory?

Consider Belloc's dinotherium:

> His teeth, as all the world allows,
> Were graminivorous, like a cow's.
> He therefore should have wished to pass
> Long peaceful nights upon the Grass,
> But being mad the brute preferred
> To roost in branches, like a bird.*
> A creature heavier than a whale,
> You see at once, could hardly fail
> To suffer badly when he slid.
> And tumbled
>   (as he always did).
> His fossil therefore, comes to light
> All broken up: and serve him right.

As an explanation for the fragmented state of dinosoaur remains, this has the merit of originality, but probably strikes the thoughtful reader as implausible. Even Belloc's justificatory footnote:

> *We have good reason to suppose
> He did so from his claw-like toes.

is unlikely to convince the experienced palaeontologist. Our scepticism derives from our folk theory of physics. However unable we may be to articulate that physics, we are reasonably convinced that animals do not climb trees several times smaller than themselves, and that the whole basis for Belloc's position is fatally flawed. Given time and some formal training in the relevant disciplines, we could probably come up with better and more rigorous arguments; but even unformalized theories constrain possible explanations, largely by excluding a wide range of plausible but ultimately untenable hypotheses, on the grounds of their incompatibility with other of our beliefs and assumptions. One role of the scientist is to make explicit, revise, refine and test our folk theories. Theories in this sense are ubiquitous, and one may object that views as vague as this are not worthy of the name 'theory'. But the hallmark of a (scientific) theory is that it give rise to hypotheses which can be the object of rational argumentation: if you are prepared to give up your belief in the habits of dinotherium because they conflict with other assumptions you have come to be aware of, then you are in possession of an embryonic theory. If you hold to your view whatever it is confronted with, it is more akin to a religious dogma than a rational belief. Rational discussion of language and linguistics is sometimes frustrated by the fact that for many people beliefs about certain aspects of language come in the former category rather than the latter, with the result that theories are deemed inappropriate.

But there is hope. Nearly everyone would agree that 'How much does this sentence weigh?' is misconceived, because sentences aren't the sort of thing that can weigh anything at all. To share such a view provides a basis for progress; by taking less implausible suggestions and isolating the presuppositions they contain, we may get closer to an understanding of why theories are useful even in language. Apart from providing overarching frameworks for making sense of a whole domain of knowledge, theories are prerequisite to asking coherent questions, to providing rational answers to those questions, and to allowing the statement of intuitively sensible generalizations. Consider the following three propositions:

Some languages have no vowels.
Languages are either tonal or intonational.
Cognitive factors influence sentence planning.

Reaction to the first of these claims is likely to be uncomplicated: either indifference or a mildly interested request for an example.

Provided your interlocutor knows what 'tonal' means, the second assertion is unlikely to cause much difficulty either, but the last one will probably elicit the Joadian response 'It all depends what you mean by "cognitive" and "planning"'. In fact, none of them is straightforward; all of them require theoretical elucidation before they can be evaluated.

What precisely does it mean to say that a language has no vowels? Or to put it more directly, just what is a vowel, the absence of which has been claimed to characterize some languages? Is the implicit suggestion that some languages can get by with only consonants on a par with Belloc's claim about the nesting habits of dinotherium, or is it a serious possibility? Initial acceptance of the claim is probably due to the fact that our orthography distinguishes the vowels 'a, e, i, o, u' from the consonants, and that a few words in English have no vowel in the spelling: ('wry, pyx, cwm') and so on. From this it is easy to imagine a writing system in which all the vowel sounds are represented by what we call consonants, or in which (like Arabic) the vowels are generally omitted, so the claim is not implausible. We might even be persuaded that some language is like that in Calvino's *Cosmicomics*, whose hero is called Qfwfq, and whose other characters rejoice in such names as: Vhd Vhd, Xlthlx, Bb'b, G'd(w)^n, Rwzfs, Hnw and Kgwgk. But this is not what is usually meant at all. Traditional phonological theory makes two distinctions relevant to the issue: first a difference between consonants and vowels as speech sounds rather than orthographic symbols; second a difference between two levels of representation – the phonemic and the phonetic. Although there are problems in how formally to define consonants and vowels, we can accept the first distinction as being intuitively sensible and almost uncontroversial: the nature of the orthography has little bearing on the sound system of the language. The second contrast – between phonemic and phonetic is more crucial to evaluating both the sense and the truth of the claim about vowel-free languages.

Words are pronounced differently in different contexts and on different occasions. 'Sane' and 'same' differ in their final consonant when spoken in isolation, but may be identical when uttered before 'people': they are phonemically distinct even if, in this latter condition they become phonetically the same. Conversely, the first and last sounds in 'six' are both considered to be

instances of the phoneme /s/, despite the fact that they are
phonetically somewhat different. How something is actually
pronounced, its phonetic representation is determined in part by
its phonemic make-up and in part by factors such as its position
in the word, its place in the structure of the sentence, the
characteristics of the person speaking, and so on. In some
circumstances whole vowels or consonants may be inserted or
deleted in the transition from phonemic to phonetic. The sequence
'soft toys' usually loses its first /t/ in informal speech, for instance;
and words like 'film' and 'athletic' are sometimes given an extra
vowel in the pronunciations 'fillum' (filəm) and 'athaletic'
(aθəletik).

The claim that some languages have no vowels can now be
reformulated as the slightly less spectacular statement that at least
one language has been analysed as having no vowels at the
phonemic level of representation, even though it does have
phonetic vowels, these being filled in by rule in particular
environments. The language concerned is the Caucasian language
Kabardian, and the suggestion came from Kuipers. That different
languages have different numbers of contrastive vowels is
reasonably clear. Even within 'English' different dialects make
more or fewer contrasts – as between 'book' and 'buck' for
instance, which are distinct in southern British dialects, but the
same in most Northern dialects, where they both have a
pronunciation approximating that of the southern 'book'.

Some of the Caucasian languages have extremely rich consonant systems and relatively impoverished vowel systems; in
some cases resulting in languages with only two or three phonemic
vowels. Kuipers took the extreme position that even these
remnants were predictable, and so could be ignored at the
phonemic level. The validity of the claim is dependent not only on
the difference between phonemics and phonetics, but even at the
phonemic level, on the possibility of leaving out one element in any
analysis. A comparable claim for English would be that 'a' (either
orthographic or phonemic as in 'hat') is unnecessary because we
can always replace it with a blank instead: 'The cat sat on the
mat' would come out as 'The c-t s-t on the m-t'. This is clearly a
possibility, but most people find the analysis rather lacking in
cogency, because the choice of item to leave out, in this case 'a', is
entirely arbitrary: we could equally well have chosen 'i' or 'q'.

Indeed, once such a device is allowed, one could get rid of all the vowels in English as well as Kabardian: 'a' could be replaced by '–', 'e' by '—', 'i' by '——', and so on. The hypothesis that there is a language without vowels can be made to be true, but at the expense of trivializing it, because it would apply to any and every language. What is needed to obviate this undesirable result is a (theoretical) constraint that forbids the kind of arbitrary, abstract replacement of vowels (or consonants, or anything else) by '–'. But to do that presupposes a theory of the relationship between phonetics and phonology. That is, we need a theory both to make sense of the original claim, and to exclude silly analyses once we've made sense of it.

The second claim, that languages are tonal or intonational, is hardly a matter for disagreement. What is of more interest on this occasion is whether our theories can provide a satisfactory way of characterizing this basic typological distinction.

All languages use variations in pitch to signal grammatical or attitudinal differences, as witness the pronunciation of the segmentally identical sentences in (1):

1 Marvin's a Patagonian rabbi.
   Marvin's a Patagonian rabbi?
   Marvin's a Patagonian rabbi!

Tone languages are those like Chinese or Nupe in which the domain of pitch variation is the word rather than the sentence, so that in Nupe, for instance, *bá*, spoken on a relatively high pitch means 'to be sour', *ba* spoken on a mid-pitch means 'to cut', *bà* spoken on a low pitch means 'to count', *bǎ* spoken on a rising pitch means 'really', and *bâ* spoken on a falling pitch means 'defamation'. Intonational languages are those like English or Hindi in which the domain of pitch variation is the sentence. In fact, all tone languages are also intonational languages in that they use pitch variation at both word and sentence level, but the contrast is none the less real and useful. Innumerable questions immediately suggest themselves, but I want to look at merely one: How is tone to be described?

The Standard Theory of generative phonology developed in the 1960s described every segment as a bundle of properties called 'distinctive features'. The 'P' at the beginning of 'Patagonian' or 'pig' is specified as in (2):

2   $\begin{bmatrix} +\text{consonantal} \\ -\text{vocalic} \\ -\text{coronal} \\ +\text{anterior} \\ -\text{voiced} \end{bmatrix}$

Consonants are [+consonantal, −vocalic], vowels are [−consonantal, +vocalic]; the lack of voicing ([−voiced]) distinguishes 'p' from the voiced 'b', the specification [+anterior] separates it from 'k', and so on; other details are irrelevant. To accommodate tonal differences, the theory simply added a few more features, so the á in the Nupe example bá would be specified as in (3):

3   $\begin{bmatrix} -\text{consonantal} \\ +\text{vocalic} \\ +\text{low} \\ +\text{High Tone} \end{bmatrix}$

The system works, but that is about the best that can be said for it. In particular, it provides no basis for explaining why tone is in any way special: why, that is, we have 'tone' languages and 'non-tone' languages but not 'anterior' languages and 'non-anterior' languages. As far as the standard theory was concerned, none of the distinctive features was in any way privileged, so there was no way of reconstructing the traditional intuition that tone languages were indeed an interesting, linguistically significant category.

In the 1970s the standard theory was subjected to a number of revisions, of which the most radical was the detachment of 'suprasegmental' properties such as pitch and stress from the linear sequence of segments (consonants and vowels) which constitute a phonological representation. What this means is that statements about the segmental make-up of words and sentences are independent of the statement about their tonal make-up. Tonal changes may take place unaffected by the segments they occur with and vice versa. In Nupe, for instance, negative sentences are marked in two ways: à (on a low tone) is added to the end of the sentence and a high tone is added to the end of the subject, irrespective of the phonological make-up of that subject. So 'it is sour' is as in (4):

4 *u bá*

and 'it isn't sour' is as in (5):

5 *u′ bá à*

'the milk I bought yesterday is sour' is:

6 *nwánwa na mi shi   tsúwó   na   bá*
   milk that I bought yesterday that sour

and 'the milk I bought yesterday isn't sour' is:

7 *nwánwa na mi shi tsúwó* na′ *bá à*

With an extra high tone after the last word of the subject *na*. The reasons for this theoretical innovation are both manifold and interesting; for present purposes their advantage is simply one that had not been explicitly considered by those who suggested them, namely that we are now provided with a theoretical basis for reconstructing our earlier intuition that 'tone language' was a sensible category. Unlike distinctive features such as [voiced] or [anterior] which function in inseparable bundles (rather like quarks), the features defining tonal properties seemed to have an independent life of their own, but this independence was unexplained and accidental within the standard theory. Within the revised theory of 'Autosegmental' Phonology, tonal phenomena do now have a special status: they define their own 'autosegmental tier', which is governed by particular rules and principles, partially distinct from those governing segmental statements. That special status can now be used to characterize the typological distinction we need.

The third proposition: that 'cognitive factors influence sentence planning', due to S. N. Sridhar, is even more in need of theoretical elucidation because it is obviously true and equally obviously nebulous. At one level this aphorism amounts to saying that what we think determines not only what we say but the way we say it. To go beyond the platitudinous it is necessary to specify the

precise nature of this influence, and to do that one has to have a
clear idea of both sentence structure and how it can vary on the
one hand, and of the representation of cognitive structures on the
other. It is the latter strand that is usually missing from any
explicit treatment of the relationship between thought and
language. In the present case, Sridhar adverts to a number of
factors including a 'principle of conceptual or motivational
salience' which he invokes among other things to account for the
marked word order one gets in passive and topicalized sentences,
for instance the difference between the active and passive
examples in (8):

8   The hijackers murdered two hostages.
    Two hostages were murdered by the hijackers.

where 'the hijackers' are more salient or prominent in the former
and 'two hostages' are more salient in the latter. He also remarks
that 'salience' is 'a vague notion' and 'a multi-factor notion', and
describes it as an example of a 'speaker-oriented principle' as
opposed to a 'listener-oriented principle'.

Many of Sridhar's observations are persuasive and each follows
individually from some particular hypothesis put forth in the
psycholinguistic literature. The trouble is that the set of
hypotheses exploited does not constitute a unified theory, but
simply an arbitrary list. However, it is possible to make 'salience'
explicit, rather than vague, and to do so without postulating quite
different principles for speakers and hearers, provided one uses
the conceptual insights provided by a unified theory of cognition
and communication, specifically Sperber's and Wilson's Relevance Theory.

The core of this theory is based on the view that attention and
thought processes turn automatically, as a matter of a general,
genetically determined, cognitive principle, to information that is
relevant, i.e. information that can yield 'contextual effects'. In the
case of communication, this means that for an utterance to be
relevant in some context it must interact with that context by
having implications which provide new information, contradict
old information or strengthen one's commitment to some
proposition. As a corollary, it is clear that the context for the
interpretation of any utterance is constructed at least in part on

the basis of that utterance itself. That is, the context is not antecedently given, but is created 'on-line' as part of the interpretive process. Furthermore, the degree of relevance of an utterance is defined in terms of a cost/benefit analysis, such that the *more* contextual effects that can be achieved or the *less* the processing cost, the more relevant that utterance is.

As part of their theory Sperber and Wilson draw a distinction between those implications of an utterance which maximize the contextual effects and those implications which minimize processing cost. Of crucial relevance for the current example is their observation that 'in general . . . an optimally relevant utterance will have its effort-saving . . . implications made available by initial constituents, and its effect-carrying . . . implications made available by its final constitutents'. This allows the construction of context as one processes an utterance to be maximally helpful: by the time the hearer reaches the end of the sentence, he will already have constructed most if not all the context required for interpretation.

Taking the active and passive sentences cited above, the former leads the hearer to assume that it will be relevant in a context about the hijackers, the latter in a context about the hostages. In a conversation about the relative merits of rival groups of religious fundamentalists who are prone to hijacking, the first sentence will have an obvious implication that, whatever their religious credentials, their moral standards are sub-human. In a conversation about the perils of air travel, the second sentence would implicate that the dangers are even worse than normally expected. The relative salience of the hijackers and the two hostages is then a result of how the utterances have been phrased to facilitate the task of processing while steering the listener to the most important conclusions first.

What is important about such examples is not the details of any particular context constructed: that will vary from occasion to occasion and according to the encyclopaedic information of those conversing, but the possibility of providing a general characterization of context construction on the basis of the syntactic structure of the sentences uttered. Relevance is a cognitive principle which constrains all information processing, and as such lends itself to an account of the inter-relationship between natural language and the language of thought. Notions such as salience should then fall out as instantiations of the optimization of relevance, rather than having to be separately specified. The only difference between this example and the simple phonological examples given earlier (or indeed the dinotherium) is in the complexity of the deductive structure of the theory. Even so the main difference is in the amount of the theory that has been presented, rather than in the amount there is. In each case, the rich interaction of a number of inter-related principles allows for the explanation of particular facts which, without that theoretical underpinning, would be either arbitrary, unmotivated or untestable.

No such principles guided Belloc in his account of Dinotherium. An explanation of the form and distribution of fossil remains requires reference to theories of sedimentation, orogenesis, plate tectonics and Darwinian evolution. But we should not be too hard on Belloc. Before the development of his ideas on natural selection, Darwin appears to have believed that extinction was the result of some kind of planned obsolescence: he was 'tempted to believe animals created for a definite time: – not extinguished by change of circumstances'. His theory of evolution allowed this earlier speculation to be replaced (in part) by something more persuasive. A century on, we can hope to replace similarly naive views about language with something a little more convincing.

Notes

p. 13   'The Dinotherium' is taken from Belloc (1899: pp. 12–14).

p. 15   C. E. M. Joad was a British philosopher and author well-known for prefacing his answer to any question with the words: 'It all depends on what you mean by . . .'

p. 15   For Arabic, cf. Haywood and Nahmad (1962).

p. 15   The bizarre names invented by Calvino occur in the first three chaps of his 1982. Characters with vowels appear in chap. 4.

p. 15   A 'phonemic' difference is one which can serve to differentiate lexical items. See the Appendix for further details.

p. 16   For Kabardian (a Caucasian language spoken in the South West Soviet Union), cf. Kuipers (1960). For discussion of his analysis, cf. Halle (1970). For Caucasian languages more generally, cf. Comrie (1981b: chap. 5).

p. 16   On English dialects, cf. Wells (1982).

p. 17   For Chinese, cf. Newham (1971); for Nupe cf. Smith (1967a,

1967b). Tonal differences are marked by accents: ' for high tone, ` for low tone, ˇ for rising tone, ^ for falling tone. Mid tone is left unmarked. Languages with different numbers of tonal contrasts demand more or less complicated systems. These marks are standard for African languages; other systems – e.g. employing numbers – are common elsewhere.

p. 17 The 'Standard Theory' refers to the theory put forth in Chomsky and Halle (1968), *The Sound Pattern of English*. Although published in 1968, the book had been announced as forthcoming in 1959.

p. 17 'Generative Phonology' refers to the phonology used in Generative Grammar.

For more on distinctive features, cf. the Appendix and essays 4 'The Puzzle Puzzle', 11 'Lellow Lollies', 15 'Clive', and especially 9 'Y'.

p. 19 Despite its translation as 'be sour', Nupe *bá* is a verb. Relative clauses in Nupe are marked by *na* at the beginning and the end of the clause.

p. 19 For 'Autosegmental Phonology', cf. van der Hulst and Smith (1982, 1985) and Goldsmith (1979). Autosegmental phonology is one kind of 'non-linear' phonology: i.e. a phonology which does not restrict itself to a single linear sequence of segments. The word is supposed to suggest the *auto*nomy of *segmental* phenomena from 'suprasegmental' ones like pitch and stress.

p. 19 The claim that 'cognitive factors influence sentence planning' is from Sridhar (1988: p. 86). The 'principle of conceptual or motivational salience' is from p. 8; that salience is a 'vague' notion from p. 9; that it is a 'multi-factor notion' from p. 38, and a 'speaker-oriented principle' from p. 19.

p. 20 Sperber and Wilson's Theory of Relevance is given its fullest exegesis in their (1986a). A useful precis, multi-authored critique and reply are in their (1987). The different kinds of implication referred to are discussed on pp. 209ff. of their (1986a) with the designation 'foreground' and 'background' implications. More details of their theory can be found in essays 7 'Wilt Thou have this Man to thy wedded Wife?', and 14 'In my Language we SHOUT'.

p. 21 The 'Language of Thought' refers to Fodor's (1975) book of that title.

p. 22 Darwin's remark is from the *Red Notebook*, and is cited on p. 32 of Burkhardt and Smith (1986). I say 'in part' because of Gould's essay on sundry theories of extinction: 'O Grave, Where is Thy Victory?', (in his 1984).

3

Grammar and Gravity

In *Babel-17* Delany describes a language from the furthest reaches of the Galaxy which is beyond human understanding, though his humanoid creations have only temporary difficulty in analysing it according to traditional linguistic principles and then explaining it to the humans. In the same book, when his heroes are not defying the laws of physics by travelling faster than the speed of light or coming conveniently alive again, they indulge in prolonged disquisitions on the properties of sundry possible and impossible languages: languages without words for 'you' and 'me'; languages where the word for 'I' differs according to the temperature . . . It's fun but is it plausible? How far can languags differ from each other? Is the apparent absence on earth of languages with these properties an accident, a logical necessity, or a reflection of our ignorance? Is it even the case that there are limits on the variability among sublunary languages, and if so how can we find out?

There are two obvious strategies one might adopt in attempting to provide a reply to such qustions: first, check out all the known languages on earth, catalogue their properties and produce a list of all the possibilities – we can call this the inductive or taxonomic approach; second, construct on the basis of as representative a sample as possible a general characterization of what any language must be like and predict the properties of other languages from this – we can call this the deductive or theoretical approach. Both approaches are desirable, indeed the second presupposes a modicum of success in the former, but they tend to be seen as rivals, and the current linguistic scene is littered with the offprints of the opposing camps trying to demolish their opponents.

Unlike in the stereotypes of sci-fi, the contest is not one between 'good and evil', but between 'good and better' portrayed as 'good and evil' – or vice versa depending on your point of view. The lines are usually drawn on the basis of attitudes to universals of language and what is the best way of capturing them, with one faction concentrating on the amassing of as many data as possible from as wide a range of unrelated languages as possible, and the other on the construction of ever deeper and more intricate analyses of a very few languages or even just one, normally English. The first position is associated with Joseph Greenberg and his followers, the second with Chomsky and his.

If one is interested in universals it may seem just common-sense that the correct procedure is the Greenbergian one. If one takes the universe of human languages as one's domain, then the more of them one studies the better. More cogently still, there are some implicational universals which it is impossible to state unless one takes into consideration a range of different languages. For instance, nearly all languages have relative clauses (the only exceptions are certain South American languages, such as Hixkaryana, spoken along the Amazon) but can deploy them in different circumstances according to a rigid, universally defined hierarchy. A relative clause is one such as 'who likes women' which can modify a 'head' noun like *man* in expressions such as (1):

1   A man *who likes women* is coming to dinner.

In this example, 'who likes women' modifies the subject, but could equally well be used to modify the direct object as in (2):

2   I know a man *who likes women.*

or an indirect object as in (3):

3   I gave it to the man *who likes women.*

or even the object of a comparative as in (4):

4   Fred is taller than the man *who likes women.*

This probably seems too trivial to be worth comment. What is of interest is that not all languages display the same range of possibilities. In Malagasy, spoken in Madagascar, only subjects can be modified by relative clauses, and the equivalents of the other sentences would be ungrammatical. In other languages subjects and direct objects may be modified by relative clauses but no other objects may be; in yet others subjects, direct objects and indirect objects may be modified but objects of comparatives can not. What never happens in any language is that indirect objects and objects of comparatives but not subjects can be modified, or that subjects and indirect objects but not direct objects may feature in relative clause constructions. We can set up a hierarchy (known as the 'accessibility hierarchy' first observed by Keenan and Comrie) representable as in (5):

5 Subject > Direct Object > Indirect Object > Object of Comparative

with the property that the ability to form relative clauses on any one element entails the ability to form relative clauses on any element to the left, but *not* vice versa. It is this kind of implicational statement which gives such statements their usual designation of 'implicational', rather than 'absolute' universals. Thus, a language like English which permits the relativization of the object of a comparative necessarily allows relativization on *all* the other categories; a language like Malagasy stops at the Subject; no language can form relative clauses on subjects and indirect objects but not direct objects, and so on. The relevance of the example is simply that it is manifestly impossible to infer such a surprising and significant universal on the basis of evidence from just one or even a few languages. Rather it necessitates the gathering and analysis of a range of subtle data from some dozens of languages. The Greenbergians seem to be completely vindicated.

Moreover they have another form of argument at their disposal. Linguistics likes to think of itself as a science in the sense that it makes *testable*, i.e. potentially falsifiable, statements or predictions. In the present case it is clear that the accessibility hierarchy makes very explicit predictions which could be falsified by the next language to be studied if it turned out to have relative clauses on direct objects and the objects of comparatives, but not on subjects or indirect objects. In contrast, the objection is often raised against the Chomskyans that their abstract analyses of individual languages are so abstract, and dispose of so many possible escape routes that falsification is inherently impossible. Given our devotion to the

Gospel according to Popper, such analyses are *ipso facto* non-scientific.

Finally, the Greenbergians rub home their advantage by criticizing the innatist basis of Chomskyan explanations, replacing them with *perceptual, functional* and *pragmatic* explanations. Typical examples of each are provided by the following. Most of the world's languages have a dominant word-order in which the subject precedes the object; so Subject–Verb–Object, Subject–Object–Verb and Verb–Subject–Object account for perhaps ninety per cent of the documented languages, whereas Verb–Object–Subject and to an even less extent Object–Subject–Verb and Object–Verb–Subject account for the remaining ten per cent. The reason is said to be that subjects, in virtue of their normal correlation with agents, are perceptually salient and are hence put before objects in the sentence. Perceptual salience is similarly invoked to account for the ordering of the 'animacy hierarchy' – which determines the characteristics of the morpho-syntactic systems of a number of languages such that humans take precedence over other animate entities, animates over inanimates, and so on. For instance, in Navajo, verbs are marked with prefixes indicating the relative degree of control over the situation of the participants in that situation. Sentences in which control is imputed to an entity lower on the animacy hierarchy than some other participant are of dubious acceptability. It is as though one could say in English either of the sentences in (6) but neither of the sentences in (7):

6a   The man kicked the horse.
6b   The horse was kicked by the man.

7a   The horse kicked the man.
7b   The man was kicked by the horse.

because only the man – higher in the animacy hierarchy – is viewed as being in command of the situation.

Functional considerations are invoked to account for such phenomena as the retention of pronouns in relative clauses: regularly in many languages, where the normal form of a relative clause is exemplified in (8):

8   The girl *that I know her* is coming.

And even in English where complex constructions can give rise to a pressure for including an excrescent and strictly ungrammatical pronoun in examples such as (9):

9   The man that everyone knows you're bigger than *him* is coming.

The claim is that 'retention of the pronoun is found with positions that are more difficult to relativize', because a 'construction that preserves the pronoun provides more access to the semantic information contained in the sentence'. That is the presence of the pronoun has a semantically facilitatory function.

Pragmatic explanations are appealed to in order to account for such facts as that the linear order of clauses frequently mirrors the temporal order of events. We are more likely to say (10) than (11):

10   John came in and sat down.
11   Before sitting down John came in.

The common-sense conclusion seems to have been confirmed beyond dispute, but in fact the result is not quite as clear-cut as might be imagined. Appeals to common-sense are rarely unequivocal, as a moment's thought about 'sunrise' should tell us. In the present context there are equally good reasons for thinking not that the Greenbergian paradigm is wrong or unnecessary, but that it is essentially incomplete and only a theoretical, deductive, treatment of the phenomena has any hope of success.

Consider again the case of implicational universals and the necessity for taking account of a wide range of languages in setting them up. The logic so far is impeccable, but omits mention of the most interesting aspect: What is the basis for such universals? Are they a part of our linguistic knowledge or simply an accident on a par with the presumably fortuitous fact that the Nupe for 'eye' is spelt *eyé*? The most plausible conclusion is that the accessibility hierarchy, for instance, represents a significant and not merely accidental generalization about the world's languages and hence about the grammars that underlie them: this is certainly the view of its proponents. But if implicational universals are somehow exploited by the language user and are not just figments of the linguist's brain, then they must be mentally represented just as are the rules of the grammar which tell us that this sentence ungrammatical is, or that *blook* is a possible, though non-existent, word of English, while *lbook* not only isn't a word of English but couldn't be.

Moreover, if the facts about the accessibility hierarchy are mentally represented, we can ask how individuals come to know them. There are two possibilities: either they learn them or they know them without learning them. By hypothesis they cannot be learned because most speakers do not have knowledge of a wide enough sample of languages on the basis of which they could induce them. Even if the majority of the world's population is multi-lingual, the average child is not so polyglot that it could establish the implicational generalizations encapsulated in (5). It seems to follow that these facts must be known without being learned: that is, they are innate; or to use a less tendentious expression they must be genetically determined. It is faintly ironic that a class of examples which is prototypical of the taxonomists' position should in fact lend equally strong support to a position on innateness with which they usually vociferously disagree. It is also important to note that examples such as that of the accessibility hierarchy still need to be incorporated into an explicit deductive theory. The fact that their mere existence can be used to support a particular theoretical conclusion: in this case that of innateness, does not relieve the theoreticians of the obligation to produce a proper account. An indication of how this can be done is given within the theory of Parametric Variation.

The question of disconfirmability is equally inconclusive. The Chomskyans have two standard rejoinders to criticisms of this kind. First, they observe that not only is the taxonomic analysis falsifiable but, less desirably, it is false. Secondly, they can claim with some plausibility that their own position is indeed falsifiable, but because of the different domain of their generalizations and because of the depth of structure in their theory, falsification is possible only on the basis of a superior theory-based analysis and not merely on the basis of some recalcitrant piece of data. The advance in the perihelion of Mercury, first discovered in 1845, was an anomaly for Newtonian physics and a challenge to the ingenuity of astronomers. It only became evidence against the Newtonian theory with the advent of Einstein's general theory of relativity, which *predicted* precisely such an advance. Puzzling or exceptional data by themselves do not falsify a theory; they do that only when they are seen to follow from an alternative theory whose explanatory power is elsewhere as great.

The major difference between the two positions I have outlined is that the taxonomists state their generalizations over (sets of) data, whilst the theoreticians state their generalizations over (sets of) rules – i.e. grammars – responsible for generating those data. As a result, the taxonomists' claims are open to disconfirmation by the observation of further facts of the same kind. As an example consider the correlation of verb-initial word-order with prepositions and of verb-final word-order with postpositions. The correlation is so striking that it must have an explanation. However, there are exceptions – extremely rare exceptions, but ones which falsify the usual claim that languages with initial verbs have (only) prepositions and languages with final verbs have (only) postpositions. The taxonomists are reduced to saying either that there is a 'tendency' towards the correlation or giving up the universal claim altogether. In fact the standard form of words is something like 'with overwhelmingly greater than chance frequency', but studies which back such claims up with hard statistical evidence are rare.

The situation with the theoreticians is somewhat less pernicious. Any piece of data is the joint product of both linguistic and non-linguistic systems and, within the linguistic module, of a number of sub-theories conspiring to produce particular effects. Accordingly, the appearance of recalcitrant data can be handled by reference to any one or more of these different components. The result is generally viewed as cheating by non-theoreticians: if your theory gives you the wrong result you change (one tiny sub-part of) your theory. This of course is the normal means of scientific progress. It is not pernicious precisely because change in any one sub-part causes a vast number of concomitant changes elsewhere in the theory and makes an even vaster number of predictions. A parallel with physics suggests itself: if your theory predicts that the universe should contain more mass than it does, make a slight – but very far-reaching – change: assume that the neutrino instead of being mass-less in fact has some minute but not negligible mass. The check on such an apparently wilful piece of manipulation is that nearly every other claim in the whole theory will need reinterpreting. If that can be done consistently while preserving a sufficient number of the correct old generalizations then the revision may be justified. What is not possible is for some single datum to invalidate the whole scientific edifice: 'naive falsificationism' in Lakatos' happy expression is dead. This does not mean that the theory is evading its responsibilities; rather it is by taking on more interesting responsibilities that *explanations* are arrived at.

What about the final claim of the taxonomists that innatist explanations should give way to functionalist, perceptual or pragmatic explanations, because the former are inherently 'dead-ends'? Two points need to be made: first, the two kinds of explanation are not mutually incompatible. Secondly, innatist explanations are not so much a dead-end as an invitation to two different kinds of researcher: other linguists to extend the work and specify precisely what it is that is innate (much of Chomsky's own work in syntax comes under this heading); and those in related disciplines – psychology, neurology, physiology, and so on, to characterize the non-linguistic underpinning of this genetically determined body of knowledge.

It is also not irrelevant that the actual explanations offered are rarely as convincing on close appraisal as they may appear at first blush. Perceptual salience sounds fine, but what does it actually mean? If we take the case of the animacy hierarchy mentioned above, it would be hard to disagree that humans are generally more perceptually salient than cobwebs or cobblestones. Unfortunately the linguistic category of animacy turns out not to coincide with the concept animate. As Comrie himself admits:

animacy seems to be one of the main parameters determining a split in the morphological system . . . in many instances the particular oppositions found seem to have no inherent connection with animacy . . . we might refer to these as arbitrary structural correlates of animacy. The fact that such arbitrary correlations are so widespread . . . is good testimony to the salience of animacy.

But if the correlations are arbitrary the explanatory power of perceptual salience is trivialized and becomes merely terminological.

The kind of functional explanation used to account for pronoun retention is plausible, but as the relative difficulty of relativization is defined cross-linguistically, and whether a language uses pronominal copies at all is apparently arbitrary, the explanation is only convincing if it is conjoined with the assumption that the hierarchy is innately specified. Even then, the notion of having 'direct access to the semantic information' is not a simple one; (12) is not noticeably simpler to understand than (13):

12 John intended himself to win.
13 John intended to win.

despite the former providing in *himself* an overt indication of the semantic (argument) structure of the sentence. Pragmatic explanations look more promising, but only because in pragmatics we have the beginnings of an explicit theory which can interact with the principles of grammar to provide real explanations. In the case discussed briefly above the fact that clause order normally reflects the order of events follows from Grice's principle of 'Orderliness', which in turn can be deduced from Sperber and Wilson's Principle of Relevance. What is important is that such explanations be deducible from theoretical principles rather than being stipulated *ad hoc* for each phenomenon individually. If they don't follow from general principles, there is no difference in status between a stipulation to the effect that clauses reflect temporal order and the opposite stipulation that they invert the temporal order.

We seem to have turned the tables on the taxonomists, but there remains the puzzle of why theoretical explanations are not more widely pursued. The reasons are a combination of an unjustified belief in the possiblity of an interesting linguistics which is theory-neutral or theory-less; a misapprehension of the domain of the subject as between languages and grammars; a misunderstanding of the notion disconfirmation; and a confusion of theories and laws.

Any attempt to provide explanations presupposes a theory. The difference between so-called theory-neutral and theoretically based explanations is not really one between the presence and absence of an appeal to theory, but a difference in the sophistication and depth of the two theories involved. Even at the simplest possible level of description, the claim that subjects precede objects or that, in English, articles precede the noun they modify, are statements that presuppose a theoretical vocabulary containing such terms as subject, object and noun. We are conditioned by our education to accept such categories, but they are neither self-evidently appropriate to the description of all or even any languages, nor is it obvious to what they actually refer in individual cases. It is often claimed that not all languages exploit the notion 'subject', and occasionally that some languages do not even distinguish nouns and verbs. Without a theory of what exactly subjects are, or what the possible differences between nouns and verbs are, these claims are uninterpretable. The disentangled claim of the taxonomists is then that the theory with which they wish to work is one which does not make use of many of the constructs that a generative grammarian for instance would wish to: most obviously, a distinction between different levels of representation in syntactic or phonological structure. Without such a theory, the claims made are simply anecdotal – not necessarily wrong, but unrevealing.

The second point leads on from this. There is to my knowledge no theory of baked bean consumption or of candlesticks or of enjoyable events. The reason is simply that these are not domains over which it is possible to make interesting generalizations as a basis for the construction of explanations about why these generalizations exist. One of Chomsky's more radical suggestions is that the same applies to 'language': it is not a proper domain for scientific enquiry. This is emphatically not the same claim as the romantic poet's assertion that investigating language rigorously destroys its soul. Rather it is the claim that linguistic phenomena need to be approached through a study of the principles and properties that give rise to these phenomena: mentally represented grammars.

The reasons are numerous: languages are geographically or politically defined entities, not 'linguistically' defined entities. There is no non-arbitrary grammatical criterion by reference to which one can adjudge that Chinese is one language but Norwegian and Swedish two; no general continuity between the English of *Beowulf* and the English of P. G. Wodehouse that motivates their joint inclusion within 'English Literature'. Even if one prescinds away from such abstractions to concentrate on what one Englishman might say or accept at one time, there is still the problem of reconciling his competence with his performance, which might raise trivial difficulties of what to do with slips of the tongue and more profound ones of indeterminate acceptability. It is easier to see a natural domain in the linguistic knowledge one disposes of: the set of rules which constitute the grammar underpinning 'knowledge of language' which itself interacts with pragmatic and encyclopaedic information to produce actual utterances.

This highlights the next misapprehension. Even if some 'beautiful hypotheses' are slain by 'ugly facts', as Huxley has it, the theories from which the hypotheses derive are not necessarily demolished along with them. Chomsky sums it up nicely when he says:

linguistic principles of any real significance generally deal with properties of rule systems, not observed phenomena, and can thus be confirmed or refuted only indirectly through the construction of grammars, a task that goes well beyond even substantial accumulation and organization of observation.

The most famous example of what is meant here is provided by so-called 'locality' principles which constrain how far constituents can move within a sentence. For instance, in (14):

14   The suit which I bought is big for me.

'The suit' is both the subject of the whole sentence and the direct object of 'bought', from which it is separated by the relative clause introduced by *which* – compare the example in (15) where 'bought' and 'a suit' are adjacent:

15   I bought a suit which was too big for me.

With a sentence like (16):

16   He knows where I bought a suit which was too big for me.

which is perfectly grammatical, such movement is impossible, and the sequence in (17):

17   *The suit which he knows where I bought is big for me.

is hopelessly ungrammatical. The explanation is standardly attributed to the locality principle known as 'subjacency' which is considered to be universal. However, in some languages the literal translation of (17) above is perfectly well-formed, apparently refuting the universal claim. In fact the principle is not refuted by such sentences (in Italian or the Philippine language Hiligaynon). Rather the principle is refined to accommodate both sets of possibilities. In English subjacency prohibits movement in one class of environments, in Hiligaynon subjacency prohibits movement in an overlapping but slightly different class of environments. The situation is analogous to that concerning the incest taboo in society. All societies have an incest taboo, even if they define it slightly differently: the fact that your society does but my society does not allow cross-cousin marriage is not a refutation of the universality of the principle that sexual relations are constrained in *all* societies, but an indication of the complexity of what appears to be a simple notion.

Ultimately, I suspect that the reason for the tendency among linguists and lay-people alike to assume that simple observation can overturn a whole theoretical edifice is a confusion between theories and laws.

The difference can be illustrated by reference to gravity. For his theory of gravitation, Newton *assumed* an unmediated attractive force between all massive bodies, and accounted for the detailed quantitative observations of the movements of the heavenly bodies by exploiting his earlier law of inertia, and deducing that the attraction was subject to the inverse-square law: that is, that the gravitational force between bodies decreases as the inverse square of the distance between them. This law is simply the mathematical expression of an observed regularity whose simplicity is such that it is unlikely to be accidental (an inverse-power 1.73 law is not a good candidate for widespread significance). This theory of gravitation presumed that the attractive force was propagated instantaneously, thus falling foul of Einstein's theory of Relativity, and leading in due course to current field theories of gravitation. For present purposes, it is sufficient to distinguish between the laws Newton exploited and the general framework into which they were incorporated. A theory embodies laws concerning *observed* regularities, but crucially also involves the postulation of ideas which do not correspond to directly observable events but provide the glue holding the laws together and explaining *why* they obtain. A theory is an imaginative construction of the human mind, making connections and predictions beyond those of the laws which fall under its scope. As such a theory is not refutable in the way that a law is, but only replaceable by a superior theory, a theory which may indeed maintain some if not all the laws of the earlier theory. Newton's theory made the wrong predictions about the movement of the planets. In one case (the perturbations in the orbit of Uranus) this resulted in the discovery of Neptune; in another (the precession in the orbit of Mercury mentioned above) this resulted in confirmation of the validity of Einstein's alternative relativistic theory – a theory in which most of Newton's claims are none the less maintained.

As in gravity so in grammar. Taxonomic grammar postulates laws which state that subjects generally precede objects, that subjects are more accessible than objects, and so on. The theory from which these laws are supposed to follow is never made explicit, but includes the tacit assumption (an explicit assumption in some recent work) that languages are autonomous, quasi-Platonic entities which have mathematical properties independently of the properties of any putative speakers of those languages. Exceptions to the laws are attributed to notions such as the relative consistency or harmony of the languages concerned: properties of the systems themselves. Generative Grammar, by contrast, looks for its laws in the mentally represented principles of speakers of languages rather than in the data structures of the languages themselves. If subjects precede objects in the majority of cases, this is due to the instantiaton of a universal principle governing the child's acquisition of grammar: a principle which, by interacting with other principles, may in a minority of cases give rise to deviations from this pattern. The observational laws are not dissimilar in content; they are radically dissimilar in ontological presupposition and in theoretical commitment.

Where does this leave us with *Babel-17*? For the taxonomists the facts of Delany's 'extra-terrestrial tongues' would simply be more data to add to the list; for the theoreticians concerned with characterizing the notion 'human language', the facts would probably be simply ignored as irrelevant, though clearly inherently fascinating and of concern to anyone theorizing about possible languages more generally. In fact, like most sci-fi writers, Delany makes fairly minimal modifications to his human templates. His creatures/creations are all strikingly similar to humans in their linguistic abilities: to the extent that translation between his various imaginary languages needs nothing more than a linguist who can identify syncope, understand speakers who leave out (nearly) all labials and, most impressively, discuss personal identity with a being whose language has no word for 'I' or 'you'. It would be slightly surprising to find that real aliens had evolved languages quite so similar to human ones, almost as surprising as to find that gravity didn't apply in adjacent galaxies: 'universals' are both more universal and less universal than we thought.

Notes

p. 24   Delany's *Babel-17* (1967) is one of several novels which deal
     interestingly, if not always very realistically, with problems of

language and linguistics. Good examples are Elgin (1984), Golding (1955), Vance (1974) and Watson (1975).

p. 25   The *locus classicus* for Greenbergian typology is Greenberg (1963). A good account in the same tradition is Comrie (1981a). Clear statements of Chomsky's position can be found in Chomsky (1980a, 1981c), and Smith (1987a). The best comparison is Hawkins' introduction to his (1988a).

p. 25   The philosopher Montague is on record as expressing his puzzlement at why generative grammarians should profess to be uninterested in Martian. If linguistics is a sub-part of (human) psychology, the answer should be clear. Personally, I would love to do field-work on Martian.

p. 25   For Hixkaryana, cf. Derbyshire (1985); for Malagasy, cf. Keenan (1976).

p. 26   The 'accessibility hierarchy' in (5) is a somewhat simplified version. Cf. Keenan and Comrie (1977) for the full statement. There has been considerable discussion in the literature of the details of the hierarchy, with the result that some of the observations would now need to be hedged. Nothing in the account here is crucially affected by these refinements.

p. 27   The most accessible account of Popper's philosophy is his (1963). For detailed discussion and criticism of 'naive falsificationism', cf. Lakatos (1970).

p. 27   On innatist explanations and alternatives to them, cf. Putnam (1980), Chomsky (1980c), Comrie (1981a, 1983), Smith (1982b, 1983c). Much of the discussion here is modified from Smith (1982b). Not all Greenbergians eschew innatist explanations *in toto*, but they are at best considered a last resort.

p. 27   On the 'animacy hierarchy' cf. Comrie (1981a), Silverstein (1976). The Navajo example is derived from Hill (1988: p. 19).

p. 28   The quotation on pronoun retention is from Comrie (1981a: p. 26).

p. 29   On parametric variation, cf. Chomsky (1981c, 1986) and essay 6 'The Oats have eaten the Horses'.

p. 30   The form of words 'with overwhelmingly greater than chance frequency' occurs several times in Greenberg (1963). The most sophisticated quantificational work on typology is that of Hawkins, e.g. his (1980), or Hawkins and Gilligan (1988). Cf. also essay 16 'The Numbers Game'.

p. 30   On the neutrino, cf. Sutton (1988).

p. 31   The expression 'dead-end' in this context is from Foley and van Valin (1984: p. 13).

p. 31   The quotation on 'animacy' is from Comrie (1981a: p. 181).

p. 32   Grice's principle of 'Orderliness' is from his (1975). For Sperber's and Wilson's 'Principle of Relevance' cf. their (1986a) and essay 7 'Wilt Thou have this Man to thy wedded Wife?'.

p. 32   The clearest discussion of the need for theories in science is Chalmers (1982). There is also interesting discussion in Chomsky (1987b: pp. 49ff).

p. 32   For the claim that not all languages use the notion 'Subject', Cf. Li and Thompson (1976). For the claim that not all languages distinguish nouns and verbs, cf. Innes (1962).

p. 33   Chomsky's claim about language not being a sensible domain of inquiry has been repeated several times: cf. e.g. his (1986).

p. 33   On the competence/performance distinction, cf. the Introduction above and essay 5, 'Quails and Oysters'. The distinction was introduced explicitly in Chomsky (1965).

p. 33   On slips of the tongue, cf. Fromkin (1973).

p. 33   On the problem of sentences of indeterminate acceptability see most recently Chomsky's (1987b).

p. 33   The 'beautiful hypotheses' and 'ugly facts' are from Huxley's essay 'Biogenesis and Abiogenesis', p. 244.

p. 34   The quotation from Chomsky is from his (1980b: p. 2).

p. 34   The locality constraint of 'subjacency' was first introduced in Chomsky's (1973). There is some discussion in Smith (1987a). For Hiligaynon, cf. Sebastian (1983). The refinement of subjacency mentioned here was first suggested by Rizzi (1982).

p. 34   On the incest taboo, cf. van der Berghe (1983).

p. 35   On Newtonian theory, cf. Cohen (1980). On Einstein, cf. Pais (1982). For a discussion of the replacement of theories, cf. Field (1973).

p. 36   On languages as Platonic abstract objects, cf. Katz (1981) and, for critical discussion, Chomsky (1986) esp. p. 33.

p. 36   On 'consistency' or harmony of languages, cf. Greenberg (1963), Lehmann (1978), Smith (1980, 1981a).

p. 36   There are other parallels between Newtonian and Chomskyan theory, in particular with regard to the nature of the causal mechanisms which can implement the relations between the mentally represented principles and their law-like linguistic effects on the one hand, and between the mathematically specified but physically unmediated gravitational effects on the other. A treatment of these similarities and differences presupposes an account of the differences between mathematical, physical and psychological theories, which takes us beyond the present problem.

4

The Puzzle Puzzle

When he was a little over two and a half years' old my elder son's speech was noticeably different from that of his parents. Like all young children, Amahl took some time to achieve mastery of the intricacies of the English sound system, and to while away the hours of baby-sitting I had decided to keep a detailed record of what he could and could not do. Many of the observations were commonplace and expected. Like many children he had problems with words like 'bottle' and 'puddle', pronouncing them as '*bockle*' [bɔkəl] and '*puggle*' [pʌgəl]. Like many children he found words like 'mouth' and 'mouse' difficult and rendered them both as '*mout*' [maut]. The obvious explanations were either that he was unable to produce the 'correct' sounds or sound sequences, or that he was unable to hear the difference between pairs of sounds such as 's' and 'th', or both.

Neither of these hypotheses, alone or together, was sufficient to account for some of his behaviour. In particular, when he learnt the word 'puzzle' he pronounced it as '*puddle*' [pʌdəl]. Why should a child say '*puddle*' when he meant 'puzzle' but '*puggle*' when he meant 'puddle'? He was obviously capable of producing the sounds in 'puddle', because he actually said the word for something else. Equally, he could obviously hear the difference between them because they had consistently different, albeit incorrect, pronunciations for him, and moreover he kept them apart with perfect regularity in his own production. This was my 'puzzle' puzzle.

It was first necessary to establish beyond doubt that his pronunciation was regular and hence *rule-governed*, rather than random. Exceptions and irregularities always exist, but Amahl's consistency was so great that it was possible to predict with almost complete accuracy what his pronunciation would be for a new word that he had never heard before. For instance, his early speech was characterized by two regular processes, illustrated by the examples 'bank' produced as '*back*' [bak] and 'duck' produced as '*guck*' [gʌk]. I had established that he always left out a nasal (m, n or ng) before p, t and k, hence his pronunciation of 'bank', as well as that of 'tent' as '*det*', 'bump' as '*bup*' and so on; and that he often pronounced an initial 't, d, s' as a velar '*g*' if another velar followed in the same syllable, hence his pronunciation of 'duck', as well as that of 'tiger' as '*giger*', 'sing' as '*ging*', and many more. What I was not sure about was which sounds assimilated in this way to a velar pronunciation and which did not. That not all consonants assimilated can be seen from the contrast between 'back' and 'duck', but there was good reason to believe that 'z' would be one that did. Unfortunately, the number of words in English which are in a two-year-old's vocabulary, which begin with 'z' and end with a velar, is rather small. Accordingly I taught Amahl 'zinc' by giving him as a toy a piece of metal, called a 'zinc'. If the processes I thought were operating in the mapping from the adult form to his pronunciation were as regular as I believed, then he should simply drop the 'n' and convert the initial 'z' to a '*g*'. Sure enough the child's pronunciation was '*gik*' [gik]. There were several hundred examples of this kind where his pronunciation was regular enough to be predictable. These included new forms as well as old ones, showing that his pronunciation could not be simply the product of a sophisticated imitative memory, and demonstrated conclusively that his behaviour was rule-governed.

The next question was what form the rules should take. The output was clear from his pronunciation, but the input was not obvious. That is, how had he stored an item like 'puzzle' in his mind? Was it the same way that he pronounced it – with a 'd' in the middle? Or the way the adults around him pronounced it – with a 'z'? Or as both of these, so that he had two mental representations for the word where we only have one? Or as none of these possibilities, perhaps with some representation neutral as between 'z' and 'd'? I took it for granted that where his pronunciation was consistently the same as the adult form and hence 'correct' (i.e. in correspondence with the form of the language he was putatively learning), his mental representation was the same as the adult's. In the present case for instance, it seemed clear that he knew correctly that 'puzzle' and 'puddle' both began with 'p'. Did he know that they had a 'z' and a 'd' respectively in the middle? Clearly he didn't *know* consciously in the way that a literate adult knows that these are the correct spellings. The question is one of his competence – his tacit knowledge of the grammar of his language, as opposed to his performance – the way he produced or perceived examples of his language. In production he was quite incapable of producing 'z' at all: he pronounced 'zoo' as *'doo'* [du:], 'lazy' as *'dady'* [deidi:], and so on. Similarly he was incapable of producing 'th' [θ] as in 'thick' or 'mouth', so it is clear that part of the reason for the difference between his speech and the speech of the adults around him was simply the pedestrian one that he couldn't make some of the appropriate sounds. The questions of his perceptual ability was less clear-cut. The fact that he differentiated 'puzzle' and 'puddle' in his production meant that he perceived them differently, not necessarily that he perceived them correctly: that is, in terms of the *same* phonological contrasts as the adults in the community. However, a number of considerations made it appear plausible that his perception was essentially perfect.

Given that he pronounced 'mouth' and 'mouse' identically, I put pictures of each in one room and asked him, in a different room, to bring me either the picture of the mouth or the picture of the mouse. He always succeeded in bringing the right one, confirming that his discrimination was perfect and suggesting that the simplest hypothesis was that his perceptual abilities were exploiting the same categories as adults do. Further, like many children Amahl would react angrily to imitations of his mis-pronunciations, accepting only the correct adult form. The standard example in the literature is 'fish': a child who pronounces this *'fis'* will object to adults pronouncing it the same way but will accept the correct 'fish' unhesitatingly; quite often responding along the lines: 'Yes, "fis" not *"fis"* ', indicating clearly that he can appreciate the correct form even while unable to replicate it and being, perhaps, unaware that he is not making the contrast appropriately. In fact my son showed considerable conscious awareness of his limitations in this respect. Curious to know why he produced the 'n' in 'hand' but not the 'm' in 'jump',

I repeatedly asked him to say 'jump' and got the perceptive response: 'Only Daddy can say "*dup*" '.

Finally, when he did learn to produce sounds correctly, they appeared appropriately 'across-the-board': that is in all and only the words in the adult language containing them. For instance, Amahl pronounced both 'f' and 'w' as '*w*' [w], so that 'feet' was pronounced '*weet*' [wiːt], 'finger' and 'fire' were pronounced '*winger*' [wiŋə] and '*wire*' [wæː], with the same initial sound as 'window', pronounced '*winnu*' [winuː], and 'wash', pronounced '*watt*' [wɔt], and so on. When he learnt to produce 'f' correctly, it was substituted at essentially the same time for all the words beginning with 'f' in the adult language, and for none of those beginning with 'w'. If his representation for 'f' had been the same as his pronunciation, such consistency would have been inexplicable. Again, this is not proof that his mental representation was the same as the adult's but the evidence converges on that being the simplest hypothesis to explain all the data.

If perception is not an explanation for the child's divergences from the adult norm, and productive difficulty is only a very partial explanation, we still have to account for Amahl's failure to pronounce 'puddle' correctly given that he could say '*puddle*' for 'puzzle'. I assumed on the basis of the kind of evidence already mentioned that his representations of the words of his language were equivalent to the forms he heard from the adults around him, and that he mapped these representations onto his own pronunciation via a series of rules. Typical examples of such rules are informally stated and illustrated below:

1 A rule turning adult alveolars ('t, d, s, z') etc. to 'g' in words where these were followed by a velar ('k, g, ng'). For example:

   duck   → *guck* [gʌk]
   sing   → *ging* [giŋ]
   doggie → *goggie* [gɔgiː]

2 A rule eliminating consonant clusters in the child's speech by getting rid of 'l, r, y' after another consonant. For example:

   blue → *boo* [buː]
   green → *geen* [giːn]
   new   → *noo* [nuː]

3 A rule neutralizing a number of adult alveolar consonants
into an undifferentiated 't' or 'd': ('t' finally, 'd' elsewhere)

bus   → *but* [bʌt]
brush → *but* [bʌt]
church → *durt* [dəːt]
mouth → *mout* [maut]

In all about thirty such rules were necessary to capture all the
regularities in the child's speech and make it possible to predict
the way he would pronounce any word of the adult language with
which he was confronted. One of these additional rules was
similar to rule (1) in converting an alveolar into a velar before a
so-called 'dark l', [ł], and it was this rule that caused 'puddle',
'pedal', 'bottle' and so on to appear in their modified form in the
child's speech. We can now identify the differences in Amahl's
pronunciation of 'puzzle' and 'puddle' with the different rules they
were subject to, as shown in (4):

4 puddle → puggle [pʌgəl] {by the 'dark l' rule}
   puzzle → puddle [pʌdəl] {by rule (3)}

The trouble with this solution is that such a plethora of rules
might seem arbitrary and unexplanatory – as well as being rather
daunting to decipher when formalized. It is very easy to write
phonological rules, but rather difficult to stop them doing things
that no grammar should countenance: like changing consonants
into vowels, or reversing the order of segments in a word.
However, the rules postulated here have interesting properties
which make them less trivial than might appear. First, it is not the
case that they are unconstrained: they can only do certain things.
Rule (1) is one of a type which brings about what is called
'consonant harmony': whereas the two consonants in the adult
word 'duck' are pronounced in different parts of the mouth (an
alveolar and a velar, the child's pronunciation makes both of them
the same (velar): i.e. they are in harmony. Rules implementing
consonant (and vowel) harmony are common in the developing
phonologies of young children; rules implementing the opposite
tendency where the adult word has consonants with the same
place of articulation, but the child pronounces them with different
articulations, are essentially unknown. So no child regularly

pronounces 'Daddy' as '*Daggy*', though lots of children pronounce 'doggie' as '*goggie*'. This is not, of course, to say that all children will have the same rules. My nephew, Robin, had consonant harmony like his cousin, but it ranged over different consonants. In both children the harmonization was to a velar ('k'), but whereas Amahl harmonized 's' (and other alveolars) but not 'f' (or other labials), his cousin had precisely the reverse pattern giving rise to the data in (5):

5   Amahl   Robin
   sock → *gock* [gɔk]   sock → *dock* [dɔk]
   fork → *walk* [wɔ:k]   fork → *gork* [gɔ:k]

(Recall that for Amahl all 'f's became 'w' at this stage. For Robin all 's's became 'd').

Rule (2) was one of a type which simplified sequences of consonants and vowels so that all the words in the child's own pronunciation consisted of an alternating C V C V . . . pattern. Rule (3) was one of a type which eliminated contrasts in the adult language, resulting in the child having a smaller inventory of sounds than his parents. There were several rules of each type in Amahl's phonology, and again all children have rules of precisely these types but with idiosyncratic differences of detail. Moreover, it turned out that rules of the first two types always operated before rules of the third type. That is, if the transition from the adult form necessitated the application of more than one rule, as in the case of 'zinc' mentioned above, then it was always the case that rules of consonant harmony, for instance, preceded rules of neutralization. This observation (which was independently motivated by a number of phenomena) immediately provided an explanation for the puzzling failure of the child to pronounce 'puddle' correctly even though he could say the correct sequence of sounds when uttering 'puzzle'. The rule collapsing 'z' with 's, t, ch, th' and so on, had to *follow* the rule of harmony which converted 'd' to 'g' and 't' to 'k' in 'puddle' and 'bottle'. Thus we had the situation depicted in (4), where 'puddle' became '*puggle*' ('d' harmonizes to 'g' because of the dark l) but 'puzzle' is unaffected, because only 'stops', such as 't' and 'd', but not 'fricatives', such as 's' and 'z', harmonized; then 'z' was converted to 'd' by a different rule *after* all harmonization processes were complete: i.e. the form '*puddle*' resulting from the child's attempt to say 'puzzle' was 'too late' to be itself harmonized to '*puggle*'.

The explanation looked neat. The assumption that the child's perceptual ability was perfect and that he had some expected production difficulties with complicated sounds, together with the hypothesis that the organizing principles he brought to bear on the learning task – principles which resulted in the need for ordering one type of rule universally before another, seemed adequate to describe the facts and even explain a puzzling puzzle. I was rather pleased with myself, until Marcie Macken of Stanford proved that the child's perception really was crucially involved, contrary to my explicit claim. What was nice about Macken's demonstration was that it was based on precisely the same data as those I had used to argue the opposite. She took my own material and showed that to account for other regularities I had overlooked, it was necessary to assume that Amahl had limited but real perceptual difficulties.

The usual conception of scientific progress is one in which the appearance of new data provides the impetus for a re-evaluation of old ideas. The discovery of a new fossil in the Olduvai Gorge suggests that *Homo habilis* was more ape-like and less human than was previously thought, for instance. Given such new information, it is relatively easy to construct a counter-argument to an old theory; to construct one on the same data as one's 'adversary' is always more satisfying and much more convincing.

Macken showed that for some phenomena the best explanation involved the assumption that perceptual factors were influencing the child's performance. One case was provided by the contrast between words like 'jump' (pronounced without the 'm') and 'hand' (pronounced with the 'n') that I have already mentioned. A minimal pair was provided by 'meant' pronounced as '*met*' [met] and 'mend' pronounced as '*men*' [men]. Although Amahl differentiated these in his pronunciation, it was plausible to claim that the reason the nasal was omitted in one case and included in the other was because of its perceptual salience in different environments. Specifically, before a voiceless consonant like 'p' or 't' the nasal is very short, and hence relatively inaudible; before a voiced consonant like 'd' the nasal is comparatively long and hence relatively audible. That the child actually distinguished the two words in his own pronunciation had made me think that perception could at best be only marginally relevant, but in the case of the 'puddle' class of examples Macken's analysis demonstrated that while Amahl could indeed perceive the difference between 'puddle' and 'puzzle' he very probably couldn't (or at least didn't) consistently perceive the difference between examples like 'riddle' and 'wriggle', or 'puddle' and 'puggle'. As 'puggle' is not a word of English, he had never been exposed to it as a test of his perceptual ability, but there were enough examples in the data of words like 'puddle' and 'pickle' to make it clear that her analysis was plausible. If Amahl's mental representations for all those examples were the same as their adult pronunciations, then *his* pronunciation for any particular word should diverge from the adult's only if some regular process, like the rules in (1) to (3), affected it. In the case of words like 'puddle', where the alveolar 'd' preceded a dark l, there was indeed a rule acting completely consistently to produce the pronunciation '*puggle*'. For words like 'pickle', however, there was no rule converting the velar 'ck' to anything else at all. Crucially, though, he sometimes mispronounced it as '*pittle*' [pitəl], making it clear that his mental representation was not the same as the adult form, presumably because he had misperceived that form. Accordingly, it was necessary to complicate my analysis by including some kind of 'perceptual filter' between the adult's pronunciation and the form the child set up as his mental representation of the words of his language.

I had proposed and defended a maximally simple model of the child's phonological representation roughly of the form in (6):

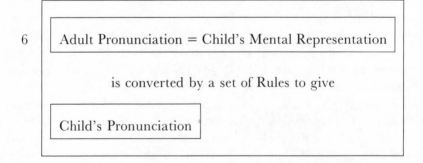

6   Adult Pronunciation = Child's Mental Representation

is converted by a set of Rules to give

Child's Pronunciation

where all the work was done by a single set of rules which had precisely defined formal properties accounting for the way they interacted (or failed to interact) with each other. Given Macken's arguments, I had to accept that a more adequate account was provided by a model of the form in (7):

7

Adult Pronunciation

is passed through a Perceptual Filter to give

Child's Mental Representation

which is then converted by a slightly smaller set of rules to give

Child's Pronunciation

The new hypothesis is in some sense more complicated than the old one, but it has the great advantage of being right. Scientific hypotheses are supposed – in virtue of being 'scientific' – to be refutable or falsifiable. One always hopes that one's own hypotheses will be confirmed rather than refuted, but it is only by refuting a partially adequate theory and replacing it with a better one that progress can be made. By being wrong sufficiently explicitly for Macken to demonstrate the fact, I had made it possible for a better theory to be formulated. It is still the case that the kind of rules I had postulated, together with the majority of their formal properties, serve to account appropriately for the phonological development of Amahl and other children. More importantly, current research will certainly bring about yet further modifications to the system. Thus many suggestions have been made to complicate the diagram in (7) still further, for instance, by proposing that the child be ascribed quite separate mental representations for production and perception; and detailed proposals have been made to reformulate the rules exemplified in (1) to (3) to accommodate changes in linguistic theory more generally. I am convinced by the latter, so far not by the former. Who is right and who wrong is largely irrelevant – the 'puzzle' puzzle is clearly being unravelled.

Bertrand Russell once wrote 'A logical theory may be tested by its capacity for dealing with puzzles, and it is a wholesome plan, in thinking about logic, to stock the mind with as many puzzles as possible.' Solving puzzles presupposes a theoretical framework in terms of which they can be made explicit and subjected to rigorous analysis. Only the existence of a linguistic theory which embodies the contrast between competence and performance, and which postulates the existence of rules – mentally represented and unconsciously applied – within the framework of a grammar which allows different levels of representation, makes an elucidation and explanation of this kind possible.

Even two-year-olds require a theory.

Notes

p. 40   This 'puzzle' was first aired in Smith (1971). Full details of Amahl's acquisition of phonology can be found in Smith (1973): The essays on 'Y' (9) and 'Lellow Lollies' (11) contain further examples and discussion of his language acquisition.

p. 40   The transcription of Amahl's pronunciation is simplified in minor respects, where fine phonetic detail is irrelevant. Background phonetic and phonological detail can be found in the Appendix and in the references cited. The reason for the odd form of some examples becomes apparent during the essay. For instance, 'tent' is given the pronunciation '*det*' not '*tet*' because of rule (3).

p. 41   The evidence of the child's ability to retrieve pictures of mouths and mice appropriately in fact leaves open the question of whether his phonological representations are strictly identical to those of the adult language. So, as far as I can see, is any evidence we are likely to get hold of in the foreseeable future.

p. 41   The '*fis*' phenomenon was first described in Berko and Brown (1960: p. 531).

p. 44   The reason for children manifesting different instantiations of universal tendencies – why Amahl and Robin exemplified different forms of consonant harmony, for instance – seems to be a matter of chance. Such tightly constrained variation provides a good example of Monod's (1970) contrast between chance and necessity: the child's deviations from the adult form are necessarily drawn from a small, finite set of possibilities; but within these limits there is considerable random fluctuation.

p. 45   Macken's alternative analysis appeared in her (1980); the suggestion that at least some of the data required a perceptual explanation appeared first in Braine (1976). The diagram in (7) appears (in essentials) in Smith (1978) which appeared after the Macken article.

p. 45   The remarks about fossil hominids were prompted by Wood (1987).

p. 47   On falsifiability, cf. Popper (1963). Further remarks and references appear in the essay on 'Grammar and Gravity' (3).

p. 47   For suggestions on changing the model in (7) and for updating the theoretical framework for describing phonological development, cf. Spencer (1986) and references therein. Some account of these suggestions is given in essay 11 'Lellow Lollies'.

p. 48   The quotation from Russell is from his (1905).

5

Quails and Oysters

The degradation of English continues unabated. My students can't spell 'grammar'; civil servants seem unable to use grammar, and even the less blimpish sections of the Press contain a daily dose of invective against the (mis-)use of 'hopefully', 'anticipate', and 'presently'. Worse, professional linguists remain entirely complacent. Instead of manning the ramparts against the assaults of the degenerate, they appear to condone the lapse into semi-literacy characteristic, it is claimed, of the younger generation.

The complacency is justified. As innumerable books and articles have emphasized, linguistics is *descriptive*, not *prescriptive*. But this truism tends to obscure two important points: prescriptivism is an important issue, albeit one about which linguistics has very little to say; and description is itself only a rather minor part of the subject matter of linguistics. It is a necessary part, and one which presupposes a great deal of sophisticated training and hard work, but none the less it is only a preliminary to the construction of theoretical explanations.

Linguistics has little to say about prescriptive usage because the bases for the prescription are virtually never linguistic, but social, educational or political. There is no linguistic inferiority in spelling grammar 'grammer', or splitting infinitives, or using 'presently' to mean 'now'. French, a reasonably close relative of English among the world's languages, uses 'actuellement' to mean 'now', rather than the expected 'actually'. American, a reasonably close relative of British among the world's Englishes, uses 'presently' to mean 'now', rather than the expected 'in a little while'. In each case the usage may be misleading for the monoglot

Englishman, but the Americanism is no more reprehensible than the Gallicism.

It is clearly desirable that we be able to understand speakers of other languages and dialects, and it is perhaps occasionally confusing to intercalate words from a different language or dialect into one's conversion (though 'code-switching' as such behaviour is called is characteristic of the majority of the world's communities), but there is nothing intrinsically wrong with either usage. What is offensive to the blimps and educators are the social connotations of using a particular form and being identified with those awful Americans/Etonians/Blacks/Bosses/Illiterates or whatever.

Linguistics has only two roles in all this: to provide an account of the facts – and in most of the cases that attract public attention the facts are already very well-known: does anyone not know about 'hopefully'? – and perhaps to provide guidance as to which bits of this description are matters of public consent and which are private. Consider the reaction of someone who is told not to continually split infinitives, and to cease spelling 'idiosyncrasy' as 'idiosyncracy'. The most likely response to the former injunction is a sullen 'Why not, everyone else does?' but to the latter a slightly bemused 'Is that really how it is spelt?' An honest descriptivist has to admit that a majority of educated men in the street spell 'idiosyncrasy' (incorrectly) with a 'c'. There is none the less a reasonable consensus (with an 's') that the correct form is the one found in reputable dictionaries, and that one should try to conform to their usage. There is no such tolerance of the instructions about split infinitives or ending sentences with prepositions. Again the majority violate these precepts, but only the severely brain-washed feel the need to conform to authority in these cases. Our knowledge of spelling is a kind of encyclopaedic or public knowledge on which we are happy to defer to experts, in particular to dictionary compilers. Our knowledge of where prepositions and adverbs can go in sentences is part of our linguistic knowledge proper, etched in our minds in a way distinct from our knowledge of facts. It is non-propositional whereas our knowledge of spelling is propositional, conscious and available to introspection.

Some of our purely linguistic knowledge can be brought to awareness indirectly via the sentences and structures generated by the rules of our grammar, and it is these which educational pundits seize on as the objects of their strictures. Some dialects allow split infinitives (all dialects of spoken English allow some splitting: 'I want to sort of get this point over somehow'); some prohibit them in all formal styles either because they are genuinely not a possible product of the grammar or because they have been stigmatized by Latinizing school-teachers. It is the social cachet associated with being a speaker of one of these dialects that causes the judgement, and the consequent resentment, not the form of the unconscious linguistic rules which underlie the differences.

The linguist's task is in part to describe and formalize the rules which characterize individual speakers' grammars. Much of this work is obviously dependent on knowing which sentences are grammatical or acceptable in the language one is describing, and which are not. Even this, however, is not a simple matter to decide. Facts of language do not come with their status emblazoned across them any more than do facts of geology or economics. Everyone agrees that this sentence is acceptable. Everyone agrees that there is wrong something with this one. The existence and recognition of such mistakes is one of the reasons for concluding that language is rule-governed. Clearly though, mistakes happen and it is not always easy to identify them, especially when judgements are uncertain: you may have had doubts about whether the example cited earlier: 'I want to sort of get this point over somehow' is or is not part of your natural speech.

One handle on this problem is provided by a central notion in Chomskyan theory: the difference between competence and performance. Competence is, by definition, our knowledge of language; performance, how we put that knowledge to use in understanding and uttering sentences in context. 'Knowledge of language' here refers to the kind of property we have in virtue of which we can judge that an example like (1):

1   Fred fried an egg.

is, however banal, part of our language, whereas (2):

2   Fried Fred an egg?

however transparent in meaning, is not. It does not refer to the kind of knowledge we might fortuitously have *about* languages, either others or our own: such as that Hawaiian only has eight consonants, or that English is spoken by two billion people. This is not the kind of knowledge that determines either our ability to speak and understand, or our judgements about what we hear: judgements such as that (3):

3 I saw the wood.

is multiply ambiguous; that (4):

4 I persuaded him of going.

is wrong, and so on. The contrast between competence and performance can be illustrated by means of an analogy from arithmetic. Any minimally numerate person can multiply 7 by 17 and (probably) come up with the answer 119. Even if they failed to come up with this answer and suggested 129 instead, we would be unlikely either to think that they did not know the rules of arithmetic or that those rules should be changed. Rather we would assume that they had made a simple performance error despite their knowledge of the rules of multiplication. Similar remarks obtain with regard to the example I gave above about there being wrong something with this sentence. The occurrence of such an example has to be identified as a mistake (a deliberate one in this case) if we are not to misrepresent both your and my knowledge of the language.

The standard concomitant of the competence/performance distinction is one between grammaticality and acceptability. Sentences are grammatical, by definition, if they are generated by a grammar: that is if the set of rules constituting the grammar has that sentence as part of its output. They are ungrammatical if the grammar does not so generate them. In the uninteresting cases, that just means that sentences are ungrammatical because the grammar is incomplete and no-one has got round to writing rules (of a perhaps obvious kind) to generate them. In the more interesting cases, sentences are generated or not for a principled reason. The usual reason for wanting the grammar to generate some class of sentences is that they are immediately acceptable to native speakers of the language concerned. Similarly, the usual reason for writing the rules of the grammar to exclude (i.e. not to generate) some class of sentences is because they are immediately unacceptable to native speakers. There are, however, more problematic cases where a sentence may on the one hand be deemed acceptable despite its obvious ungrammaticality, or unacceptable despite the fact that an optimal grammar has to define it as grammatical. Postulating such examples clearly needs to be justified, so I shall select some of the more plausible candidates to illustrate the range of possibilities that have to be accounted for. Consider the following quails and oysters, or rather the sentences containing them in (5) and (6):

5   And no quails tumbling from the cloud.
6   Oysters oysters oysters split split split.

I want to argue that (5) is strictly speaking ungrammatical but may nevertheless be acceptable in some contexts; and that (6), despite its apparently impenetrable unacceptability, is really grammatical.

The reason for objecting to the quails is not that the sentence containing them begins with 'and' – so do innumerable sentences in the Bible, but that it contains no finite verb, a basic prerequisite for the grammaticality of a complete sentence. So 'And no quails tumbled from the cloud' would be a well-formed, complete, grammatical sentence, whereas the example with 'tumbling' could only be a subordinate participial clause. The reason I none the less think it is acceptable in the appropriate context is that it is a line (separated off as a sentence) in Ted Hughes' poem 'Einstein plays Bach'.

There are other kinds of examples which are often cited as being acceptable despite their ungrammaticality. The mixture of languages seen in (7):

7   According to Bismarck a Bavarian was *eine Kreuzung zwischen Oesterreicher und Mensch.*

is supposed to make it necessarily ungrammatical as, by hypothesis, a grammar generates the sentences of a single language. Unfortunately, such examples could equally well be taken as potential refutations of the hypothesis that grammars are unitary. The literature on code-switching and code-mixing indicates that there are dependencies between words occurring in two different languages within the same sentence, suggesting that the speaker is manipulating a system which subsumes both grammars simultaneously. If one's competence is by definition one's linguistic knowledge, and if that knowledge is to be characterised by the rules of a grammar, and if those rules make crucial reference to each other despite being apparently drawn from different systems, the conclusion one is led to draw is that the rules (and hence the sentences generated by them) constitute a unit, and that the examples of language mixture are grammatical after all. It should be emphasized that this conclusion has no further effects on Chomskyan theory than to suggest that one of the idealizations it makes (to the homogeneity of the speech community) is just that: an idealization. There is no evidence that any of the universal principles or claims of the theory are jeopardized by the phenomenon of code-switching: on the contrary, the fact that dependencies of the sort mentioned can be stated in terms of, say, the Binding Theory provide further support for that theory.

Other examples of the same ungrammatical yet acceptable kind are provided by phenomena of repetition, hesitation, anacoluthon, impropriety, and so on: all of which are illustrated in (8):

8　The square on the on the hypotenuse is – come in! – equal to, the sum of the – um – squares on the other two bloody sides.

This is a typical (well, not untypical) specimen of spoken English, but no-one would want the grammar to insert 'ums' or repetitions at random points among the constituents of a sentence, so the example is strictly ungrammatical, though acceptable and unobjectionable in the appropriate context. This conclusion remains untouched by the observation that the grammar may well define those places where interruptions and repetitions are most likely to occur. The actual occurrence of such intercalations is still a matter of performance, where, as usual, this is in some sense parasitic on competence.

The reason for claiming that the oysters in (6), despite their

blatant unacceptability, are grammatical is that to claim otherwise would make the grammar significantly more complicated,
and there is in any case a superior, alternative, explanation for
our reaction to them. The structure of the sentence concerned is
parallel to that of the perhaps inelegant but comprehensible and
acceptable example in (9):

9   The game those boys I met invented resembles chess.

more transparently expressed in (10):

10   The game that was invented by those boys whom I met
     resembles chess.

Both (6) and (9) consist of a sequence of three Noun Phrases
followed by three Verb Phrases, where each pair of a Noun Phrase
and a Verb Phrase constitutes a clause. The three clauses are then
'embedded' one inside the other. That is, 'the game' is a Noun
Phrase which is the subject of the Verb Phrase 'resembles chess',
as shown in the labelled bracket in (11), where the clause is
marked with 'S' for 'Sentence':

11   $_S$[$_{NP}$[The game] $_{VP}$[resembles chess]]

This subject is modified by the relative clause '(which) those boys
invented', itself composed of a Noun Phrase 'those boys' followed
by a Verb Phrase 'invented', whose object is represented by the
optional 'which' at the beginning of the clause. That is, we have
the structure shown in (12):

12   $_S$[$_{NP}$[$_{NP}$[The   game] $_S$[(which) $_{NP}$[those   boys]
     $_{VP}$[invented]]] $_{VP}$[resembles chess]]

'Those boys' is in turn modified by a further relative clause
'(whom) I met', which again consists of a Noun Phrase 'I'
followed by a Verb Phrase 'met' whose object is likewise
optionally represented by 'whom' at the front of the clause.
Missing out the optional 'which' and 'whom', we have the
structure in (13):

13    $_S[_{NP}[_{NP}[\text{The game}]$ $_S[_{NP}[_{NP}[\text{those boys}]$ $_S[_{NP}[\text{I}]$ $_{VP}[\text{met}]]]$
      $_{VP}[\text{invented}]]]$ $_{VP}[\text{resembles chess}]]$

The resulting structure is called 'centre-embedded' and is notoriously difficult to understand despite its formal simplicity.

Mathematically it is extremely easy to characterize a structure of this kind, and with a single level of embedding it is equally easy to understand: no-one has problems with 'The girl I kissed loves me'. Accordingly it is necessary to ensure that the grammar allow for the possibility of a relative clause modification of this type. But if it does so then it will automatically also allow for the kind of monstrosity seen in the 'oysters' example. 'Oysters split' is a laconic but perfectly acceptable comment on the fissiparous nature of certain shell-fish. As 'split' can be either transitive or intransitive (it can occur with or without an object), we could equally well describe the internecine behaviour of these bivalves as in (14):

14   Oysters split oysters.

or, if you prefer a more prolix version, as in (15):

15   Some oysters split other oysters.

This gives rise in turn to the possibility of (16):

16   Oysters that are split by other oysters then split themselves.

or more briefly (17):

17   Oysters (that) oysters split split (themselves).

from which it is but a brief step to the iterated mayhem we started with. The big difference between this example and the chess one is that in the latter I carefully chose Noun Phrases and Verb Phrases that were maximally different from each other: a singular Noun Phrase ('The game') followed by a plural one ('those boys'), where moreover the plurality is marked on both elements of the phrase, in turn followed by a singular pronoun ('I'); the Verb

Phrases are of radically different meaning and involve no ambiguity, and so on. In the oysters sentences, none of these desiderata are satisfied. We have not only three Noun Phrases of the same structure, something which gives rise to difficulty anyway, as can be seen in (18):

18　Essays linguists psychologists respect write are hard to understand.

but identical Noun Phrases. The human processing mechanism is too confused to cope. It is not the grammaticality of the examples that causes the difficulty but the problem caused by the repetition of structurally undifferentiated phrases whose relations are therefore opaque.

The same kind of difficulty is provided by any kind of iteration and is exacerbated by centre-embedding, in particular because this causes discontinuities, where you have to wait for a long time to discover what the verb associated with a particular Noun Phrase is. English has a well-known construction in which a particle can be detached from its associated verb and moved to the end of the sentence, so we can say either (19) or (20):

19　I picked up the child.
20　I picked the child up.

If this process is repeated the effect is either comical or confusing: (21) is fine, but (22) is only marginally acceptable:

21　He put down the child that had sat down.
22　He put the child that had sat down down.

and if we complicate matters with further homonyms such as 'down' in the sense of feathers or 'Down' the city, the result is again impenetrable:

23　He put the child who got the Down down down down.

even though the structure of (23) is the same as that of the scarcely felicitous but hardly unacceptable (24):

24   He picked the child who got the London feathers together
      up.

Examples could be multiplied: I have been told indignantly that
Hofstadter's example in (25):

25   Is a sentence without a subject is a sentence without a
      subject.

is impossible to construe acceptably and should be ungrammatical; but when suitable inverted commas are inserted,
indicating that the first half is a quotation functioning as the
subject of the second half:

26   'Is a sentence without a subject' is a sentence without a
      subject.

it becomes not only acceptable and grammatical but simultaneously both true and false as well!

Grammaticality is only one of many determinants of acceptability. A grammatical sentence may be entirely inappropriate or
irrelevant or obscene, and be unacceptable as a result; an
ungrammatical sequence may in special circumstances be acceptable, without one therefore wishing to say that the grammar
which partly defines one's language has to be modified to
accommodate the offending string. The possibility of making
deliberate mistakes (as linguistic examples for instance), without
thereby changing the grammar is sufficient indication that mere
occurrence is no guarantee of grammaticality. There are of course
serious problems in deciding what the facts that your grammar
has to account for are. Acceptability is a gradient notion:
sentences may be more or less acceptable depending on myriad
factors. Grammaticality on the other hand is a technical notion of
the theory of grammar, and the traditional view was that a
sentence is either grammatical or ungrammatical with no further
possibilities.

Early in the history of generative grammar Chomsky developed
a gradient notion of grammaticality to underlie the cline of
acceptability. This idea fell into desuetude for a generation largely
because it sat uneasily with the rule-based grammars that were

characteristic of transformational generative theory. In the past few years Chomsky has suggested that there are no rules as such but that all one needs is a set of universal principles (subject to some language specific 'Parametric' Variation) and entries for individual lexical items. These principle characterize sub-theories such as binding and bounding which interact to give the complex data we are confronted with when analysing language. It is still important to note that the overall acceptability of a sentence will still be a joint function of such principles and principles which are entirely non-linguistic in the sense defined at the beginning of this essay. We have then the possibility of a sentence being fully well-formed grammatically, in violation of one or more grammatical constraints, or totally deviant. The acceptability of that sentence will normally decrease accordingly, but the possibility remains that intuitive notions of what is acceptable in a more general sense will over-rule the purely grammatical. The opinion that English and other languages are degenerate is rarely a result of grammatical considerations, merely a function of failing to distinguish different aspects of language. Ambrose Bierce describes a dictionary as 'A malevolent literary device for cramping the growth of a language and making it hard and inelastic.' In fact languages, or rather the speakers of languages, are remarkably resistant to the stricture of the prescriptivists, and beautifully elastic in their ability to describe the innovations of science and technology. The only real danger of 'degradation' is much more insidious and resides in the politicians' newspeak, where 'democracy' is applied mindlessly to the regimes of our friends and 'dictatorship' to those of our enemies, irrespective of political reality. Again, linguists have little to say on the matter, except perhaps to warn the community of what is going on. Here complacency is not justified.

Notes

p. 50   On prescriptivism vs descriptivism, cf. Palmer (1984: pp. 15ff), and most introductions to linguistics.

p. 51   On code-switching, cf. Hudson, 1980.

p. 51   The stigmatized use of 'hopefully' to mean 'it is hoped that' is parallel to that of German '*hoffentlich*'. The *OED* doesn't give it; Collins describes it as 'informal'.

p. 51   On public knowledge, cf. Sperber, 1985.

p. 52   The competence/performance distinction was introduced in Chomsky, 1965. For discussion of both this dichotomy and the grammaticality/acceptability distinction, cf. Smith and Wilson, 1979, esp. chap. 2.

p. 53   For Hawaiian, cf. Ruhlen (1976: p. 204). If you exclude the semi-vowel /w/, Hawaiian has only 7 phonemically distinctive consonants.

p. 53   The analogy with arithmetic is only partially cogent, because our knowledge of the rules of arithmetic is conscious whereas our knowledge of the rules of our grammar is unconscious.

p. 54   Example (5) is from Hughes (1967: p. 175). Whether it is strictly speaking a sentence or a constituent of some other type is irrelevant to the point being made: that it is acceptable – in context – despite its obvious deviation from full grammaticality.

p. 54   Example (6) is taken from a lecture by Bever. He discusses comparable examples (but without any oysters) in his 1976.

p. 54   Innumerable sentences begin with 'and' in the Authorized Version (1611) of the Bible. The New English Bible (1970) has done away with them.

p. 55   For an interesting example of the interaction of two grammars in one head, cf. Sridhar and Sridhar (1980).

p. 55   For Binding Theory, cf. Chomsky (1981a), and essay 12, 'Data, Evidence and Theory Change'.

p. 55   On hesitation phenomena, cf. Goldman-Eisler (1958).

p. 56   On centre-embedding, cf. Miller and Chomsky (1963). For language processing more generally, cf. e.g. Frazier (1988).

p. 59   Example (26) is almost from Hofstadter (1980: p. 435).

p. 59   Chomsky introduced the idea of degrees of grammaticality in his 1961. His most recent discussion is in his 1987b, e.g. p. 40. The suggestion that there are no rules occurs repeatedly in Chomsky's recent writing; cf. e.g. his 1986, and for discussion Smith, N. V. (1988).

p. 60   For bounding theory (alias 'subjacency'), cf. essay 3, 'Grammar and Gravity'.

p. 60   For parametric variation, cf. essay 6, 'The Oats have eaten the Horses'.

p. 60   The quotation from Bierce is part of his definition of 'dictionary' in his 1911: p. 31.

p. 60   On the degradation of political language, cf. Chomsky (1986), where it is discussed under the heading 'Orwell's Problem'; and also Chomsky, 1988b, esp. chap. 6.

6

The Oats have eaten the Horses

As part of the plan to tame his shrew, Petruchio turns everything upside down, so his servant Grumio's remark that 'the oats have eaten the hoses' is in keeping with the absurdity of the rest of the scene, even if it strikes the listener as illogical. But is there a *logical* word-order for English or human language more generally? Or does 'anything go'?

Obviously in the world we inhabit it is customary for horses to eat oats, rather than the reverse, so it is clear that what Grumio says is bizarre and that the bizzareness has been gained by switching the normal order of the words. Of itself, however, this does not make the *word-order* either logical or illogical. What we are used to because of the grammar of our own language always seems natural and inevitable; with the result that we can always raise a pitying smile by pillorying the syntax of foreigners. Everyone knows that subordinate clauses in German the verb at the end have. If you do it in English it sounds funny; if you *don't* do it in German it's ungrammatical. Similarly, in Welsh the verb comes first with the rest of the sentence trailing along behind. These are matters of grammar rather than logic. Some languages like English and French have the word-order we are used to: Subject–Verb–Object; some like Japanese, Hindi and Turkish have Subject–Object–Verb word-order; others like Welsh and Classical Arabic have Verb–Subject–Object.

For some time it was thought that the only possibilities were these three types, with perhaps a fourth category of 'free' word-order languages. Examples of such freedom are provided by highly inflected languages like Latin and Sanskrit where *any* word-order is possible because inflections on the ends of the words signal the grammatical functions of subject and object whenever they turn up. So in Latin the sentence in (1):

1   *servus occidit dominum* (the slave killed the master)

can be recast as any of the possibilities in (2):

2a   *servus dominum occidit*
2b   *dominum servus occidit*
2c   *dominum occidit servus*
2d   *occidit servus dominum*
2e   *occidit dominum servus*

with no change in meaning, because the *–us* on *servus* shows that it's the subject, and the *–um* on *dominum* shows that it's the object, irrespective of their relative positions in the sentence. In English and similar meagrely inflected languages, swapping the position of 'servant' and 'master' reverses the sense; in Latin the sense is unchanged and the difference in order can be exploited for nuances of emphasis, story construction and the like.

What is common to these three commonly occurring word-orders – Subject–Verb–Object, Subject–Object–Verb and Verb–Subject–Object – is that the subject precedes the object as, according to many, is only logical. For a time rumours of the existence of other word-orders circulated in the linguistic literature and it was soon confirmed that some languages, Malagasy for instance (spoken in Madagascar) and the Genoese dialect of Italian have the word-order Verb–Object–Subject. This successfully demolished the attractive claim that languages universally put subjects before objects, but it did leave open the possiblity that perhaps no language would be 'object-initial', having either of the orders Object–Verb–Subject or Object–Subject–Verb. Even this faint hope was dashed with the discovery by Des Derbyshire of a group of languages spoken in the Amazon jungle in which each of these unexpected orders occurred: for instance, Hixkaryana with Object–Verb–Subject and Apurinã with Object–Subject–Verb. In Hixkaryana 'the oats have eaten the horses' would be the normal way of expressing what we in English mean by 'the horses have eaten the oats'.

This discovery was embarrassing for those theories which had been carefully designed to predict the impossibility of such word-order; but still left open the possibility put forward by the distinguished psychologist C. E. Osgood, for instance, that Subject–Verb–Object was the preferred order universally; that it is indeed the logical order and that people who grow up speaking languages with word-orders different to this are intellectually disadvantaged. Unfortunately Osgood never produced any evidence in favour of this astonishing hypothesis – astonishing because it would suggest that the sixty per cent of the world's population that do not speak Subject–Verb–Object languages were in some way inferior. What is really surprising is that Osgood could ever have thought such a thing, especially as one of his main research assistants at the time was a native-speaker of Kannada, a Dravidian language of South India whose word-order is consistently Subject–Object–Verb.

All the evidence we have so far accumulated indicates that all languages are equal in the sense that anything you can say in your language I can say in mine and vice versa; and also that no language bestows material advantages or disadvantages of a conceptual nature on its speakers. This is not to deny that being brought up to speak English rather than Amharic confers very considerable economic, political and social advantages in today's world: one of our few growth industries in a period of recession and depression has been the teaching of English as a foreign language. Nor is it to deny that discussing micro-electronics is easier for someone who can read this essay than for a monoglot Mongolian. We have the relevant vocabulary, he (or she) doesn't. On the other hand if the subject of discussion is the correct way to build a *yurt*, the advantage would be reversed. In either case, however, we can easily borrow the relevant vocabulary, as I have just borrowed the Mongolian word *yurt*. It is also clear that different languages present difficulties in different areas of their overall system. The learner of English doesn't have to bother with the inflexional complexities of Latin, but then the learner of Latin doesn't have to bother with the complexities of English word-order.

To the extent that our thinking is conditioned by the categories provided by our native language (the Whorf hypothesis) so shall we be temporarily more at ease manipulating the vocabulary we are used to than recent loans, but there is no evidence that our thought processes are designed to slot more easily into the framework of one language than another. One of the more exciting hypotheses of recent work in the philosophy of language and mind is Jerry Fodor's claim that in order to learn a language you already need to know a language. To learn a new word such as *red* or *mosquito* you have to have available a representational system rich enough to formulate such concepts as *same, coloured, buzz* and so on. To avoid an infinite regress Fodor is led inexorably to the position that a large part of our linguistic ability is innately wired up: specifically all that part of our linguistic knowledge which is universal. This would include such categories as subject, object, noun, verb, etc. but presumably not the order in which these occur, as this demonstrably has to be learnt for each language. Moreover, as Dan Slobin, one of the most knowledgeable linguists working on first-language acquisition, put it: 'in terms of word-order, languages of different order types do not seem to differ in terms of ease of acquisition'.

Thus it is not the case that all children start by putting their words into, say, Subject–Verb–Object order and changing it if they find out that they are learning a Subject–Object–Verb language; rather all children learning whatever language make mistakes in part dependent and in part independent of the word-order of the language being learnt. For instance, my younger son Ivan at the age of one year eleven months produced his first sentences to contain all three of the constituents Subject, Object and Verb in the order Verb–Object–Subject, as exemplified in (3):

3a   'do that me' {= 'may I do that?'}
3b   'play Paul me' {= 'may I play with Paul?'}
3c   'do this me' {= 'let me do this'}

and examples with the 'correct' order as in (4):

4   'me do this' {= 'let me do this'}

didn't appear until a few days later.

Learning a language then must consist, in part, of relating the innate language of thought to the grammar of the language one is exposed to. It is clear that the examples in (3) provide strong evidence against Osgood's conjecture that Subject–Verb–Object is universally the preferred order. Even if one construes his remark as being about the syntax of the Language of Thought rather than the syntax of Natural Languages, there is no reason to expect the kind of mismatch displayed by Ivan, where the word-order of the child's utterance deviates both from that of the language he is learning and from that of the system he is innately endowed with. It may well be the case that learning one's 'first' language consists in replacing the language of thought by one's native language, resulting in the overwhelming feeling that one thinks in English, or whatever natural language is one's mother tongue.

Although no single word-order or sub-set of word-orders seems to be linguistically or psychologically favoured, syntactic typologists influenced by the seminal work of Greenberg have emphasized the fact that bundles of word-order properties correlate in the languages of the world. Languages which have the verb initial in the sentence have *prepositions* like English 'in', 'at' and 'to' which *precede* the noun they govern. Languages which have the verb final in the sentence have *postpositions* like English 'ago', which *follow* the noun they govern. Some languages have both prepositions and postpositions or even 'ambipositions' like *for* ——'s *sake* which flank the governed noun phrase. A wide variety of such correlations has been discovered, ranging over every aspect of word-order.

Unfortunately, no correlation has turned out to be perfect: Persian, for instance, has the word-order Subject–Object–Verb but has prepositions. Accordingly, any claim for universality would be falsified by some language somewhere; the only universal left in this particular area being that if a language is verb-initial it will have prepositions. Even this isn't as good as it looks, as the natural assumption that such a language will *not* have postpositions as well is wrong. Papago (a North American Indian language) is verb-initial, it has the word-order Verb–Subject–Object, but it has both prepositions and postpositions. Other generalizations across constructions from the world's languages have fared little better and the reason is not hard to find: It's not that languages can 'differ from each other without limit and in unpredictable ways' as Joos put it; it's that the domain of generalization is being misconceived. Greenbergian typologists try to make generalizations about *data*, when what they should be doing is making generalizations across *rule* systems.

'Language' is used in several different ways. As a political or geographical term, as in 'the Chinese language' or 'the Norwegian language' it is useful but linguistically uninteresting. At a geographically more circumscribed level one talks of the language of a speech community: the English of Barnstaple, for instance; but it is important to realise that even this constitutes an idealization in that not every member of the community speaks exactly like every other. Even within the same family people often differ from each other, albeit in relatively minor ways. For me, the sentence in (5):

5 John promised Mary to go.

is grammatical and means 'John promised Mary that he (John) would go'. For my sons and many speakers of their generation (5) is not a possible sentence at all, even if its meaning is usually transparent. Just as we can understand the Frenchman who says he speaks very well English without being committed to agreeing that what he says is grammaical, so can my sons understand me without having to admit that what I say could be said using their grammar.

The implication of this recognizable difference between individuals is that each person's language is different from everyone else's. More particularly, our linguistic activity must be rule-governed, or we couldn't make the judgements we do or recognize mistakes in our own or others' speech, and linguistics is really about the rules that we have stored somewhere in our heads, where a bundle of rules constitutes a grammar. For instance, we know immediately that in (6):

6 Ford fell over when he tried to chew gum and walk.

Ford and *he* can refer to the same person, whereas if we change the word-order to that in (7):

7 He fell over when Ford tried to chew gum and walk.

he and *Ford* cannot refer to the same person. This fact is a reflection of quite subtle linguistic rules which we use every day despite being completely unaware of them until they are drawn to our attention.

The relevance of all this to our criticism of the work of many typologists is that the set of rules we control is very large and, not surprisingly, these rules are not in 1:1 correspondence with types of sentences or phrases of English. That is, knowing whether a sentence is well-formed or ill-formed – grammatical or ungrammatical – gives us only the most elementary indication of what the rules responsible for characterizing that sentence are. Indeed it is often the case that a sentence can be described by reference to quite different sets of rules, each of which is independently needed to describe some other construction. The archetypal example of such a situation is ambiguity, where one sequence of words has two or more distinct meanings as in (8):

8   Anne likes horses more than Mark.

which is related semantically, and perhaps syntactically, to both the sentences in (9):

9a   Anne likes horses more than she does Mark.
9b   Anne likes horses more than Mark does.

But if the data of a language do not allow you to determine unambiguously what the rules of that language are, then it is highly unlikely that studying bits of data (as opposed to fragments of rule systems) from lots of languages will be revealing of deep-seated generalizations. The grammar of English has been described in far more detail than that of any other language, yet even for English there is no agreement as to the correct description of the *that* or even the *ago* in 'the girl that I loved three years ago'.

Saying that typologists have been barking up the wrong tree, while accurate is perhaps rather unsatisfactory. One would be right to feel that, however misguided, they are on to something with their notions of consistency and harmony. Surely it's not a coincidence that most languages which have Verb–Subject–Object word-order have prepositions and not postpositions, and that most languages with Subject–Object–Verb word-order have postpositions and not prepositions. The fact that I had to look as far from home as Papago to find a good counter-example may be significant.

What we need, then, is some system which is capable of making implicational or correlational statements over grammars not just over data. What has emerged over the past ten years is a system known as 'parametric variation'. The details are complex but the basic idea is simple. As the child learns its language on the basis of its innate (genetic) endowment it is constrained to make hypotheses of a particular kind about the rules of the grammar it is learning. One possible rule of grammar is to move a phrase to a different position – compare the corresponding question and answer in (10):

   10a   Is he a genius?
   10b   He is a genius.

illustrating a rule which moves the subject 'he'. One impossible rule is simply to invert the order of words from one sentence to another: that is, no language contains a rule of the kind which would convert (10b) directly into (11):

   11   Genius a is he.

This claim can be made convincingly even in the face of such pairs as those in (12):

   12a   John ran away.
   12b   Away ran John.

where the inverted word-order is not the product of a simple rule of inversion, as witness the unfortunate result one would get by inverting the minimally more complex 'Poor John ran away'. All rules are 'structure-dependent'.

One of the interesting claims of the theory of parametric variation is that rules are not arbitrary entities that have to be learned piecemeal, but are rather the reflections of general principles, which will have repercussions throughout the system. Once the child has developed one rule, this will foreclose a number of other rules, making the learning task that much easier. It won't necessarily prohibit the appearance of all the data that might have been produced by such rules, as some of those data could be produced by rules unaffected by the original choice; hence the unreliability of looking only at data and not the system responsible for generating the data. (Perhaps the germ of truth in the claims of the logical word-orderers is that the development of some rules forecloses more options than does the development of others.)

As a specific example consider the Head-first/Head-last parameter. The 'head' of a phrase is the principal, and usually only obligatory, element in that phrase. So a noun is the head of a Noun Phrase, a verb is the head of a Verb Phrase, and so on. Typically, the relative position of a head and its complements – those items dependent on it – will be the same across all phrase types. Accordingly, in (13) the complement prepositional phrase, 'at Fred', *follows* the *head*, be this verb, noun or adjective, because English is a 'Head-first' language:

13a   John *swore* at Fred.
13b   John's *amazement* at Fred.
13c   John is *mad* at Fred.

In Head-last languages (like Japanese, Hindi or Kannada) on the other hand, the parallel *post*positional phrase would *precede* the verb, noun or adjective. The claim then is that the child acquiring his or her first language needs to learn a rule for only one of the structures exemplified in (13). The development of such a rule will 'fix the parameter' for the grammar as a whole, meaning that the child who has correctly absorbed the fact that (13c) is the right way to say things will already know that (13a) and (13b) are also right. Indeed, the child could learn all of this from simply observing and understanding a sentence as simple as 'Kiss Mummy', where the Head verb 'kiss' precedes the object noun 'Mummy'. This greatly reduces the learning task for the child, and goes some way to explaining the rapidity and ease with which children develop language. In fact, it is clear that when much of the child's knowledge comes for free in this way, 'learning' is not really the appropriate expression to use, and that 'triggering' or 'growth' would be a more accurate designation.

There is still some place for learning, however. If the language the child is exposed to is of a mixed type – like Persian or Papago

– he will have to learn the exceptional constructions piecemeal. Fixing the Head parameter on the basis of just one example would, in this case, give the wrong results, predicting very specific mistakes in the child's speech. Such predictions, with their attendant risk of falsification, are a major advantage of the approach: what would just be another datum for the taxonomist is the basis for a re-evaluation of the theory for the generativist.

In fact most parameters are more abstract than the example given here, representing conditions on rules rather than rules themselves. In either case, however, we end up with a situation in which the output of our grammar assumes the inevitability of logic. Our knowledge of language is so much part of us that it colours our perception and even our reason; but the resulting 'logic' is language dependent: there is no logical word-order. At the end of *The Taming of the Shrew*, the widow says tauntingly to Kate: 'He that is giddy thinks the world turns round': it is as hard to tell reality from our perception of it in language as in love.

Notes

Some of the issues discussed in this essay are also discussed in essay 3, 'Grammar and Gravity'.

p. 62   The title of this essay is from *The Taming of the Shrew*, Act III, scene 2, line 201.

p. 62   On word-order and word-order typologies, cf. Greenberg (1963), Comrie (1981a, 1983), Hawkins (1988a, 1988b), Dryer (1988), Smith (1981a).

p. 63   For Malagasy, cf. Keenan (1976) and his contribution to Lehmann (1978). For Genoese, cf. Vattuone (1975). For Hixkaryana and Apurinã, cf. Derbyshire (1977).

p. 64   The best example of a theory predicting the impossibility of object-initial languages is Pullum (1977). Happily he was directly involved in the subsequent (re-)discovery of such languages: cf. Derbyshire and Pullum (1981).

p. 64   Osgood's remark about Subject–Verb–Object languages was made several times in lectures; it is reproduced in Osgood and Tanz (1977). For Kannada, cf. Sridhar (forthcoming).

p. 64   The Whorf hypothesis (also known as the Sapir–Whorf hypothesis) is elaborated in Whorf (1950). It has spawned a vast literature, of which a recent example with useful references is Hill (1988). Some of the remarks here are from Smith (1983a).

p. 65   Fodor's discussion of the language of thought is best summarized in his book of the same title, Fodor (1975).

p. 65   The quotation from Slobin is from his 1978: p. 7.

p. 65   The examples in (3) and (4) from Ivan were first discussed in Smith (1981a).

p. 66   For Persian, cf. Lambton (1974: pp. 5, 110).

p. 66   For Papago, cf. Greenberg (1963: p. 107). The Papago data are discussed in Comrie (1981a) and Smith (1982b).

p. 66   The quotation from Joos is from his 1957: p. 96.

p. 68   The notion of 'consistency' or 'harmony' originated with Greenberg (1963) and was emphasized by Lehmann (1978) among others. Critical discussion appears in Smith (1980, 1981a). Hawkins in recent work has refined the notion in interesting ways: see his 1988a, 1988b.

p. 69   For parametric variation, cf. Chomsky (1981a, 1981c, 1986). Interesting extensions appear in Roeper and Williams (1987). For detailed discussion, cf. Smith, A. (1988).

p. 69   For 'structure-dependence', cf. Chomsky (1972).

p. 70   For the Head-first/Head-last parameter, cf. e.g. Chomsky (1988a) p. 70.

p. 71   The last quotation from *The Taming of the Shrew* is from Act V, scene 2, line 20.

7

Wilt Thou have this Man to thy wedded Wife?

It's surprising how rarely we mean what we say. Or rather, it's remarkable how efficiently we can communicate one message by uttering something quite different. Slips of the tongue, or of the brain, represent only the most obvious and easily handled examples of a much more pervasive phenomenon.

If the Reverend Spooner really declared that 'the Lord my God is a Shoving Leopard', it is reasonably certain that no-one in the congregation will have been misled into re-categorizing him as a boisterous pantheist. Quite apart from the ready accessibility of the cliché 'Loving Shepherd', the literal interpretation is so grotesque in this context that it would be immediately rejected as irrelevant even if mildly amusing. So much is neither controversial nor problematic. What is of interest is that with the development of work in pragmatics by Sperber and Wilson we are now in a position to provide an explicit characterization of *relevance* and hence of *irrelevance*.

Intuitively, an utterance is relevant if it tells you something you didn't know, or weren't consciously aware of before. But to tell you *now* that 'Nouakchott is the capital of Mauretania' is hardly relevant, though it might be on some other occasion. So relevance is dependent on the 'context of utterance', that is, the background body of assumptions against which you interpret some utterance. If you have been asked whether you think Fred would enjoy a holiday in Nouakchott, and you already know that he loves capital cities, then the information provided certainly is relevant. Thus an utterance is relevant in a context if you can use it, together with that context, to deduce something which was apparent from neither of them taken alone: in the jargon, if the utterance has 'contextual effects', in virtue of being 'a synthesis of old and new information'. This is the foundation of Sperber and Wilson's definition or 'relevance', with the added proviso that the effort involved in making this deduction is not too great. The heart of their pragmatic theory then consists of the 'Principle of Relevance', informally defined as: 'Every utterance carries a guarantee of optimal relevance to the hearer.' That is, by claiming the hearer's attention, the speaker communicates that the utterance is relevant enough to be worth his attention. For instance, the utterance in (1):

1   That painting is by Keating.

is relevant in the context given in (2):

2   If that painting is by Keating, it is a worthless forgery.

because it allows the deduction in (3):

3   That painting is a worthless forgery.

which is deducible neither from (1) alone nor from (2) alone. Moreover, in the same context (2), example (1) is more relevant than (4):

4   That painting is by Keating, who died recently.

as (4) allows no more deductions to be made than does (1) but requires greater effort to process. Similarly, to say (5):

5   My first wife gave me this watch.

when one has only ever had one wife is grossly misleading, not because it is false – one's only wife is presumably one's first wife – but because the extra effort involved in processing 'first' could only be justified if there were some possible alternative non-first. That is, if 'first wife' is meant to refer to one's current spouse, then it is more economical simply to say 'wife', and irrelevant to mention 'first'.

Such simplified examples may give the impression that the set of propositions which constitutes the context in which an utterance is interpreted is antecedently given. In fact, one of the insights of the Sperber/Wilson theory is that the context for interpretation is constructed *ad hoc* as part of the process of interpretation of the utterance heard. The idea is that there is a small immediately accessible context consisting of the most recently processed propositions, which forms the basis for the interpretation process, and this minimal context is then expandable by reference to earlier discourse, to encyclopaedic knowledge or to sense perception. Each of these extensions of the context will, by hypothesis, be motivated by the desire to optimize the relevance of what has been said: that is, to interpret the utterance in accordance with the guarantee of relevance. For instance, B's response in (6):

6   A: Did you have a good summer?
    B: It's actually not very comfortable in Dartmoor.

requires A, if he is to understand B's response as relevant to his question, to assume a proposition to the effect that B has been in prison for the summer. This proposition was presumably unknown to A, hence could not have been antecedently available, and also involves the accessing of encyclopaedic information (Dartmoor is the name and location of a famous prison in England). Despite the unexpectedness of B's remark, the interpretation is almost inevitable, because it requires from A the minimal amount of work needed to achieve an adequate amount of relevant information. This is not to deny that other interpretations might be possible, especially if A has, and is known by B to have, further information which would require or permit a different construal, but the simplicity of this example seems not to render it atypical of natural exchanges.

Slips of the tongue generally cause no problem because the literal interpretation is irrelevant, while a different interpretation is optimally relevant, either because it allows immediate and appropriate deductions or because (in the case of ritualized language) the intended meaning is so overwhelmingly accessible.

George Eliot's gentle, if teasing, depiction of the characters in *Silas Marner* revolves at one stage around the mistake made by the rector at Mr Lammeter's wedding, where he inverts the words

'husband' and 'wife' in the marriage service, saying 'Wilt thou
have this man to thy wedded wife?' and 'Wilt thou have this
woman to thy wedded husband?'. Only Mr Macey noticed the
slip and worried about the legality of the wedding: 'Is't the
meanin' or the words as makes folks fast i' wedlock?', and is
reassured by the parson that it's neither: the 'regester' is what
matters. Whatever the legality of the wedding, the correct
interpretation of the words used is arrived at straightforwardly,
because the alternative literal interpretation is irrelevant.

The same relevance-theoretic concepts will account for a range
of other cases where we mean something other than what we say.
Consider (7) or (8):

7a The ulcer in ward 2 is to be discharged tomorrow.
7b The ham-sandwich in the corner has left a huge tip.
8a My heart is turned to stone; I strike it and it hurts my
    hand.
8b John's a cabbage (he has his heart in his head).

The sentences in (7) are typical examples of metonymy where
some property of a person is used to refer to that person. In these
cases it is clearly not possible for an ulcer to be discharged or a
ham sandwich to leave a tip, but on the assumption given by the
Principle of Relevance that that utterance is relevant, even
optimally relevant, the correct construal, on which the referent
with the most salient relevant relationship to an ulcer or a ham
sandwich is picked out, will spring immediately to mind. Apart
from colourfulness, the locutions in (7) have the bonus of being
shorter than their language of thought equivalents 'the patient
with the ulcer', 'the customer with the ham sandwich', so we have
a saving in performance both for the speaker, and even if less
obviously, for the hearer, of a kind made advantageous in any
environment where the same stereotypical situation recurs with
sufficient regularity to make the explicitness of the complete
referential expressions tedious. Hence (7a) and (7b) are typically
expressions used by medical staff or waiters rather than members
of the public.

The metaphors in (8) are false in a different way, but relevant
in much the same way. Had his heart really been petrified,
Othello would not have been in a position to utter the sentence in

(8a), but its force comes from suggesting to the listener that Othello's heart, itself a metaphor for his whole (emotional) being, now has some of the properties of a stone: hard, unyielding, insensitive and so on. Which particular attributes the hearer supplies will vary from person to person and occasion to occasion, depending on which other thoughts are uppermost in his consciousness, and hence maximally accessible. Similarly, (8b) is sufficiently opaque to allow of any number of weak associations in addition to the one provided by the parenthetical continuation.

One of the insights of the Sperber and Wilson framework is that such literary figures form a natural class with less mannered, and less calculated, examples of 'loose use'. For instance, it is more relevant (because of the processing cost to both speaker and hearer) to say you earn £20,000 per annum, rather than £19,897, even though the former claim is false and the latter true; that Wilt is 6 feet tall even though he's only 5'11.5"; that Manchester is 200 miles away when it's only 197 or 203, and so on. The fact that if Manchester is exactly 203 miles away then, traditionally, the claim that it's 200 miles away is strictly speaking true, and that if it is 197 miles away it is strictly speaking false is irrelevant to the interpretation. Such niceties could be relevant to cartographers, to those who have already walked 190 miles and are near to exhaustion, and so on, but in the usual kind of context where one wants to get a general idea of the sort of distance involved, the round number is the most relevant one in providing adequate information at minimal cost.

The same appeal to the Principle of Relevance and the maximization of contextual effects suffices to account for a range of other cases. The hyperbole in (9):

9　It's *miles* to the post-office.

spoken when in fact the place is only a few hundred yards away, gains its effect from the realization by the hearer that the speaker is being deliberately economical with the truth, and presumably is using the expression to suggest indirectly what would follow directly if the sentence were true: for instance, 'let's not bother to go there'. That is, the context against which the speaker is suggesting the hearer interpret his utterance is something like: 'If a place is miles away, it's inconvenient to go there'; 'If it's inconvenient to go, we should presumably stay here or do something else'; with the conclusion that we need do nothing.

Comparable analyses obtain for the necessarily true or necessarily false (and hence apparently uninformative) utterances in (10):

10a   It's some distance to go there.
10b   It's no distance to go there.

With (10a) the truism must, if relevant (which by hypothesis it will be construed as) be interpreted as suggesting that the distance is greater than the interlocutor appears to think. (10b) typically has the reverse interpretation. The hearer knows it is false, assumes because of the Principle of Relevance that it is none the less relevant, and is therefore forced to interpret it, for example, as elliptical for 'it's not a distance that will have any relevant effect on our plans'.

As a last, similar, example consider the use of paralipsis: the self-contradictory figure in which one explicitly denies doing what one is doing, as in (11):

11   I would not like to suggest that he is a liar.

A typical example is provided by Brodsky when he writes: 'If I refrain from stating here that Platonov is a greater writer than Joyce or Musil or Kafka . . .', where he is stating precisely that. Or rather, he is attempting to have his cake and eat it too: to suggest Platonov's superiority as though it were beyond dispute, because it emanates from someone other than himself, or is accepted knowledge. Such examples are not simply 'descriptive', describing some state of affairs in the world directly, but fall under Sperber and Wilson's rubric of 'interpretive use', where an utterance represents some state of affairs indirectly as an 'interpretation' of a thought of someone other than the speaker. This device of interpretive use is seen most clearly in ironical utterances where the speaker dissociates himself quite explicitly from the content of the proposition expressed, as when Voltaire catalogues an appalling series of disasters that befall Candide, while still reiterating that 'Everything is for the best in this best of all possible worlds.'

Perhaps the best-known phenomenon in pragmatics is the Gricean notion of 'conversational implicature'. This is illustrated by the exchange in (6) above, where B's answer leads one via the presumption of relevance to the ('conversationally implicated') conclusion that the speaker has been in penal detention, with obvious implications for the kind of summer he has had, as well as more striking ones about his life-style generally. Again, 'Relevance' provides an explanation for the operation of a well-known phenomenon by embedding it in an explicit theory which accounts for how and why particular conclusions are drawn: to optimize relevance.

At this stage one may well become suspicious. The Popperian paradigm in the philosophy of science demands that the claims one makes be falsifiable, but the refutability of the Principle of Relevance seems to be minimal. The suggestion is that, by accounting for everything, one trivializes the whole system. Just as the predictions of astrology are compatible with any conceivable state of affairs; just as, for the devout, any disaster shows the hand of God – if you are spared, God was watching over you, if you are stricken, God is either punishing you for sins unspecified or is simply inscrutable – so one might worry that Relevance Theory, by having an answer for (nearly) everything, is perniciously irrefutable.

There are several possible responses to this reaction. First, Popper's criterion of falsifiability was used to demarcate science from non-science, rather than sense from non-sense, and one can admit the insights of, say, Freudian psychology or Marxist economics without admitting them to the realm of science. Although it is not inconceivable that the Principle of Relevance is true *a priori*, and hence not subject to empirical disconfirmation, this would be an unnecessarily Pyrrhic victory. Relevance theory is both sense and science. So either it must be potentially falsifiable or the criterion of falsifiability must be inappropriate. Both propositions are probably true.

Falsifiability as a practical test is a property of specific hypotheses thrown up by the theory, and thus only indirectly a property of the theory as a whole. The core of Relevance Theory is the Principle of Relevance which makes simultaneous claims about the maximization of contextual effects and the minimization of processing costs. The theory would be jeopardized therefore if it could be shown for a range of cases that, for instance, processing cost was immaterial for the interpretation of utterances in conversation in the way it clearly is immaterial in the interpretation of sacred texts or poetry, to which people happily devote whole lifetimes. At first sight the time one is prepared to spend musing over the words of a lover might seem to be a case in point, but the contextual effects so derived themselves go on multiplying indefinitely as one thinks of more contexts in which to (re-)process them, and hence offset the effort involved.

There is, however, a more serious kind of possible counter-example, suggested by the analysis of stories in recent work by Annette Karmiloff-Smith. The problematic data are those where the speaker telling a story chooses to repeat a proper name or definite description (such as "the girl") even where the corresponding pronoun would be both unambiguous and shorter. But if it is shorter and the 'full' form adds nothing then, by hypothesis, the short, pronominal, form should be used. Karmiloff-Smith describes the case of 'discourse repairs' where the speaker 'corrects' him- or herself from the use of a pronoun to the use of a full Noun Phrase, but where there is no ambiguity or failure of reference to motivate such a correction. A good example is provided by (12), in which the pronoun *she* is totally unambiguous with regard to the identification of the only female referent:

12   'This boy and girl are playing outside. He's gone to the river and he's going to catch some fish. So he tries to steal the girl's bucket but *she* won't . . . *the girl* won't let go of it so he just grabs it out of her hand and the girl starts to cry.'

Such an example suffices to show that the theory makes empirically falsifiable predictions. It does not, of course, show that the theory, or even the relevant hypothesis, is false, because the correct response may be to save the hypothesis by attributing the deviation from the expected results to some other factor: that is, to modularize the account given of such examples, and to take cognizance not only of the Principle of Relevance but of other, stylistic, considerations as well. In this case the phenomenon is reminiscent of the rhetorical device known as 'epizeuxis'. But this is traditionally an emphatic device, and it is clear that emphasis is not relevant in the example given. Karmiloff-Smith herself attributes the repair to the 'thematic subject constraint' the effect of which 'is to pre-empt pronominalization for the thematic subject of a narrative, and to refer to subsidiary characters by a full NP in subject position even if a pronoun would *not* be ambiguous'. It is clear that no such prediction can be derived from Relevance Theory itself, so that while the theory is necessary for an explanatory analysis of stylistic effects, it does not exhaust what has to be said about them. This, of course, is exactly what one would expect.

The conclusion one comes to is that there is, in virtue of Relevance Theory, a simple treatment – and indeed *explanation* – for a range of disparate and apparently idiosyncratic phenomena: an explanation even for how we can convey what we wish to convey without saying it. As Mr Macey says a little later in the same chapter of *Silas Marner*, 'When I come to think on it, meanin' goes but a little way i' most things.'

Notes

p. 73   On slips of the tongue, cf. Fromkin (1973, 1988). For spoonerisms, which appear to have been deliberate efforts at humour rather than slips of the tongue, cf. MacKay (1973).

p. 73   Sperber and Wilson's theory is elaborated in most detail in their (1986a); cf. also their (1986b) and (1987). The quotation 'a synthesis of old and new' is from their 1986a: p. 108. The Principle of Relevance is given, in somewhat different terms, on p. 158. The *deductive* nature of the interpretation process is justified in detail on pp. 94ff.

p. 74   The exegesis of their theory here is adapted from Smith and Smith (1988).

p. 75   The incident from *Silas Marner* described here is in chap. 6.

p. 76   There is a useful discussion of metonymy in Nunberg (1978), from which the examples in (7) are modified.

p. 76   The quotation from *Othello* in (8) is from Act IV, scene 1, line 179.

p. 77   The examples of 'loose use' are modified from Sperber and Wilson (1986b).

p. 78   The example of paralipsis after (11) is from Brodsky's essay 'Catastrophes in the Air'. See his 1987: p. 280.

p. 78   The notion of 'interpretive use' is developed in Sperber and

Wilson (1986a), esp. pp. 224ff. Cf. also their 1987 for further discussion.

p. 78   Voltaire's *Candide* is a satire on Rationlist optimism, especially Leibniz's view that this is the best of all possible worlds. The words cited are repeatedly mouthed by Pangloss.

p. 79   The late Paul Grice is the father of modern pragmatics. His idea of 'conversational implicature' is presented in his 1975. For discussion of the relation of his theory to Relevance Theory, cf. Sperber and Wilson (1986a) and Wilson and Sperber (1981).

p. 79   On the Popperian paradigm, cf. Popper (1963), Lakatos (1970), and essays 3 'Grammar and Gravity' and 18 'Linguistics as a Religion'.

p. 80   The problematic example of a 'discourse repair' is from Karmiloff-Smith (forthcoming), p. 20.

8

Must and the Randy Pachyderm

What does 'must' mean?

A good dictionary will give a number of different answers: 'the newly pressed juice of grapes', 'frenzied sexual excitement in the male elephant', 'an expression of inevitability', 'an essential and necessary thing', and maybe more; 'must' is clearly ambiguous. Exactly how many ways ambiguous it is, and how one might decide such a question are not so obvious. It is not even self-evident that ambiguity, rather than vagueness, is the correct descriptive category. Traditionally, the last two examples are linked under a single heading distinct from the others. 'Must' as used in (1):

1a   John must eat his spinach.
1b   A good head for heights is an absolute must for mountaineers.

is said to be *polysemous*, it is one word with two or more related meanings. The 'must' – or rather 'musts' – in (2) and (3) on the other hand:

2   The must is ready for fermentation.
3   The elephant is in a dangerous state of must (*or* 'musth').

is (or *are*) said to be *homonymous*, different words that happen to be spelt the same way; or, if you spell the sexual frenzy one 'musth', homophonous, different words that happen to be pronounced the same way.

Homophony is the simplest case to dispose of. No-one is

tempted to claim that 'right', 'write', 'rite' and 'wright' are anything other than four different words, because the spelling, the syntax and the semantics all point in the same direction. In this case neither vagueness nor ambiguity is an appropriate concept, though if we restrict ourselves to the particular item spelt 'r-i-g-h-t', there might be some difficulty in deciding how many lexical items it is. Homophony lends itself to punning, but is otherwise not a problem. Good puns rely for their wit on using similarity of sound to evoke a *relevant*, but lexically unrelated, sense which is quite independent of ambiguity or polysemy, as when a silly ambitious feminist is described as 'a goose with delusions of gander'. Bad puns simply play on the similarity of sound with no particular relevance. This may be extremely clever, as in the well-known perfect rhyme of the French couplet in (4):

4   *Gal, amant de la reine, alla, tour magnanime,*
    Galamment de l'arène à la tour Magne, à Nîmes.

but has little trace of wit.

There is a clear intuition that necessity and inevitability have more in common than wine and sexual frenzy (at least linguistically), but is there a more solid basis for distinguishing these different kinds of ambiguity? The idea that polysemy refers to examples sharing the same meaning, while homonymy refers to examples with different meaning, gives a clue to our intuitions, but in the absence of clear criteria as to what constitutes sameness of meaning, does little more. Indeed, it still leaves unanswered the more basic question of whether we have ambiguity at all. Just because a word or sentence has two interpretations does not entail that it is ambiguous. Compare the ambiguous (5):

5   My son has grown another foot.

which, among other possibilities, can mean either that he is twelve inches taller or a freak, with the unambiguous (6):

6   My son has damaged his foot.

which, again among other possibilities (for instance, he may collect feet), can mean either that he has hurt his left foot or that he has hurt his right foot. Most people are reasonably sure that the last example is simply vague, but it would be nice to have a better reason than a popular vote.

To return to the examples with 'must', one immediate response is that there are grammatical reasons for differentiating them in this way: in one case, that of inevitability, 'must' is an auxiliary verb; in the other cases 'must' is a noun. Unfortunately, not only is this not entirely true: 'must' in (7):

7   A good head for heights is a must.

is a noun; it is irrelevant, unless one can substantiate the implicit claim that nouns with more than one meaning must be homonyms and that (auxiliary) verbs couldn't be. The latter claim might be defensible, the former is certainly false: the standard example of polysemy is 'mouth' as it pertains to humans and rivers.

A second common response is to appeal to etymology. Here as elsewhere the standard presupposition is that linguistics is pre-eminently about the origin of words and the (pre-)history of languages. Although only about one per cent of modern linguistics is actually about etymology, in this case it can be quite helpful. 'Must' in all its 'necessity' uses is indeed derived from the same source, namely Old English *moste*, with cognates in most of the Germanic languages, as for instance German '*müssen*'; whilst 'must' as in grapes comes from Latin *mustum*, 'new wine', and 'must' as in 'sexual frenzy' comes from the Urdu (ultimately the Persian) *mast* meaning 'drunk'. There is no historical connection between the vinous and the sexual meanings, despite the loose link with intoxication, just as there is no connection between either of these and the Cockney rhyming slang *elephant's* meaning 'drunk', (from 'elephant's trunk').

The reason etymology correlates with the dictionary entry is simple: dictionaries are generally constructed on 'historical' or etymological principles. However, this is inadequate as a general explanation for two reasons. First, linguistics is primarily interested in characterizing the knowledge of native speakers of a language, and generally only very few people have the etymo-logical knowledge necessary. Secondly, the criterion often does not work: that is, there are words which are etymologically connected which both dictionaries and our intuitions tell us should not be related, and conversely, there are words which are etymologically unconnected, which nevertheless fall together. Examples of the former kind are legion: 'guest' and 'host' are both derived from the Latin *hostis* (enemy); 'glamour' is originally the same as 'grammar': 'glamour' used to be used for a magic spell and owes its origin in 'grammar' to the belief that the occult was the exclusive preserve of the learned, in particular of the grammarian. We could do with some glamour and some magic in these days of cutbacks.

Examples where items should be associated despite their lack of etymological identity are harder to come by, if only because the received wisdom is that they are, by definition, not related and so are not remarked upon. However, folk etymologies and puns, however despised by the professional philologist, are good indications that the items (mis-)related are psychologically identified by the speaker; that is, they are related in his or her mental lexicon. Knowing what we do about bells and belfries, it is very hard not to make the assumption that the 'bel' bit of 'belfry' is related to 'bell', even though etymologically 'bell' is related to Old Norse *bjalla* and 'belfry' is related to the Middle High German *bercfrit* – 'fortified tower', and they have no historical connection. Similarly, nearly everyone appreciates that 'life depends on the liver' (or in French that '*La vie, c'est une matière de foi(e)*') without there being any etymological connection between the homophonous pairs 'liver' and 'liver' or 'foi' (faith) and 'foie' (liver) (pronounced the same despite the difference in spelling).

If etymology is not a reliable guide to meaning and the difference between polysemy and homonymy, there are other indicators which might prove more useful. First, however, note that 'must' as an auxiliary verb has traditionally been given at least three rather different interpretations. Consider the simple sentence in (8):

8   He must be unmarried.

In the rather high-flown parlance used by logicians, this can be construed as either *alethic* or *deontic* or *epistemic*. The first of these is what one has in (9):

9   John is a bachelor, so *he must be unmarried*.

appropriately used as a detective's deduction or the solution to a puzzle. This is the 'alethic' interpretation, (from the Greek for 'truth'), because it preserves the relation of entailment between sentences that differ only in containing either one of the items 'bachelor' and 'unmarried'. The second, epistemic, interpretation is exemplified by (10):

10 John always has plenty of spare time, *he must be unmarried.*

where the 'deduction' is not logically valid, but is a plausible assumption to add to our set of beliefs – 'epistemic' comes from the Greek for 'knowledge'. The third deontic, interpretation (from the Greek for a 'duty') can be seen in such examples as (11):

11 If John is to qualify for this job *he must be unmarried.*

In fact, as a glance at the *Oxford English Dictionary* or other major dictionary will show, this set of meanings or uses is by no means exhaustive. More interestingly, if one translates 'he must be unmarried' into French (*il doit être célibataire*) or German (*er muss unverheiratet sein*), the same range of interpretations is available, and French and German dictionaries have essentially the same range of headings for their equivalents of 'must' as do English ones. By contrast if one translates genuine homonyms into another language, the chance of their being identical is vanishingly remote. 'That *mould* is dangerous' will be translated completely differently depending on whether it is a fungus or a frame.

The criterion of translatability perhaps gives us a little guidance. Most ambiguities are lost in translation whereas a vaguely defined word with a wide range of interpretations will keep many of them in the other language. As usual, Shakespeare provides good examples. In his *double entendre* in (12), where Dromio is describing Nell as though she were a globe:

12 'Oh Sir, I did not look so low.'

'Low' can mean either 'low down spatially' or 'depraved', but its German equivalent, given in (13):

13 '*Oh Herr, so tief habe ich nicht nachgeschaut.*'

has only the former meaning, and the pun (however weak) is lost. On the other hand, if we take an example like the exchange between Emilia and Iago in (14):

14 *Emilia*: Do not you chide; I have a thing for you.
    Iago: A thing for me? It is a common thing.

the German translation in (15) retains the (obscene) dual interpretation of the English, because the vague 'Ding' has the same sexual connotations in German as the vague 'thing' does in English:

15 Emilia: *Sei nicht zu böse; hier ist ein Ding für dich.*
    Iago: *Für mich? Ein Ding woran sich jeder freut?*

Even so, the vagaries of usage make it hard to provide any hard and fast rule: different translators may exploit different associations, and in the present case may deliberately avoid 'indecent' translations. Moreover, even in the simple case of 'must' it is often impossible to use translatability, because not all languages have the relevant category, in this case of modal (auxiliary) verb; and the means used to render appropriate translations of the sentences in English (or French or German) may have to reproduce explicitly the implicit differences that we have teased out above.

At this stage, you might well ask whether it all matters. The answer will depend on whether you are attempting, on the one hand, to write a grammar (characterizing exclusively linguistic knowledge) or, on the other, to give a more general account of mental processes, including the pragmatic operations involved in the interpretation of utterances. It is again a question of linguistic versus non-linguistic knowledge. From the linguist's point of view, the relevant question is whether it is necessary to make any statement in the grammar, where of course the lexicon (or vocabulary) is a proper sub-part of the grammar, or whether the data can be predicted on the basis of other factors, e.g. encyclopaedic knowledge or general processing principles?

It is part of our general knowledge that we have two feet, so the indeterminacy between 'right' and 'left' of examples like (6), 'My son has damaged his foot', requires no account in the grammar, but can be left to extra-grammatical considerations. If, when we hear (6), it is irrelevant to us which foot is hurt, we simply construct a mental representation in which the afflicted appendage is indeterminate; if it is relevant we can seek further information. On the other hand, it is part of our lexical (hence linguistic) knowledge that 'foot' means both the thing at the end of your leg and a unit of measurement. Although the relationship between the two is transparent, there is no general principle of non-linguistic convention which enables us to predict one from the other. We have no unit of measure the 'thumb' (even though the French '*pouce*' means both 'thumb' and 'inch'). Hence we need an entry for both meanings of foot in our mental lexicon: entries which will provide the basis moreover for the syntactic differences between ordinary objects and measure phrases. 'My son has grown by another foot' is unambiguous, for instance.

How does this help with 'must'? It is clear that there is no way of predicting either of the meanings 'grape juice' or 'frenzy' from the other, despite the fact that we are invariably able to make connections between any pair of arbitrarily selected words in our language. Accordingly, each of these must be given an entry in our mental grammar. Similarly, we could not realistically expect to derive the meaning of the auxiliary 'must' from either of these, so that necessitates a third entry. The only reductive possibility is to lump all the 'necessary' uses of 'must' together, predicting the various differences (epistemic, deontic, etc.) from general principles. I shall take one particular example and see how this reduction might be made by having recourse to the Principle of Relevance. The following story is germane:

Castro visits Moscow and is taken on a tour by Brezhnev. First, they go for a drink and Castro praises the beer.

'Yes, it was provided by our good friends from Czechoslovakia.'

Next, they go for a ride in a car and Castro admires the car.

'Yes, these cars are provided by our good friends from Czechoslovakia.'

They drive to an exhibition of beautiful cut glass, which Castro greatly admires.

'Yes, this glass comes from our good friends in Czechoslovakia.'

'They must be very good friends,' says Castro.

'Yes, they must,' says Brezhnev.

Castro's last remark is to be interpreted epistemically: 'from everything I have seen and heard, there is massive evidence that the Czechoslovaks are very good friends', whereas Brezhnev's last remark is to be interpreted deontically: 'they have no option but to be good friends'. How could we derive this? For the sake of simplicity, let us restrict ourselves to these two possibilities – there is, after all, no evidence for an alethic interpretation. From our encyclopaedic knowledge, we know that Castro is dependent on his host, that one is normally polite in such circumstances, and that a deontic interpretation with its suggestion of menace would be inappropriate. Allied to the immediately preceding utterances, which are necessarily exploited in the interpretation of any sentence, this makes the epistemic gloss given overwhelming. What is more interesting is why the same epistemic interpretation is not supplied for Brezhnev's rejoinder. As a piece of silence-filling, corroborating what one's interlocutor has just said, this sentence does indeed lend itself to an epistemic interpretation, and it may well be that outside the artificial context of the joke, such a reading would be the first one arrived at and processing might stop. The punch-line of a joke, however, cannot end in such bathos and also satisfy the principle of relevance, so a further interpretation is called for. What Brezhnev literally affirms is the necessity of the proposition that the Czechoslovaks are good friends. The implication of that necessity: that it's not just evidentially forced but is a consequence of *realpolitik* is arrived at inferentially by the hearer.

A comparable process of inferencing, but leading to a quite different, ironic, interpretation accounts for the somewhat similar exchange in (16):

16   A: I went to Disneyland yesterday.
     B: That must have been fun.
     A: Yes, it must.

B's remark must again be interpreted epistemically, and again it is the final rejoinder that is of interest. This time, there is no possibility of providing a deontic interpretation, and an epistemic one is unlikely to satisfy the Principle of Relevance, because it is bizarre in much the same way that asking 'Am I happy?' is bizarre. (To enquire of someone else about one's own internal states is not impossible, but requires a very considerable elaboration of the context, and is correspondingly unlikely.) Given this, and the echoic nature of the repeated 'must', the natural interpretation arrived at is one of ironical dissociation from the proposition expressed by B.

What this implies in turn for the meaning of 'must' is that the various sub-headings provided at the beginning are unnecessary. Once one knows the syntactic category involved ('must' can be an auxiliary verb or a noun), and that its semantic force is 'necessity', everything else follows without further linguistic stipulation. One might expect that, if everything beyond the core meaning of 'necessity' follows from general principles, 'must' should have the same range of possible interpretations when used as a noun as when used as an auxiliary. Thus '. . . is a must' should be interpretable deontically as well as epistemically. In fact, the noun has only the deontic use, so that the subject of (17):

17   That John is unmarried is an absolute must.

corresponds only to the obligation sense of 'John must be unmarried' and cannot be used to reflect the result of our inferential processing.

This might seem problematic for the suggestion that everything beyond 'necessity' is derived pragmatically, but in fact it suggests that the basic, or default, meaning is deontic, and that the epistemic reading is secondary. It is not uncommon for derived forms of words to have only a subset of the readings available for the original form, and it is clear that the noun use of 'must' is derivative from the verbal reading. This suggestion would also be compatible with another mystery: the fact that 'must' has only a deontic reading when used in conditional clauses. 'If the candidate must be unmarried . . .' allows only one of the readings that are available for the simple 'the candidate must be unmarried'. Again, the complex construction allows only the basic meaning of the auxiliary: the only one that the grammar needs to specify.

So what *does* 'must' mean? Pretty much what common-sense would lead us to expect. There are separate lexical entries for the grape juice, for the randy pachyderm, and for the use of the auxiliary as a noun: you cannot replace 'must' by 'can' or 'ought' in (1b) or (17). But the triple of alethic, epistemic and deontic readings can, mercifully, be left unspecified, as the differences are arrived at on the basis of pragmatic interpretation in context. This common-sense result is, however, not without interest. One of the beauties of Relevance Theory is that it provides, with the Principle of Relevance, a reasoned basis for disambiguation. The examples of such disambiguation usually cited are typically rather gross: the difference between *admit* in the sense of 'let in' and in the sense of 'confess', for instance. The auxiliary examples here show that the theory copes equally happily with the much more subtle distinctions concocted by logicians. In most languages 'admit' would have two different translations (*hereinlassen* and *zugeben*, for instance). As far as I know, no language distinguishes with different lexical items the epistemic and deontic readings of 'must', but all languages allow one to draw such a distinction. Relevance Theory has completed another mammoth task.

Notes

p. 83   The 'good dictionaries' I used were Collins and the *OED*.

p. 83   The best source for ambiguity, and semantic relations in general, is Lyons (1977).

p. 84   The example in (4) is usually attributed to Victor Hugo. It occurs in a slightly different form in Redfern (1984: p. 100). It can be (literally) translated as: 'Gal, lover of the queen, went – a magnanimous walk/gallantly from the arena to the Magne tower at Nimes'.

p. 85   The Cockney rhyming slang example is from Franklyn (1975).

p. 86   For alethic, deontic and epistemic uses of the modals, cf. von Wright (1951). A more accessible discussion is provided by Palmer (1986).

p. 87   The Shakespearean example in (12) is from *The Comedy of Errors*, Act III, scene 2. The German equivalent in (13) is taken from the translation by Schlegel and Tieck. The English version is cited in Partridge (1955: p. 141). The example in (14), from *Othello*, Act III, scene 3, is discussed by Heinze (1977) who compares it with seven different German translations. The version in (15) is by Rothe. Most of the other versions miss the pun by translating 'thing' not by '*Ding*', but by '*etwas*'. Heinze comments more generally that 'wordplays dealing with sexually suggestive expressions are often translated literally, even though the equivalent German phrase renders them harmless' (p. iv).

p. 88 A language without modal auxiliaries is Nupe.

p. 89 The joke about Brezhnev and Castro is from Lukes and Galnoor (1987: pp. 52-3). The exchange about Disneyland was suggested to me by Annabel Cormack.

p. 89 Relevance Theory is expounded in Sperber and Wilson (1986a) and essays 7, 'Wilt Though have this Man to thy wedded Wife?' and 14 'In my Language we SHOUT'. Sperber and Wilson's treatment of irony (and interpretive use more generally) is in section 9 of chap. 4.

9

Y

Perhaps the major quest of modern linguistics is the search for universals. It is certainly the aspect of Chomsky's work which has fired the imagination of psychologists, which has revitalized the theory of innate ideas in philosophy, and which has brought linguistics to the forefront of the humanities. Talk of universals usually evokes such ideas at that of Deep Structure as a necessary level of representation in any grammar; the existence of nouns and verbs in all languages; the general need for conceptual categories such as 'physical object' in the semantic analysis of the vocabulary. In this essay my horizons are a little less ambitious: I want to look at the universal properties of 'Y'. This may seem trivial and irrelevant, but I hope to show that the issues involved are important and the method of argumentation essentially the same as when one is dealing with apparently weightier matters.

Any theory of grammar has to provide tools for the analysis of the sound systems of the world's languages. Phonological theory has accordingly developed a set of descriptive categories which can cope not only with the vowels and consonants of English but with the clicks of certain languages of Southern Africa, the tones of Chinese, and even the glottal exuberance of Cockney. At the heart of generative phonology – that is, the phonological part of a generative grammar – are distinctive features: a set of properties necessary and sufficient to characterize all the possible commonalities and contrasts in human languages.

Consider the consonants that can occur at the beginning of words in English. Restricting ourselves just to those which can immediately precede '–in' by themselves, we have *p*in, *t*in, *k*in, *ch*in, *b*in, *d*in, *g*in, *f*in, *s*in, *th*in, *w*in, *Y*in, and *M*in. By ringing the

changes on the sequences they precede or follow, we can establish
the following inventory of 'phonemes':

1	p		t	tʃ	k	as in: *p*in, *t*in, *ch*in, *k*in
	b		d	dʒ	g	as in: *b*ig, *d*ig, *j*ig, *g*ig
	f	θ	s	ʃ	h	as in: *f*in, *th*in, *s*in, *sh*in, *h*inder
	v	ð	z	ʒ		as in: *v*at, *th*at, la*z*e, lei*s*ure
	m		n		ŋ	as in: ra*m*, ra*n*, ra*ng*
	w		r l	j		as in: *w*att, *r*ot, *l*ot, *y*acht

This table is significant in being arranged not alphabetically, but
in the form standard in phonetics according to the place and
manner of articulation of the segments involved. Thus the top line
consists of 'stops' or 'plosives' (there is a complete stoppage of air
in the mouth during their articulation) which are moreover
voiceless; the second row are the same but voiced (the vocal cords
are vibrating during their articulation); the next two rows are
fricatives, voiceless and voiced respectively; the penultimate row
consists of nasals (i.e. the air escapes through the nose rather than
the mouth); and the final row are all 'sonorants'. Similarly, the
first column consists of sounds all of which are articulated with
the lips; the next two columns involve the front of the tongue
(they are not perfectly aligned in order to reflect the fact that the
tongue is involved in different ways in, say, [t] and [θ]), and the
last column includes sounds articulated with the back of the
tongue. (Again [h] is off to one side, as its pronunciation involves
no articulation with the tongue at all).

Each of the properties mentioned above is *prima facie* a
candidate for being a distinctive feature; so we have features such
as [voiced], [nasal], [sonorant] etc. each of which is traditionally
enclosed in [square brackets] and represented as being present or
absent by a '+' or '−', so [b] is [+voiced] where [p] is
[−voiced]; [m] is [+nasal] where [p] is [−nasal] and so on.
Distinctive features of this kind are said to be 'binary', each
allowing for the characterization of two classes of sound, and (if
there are n of them) jointly providing a description for 2^n
contrasts. That is, given two distinctive features one can describe
four $(=2^2)$ classes of sound; given three features one can describe
8 $(=2^3)$ classes, etc. So we can have sounds like [p] and [t] which
are [−voiced, −nasal], [b] and [d] which are [+voiced, −nasal],

[m] and [n] which are [+voiced, +nasal] and [m̥] and [ŋ̊] which
are [−voiced, −nasal]. These last do not occur in (adult) English,
but are common in the developing phonologies of young children,
and in the adult language of Burmese.

The justification for using distinctive feature theory is that it
provides a universal account of possible phonological segments,
systems and rules, and does so more elegantly and economically
than a theory just using phonemes. The major concept involved is
that of 'natural class': a class of sounds which can be
characterized by using a maximally economical description. Many
languages have rules which refer to the class of nasals. With
distinctive features this is described as the class having the
property [+nasal] which, in English means all and only the items
in the list [m,n,ŋ]. Take the form of the plural in regular English
nouns. There are three common predictably different pronunciations for the plural '−s' as found in 'cats', 'dogs' and 'horses'. In
'cats' (as in 'heaps', 'leeks', 'moths', and so on) it is pronounced
[s], voiceless like the [t] (or [p] or [k] or [θ]) immediately
preceding it. In 'dogs' (as in 'cubs', 'birds', 'lathes', and so on), it
is pronounced [z], voiced like the [g] (or [b] or [d] or [ð])
immediately preceding it. In 'horses' (as in 'fishes', 'witches',
'mazes', and so on) it is pronounced [iz], the vowel [i] being
present to separate the two 'strident' sounds which would
otherwise occur next to each other. The stridents are [s, z, ʃ, ʒ, tʃ,
dʒ]. By using distinctive features one can both describe this
situation simply: a [+voiced] sound is followed by a [+voiced]
sound; a [−voiced] sound is followed by a [−voiced] sound;
[+strident] sounds must be separated by a vowel; and do so using
the categories which are clearly articulatorily and perceptually the
appropriate ones. Listing the segments without reference to their
properties, as when one says that you get [s] after /p, t, k, θ/, but
[z] after /b, d, g, m, n . . . / and so on is accurate but
unilluminating. Moreover, the same kind of statements occur
again when one looks at the pronunciations of the past tense
'−(e)d' as exemplified in: 'walked', 'loved', and 'folded', though
the segments which are involved are slightly different for reasons
which should be clear after a little thought. As before we need
natural classes of voiceless and voiced segments, and also a class
consisting of /t/ and /d/: the alveolar plosives. This last class is
somewhat more complex than the others: it takes more features to

specify it, but it is still more natural than an 'unnatural' class like /t/ and /p/ which is extremely difficult to describe with distinctive features and is correspondingly predicted by the theory not to occur in the grammar of many (if any) languages.

The features so far used are fairly transparent, but the distinctions among the four places of articulation represented by /p, t, tʃ, k/ in English and other languages are usually described by reference to the slightly opaque features [coronal] and [anterior]. It should be clear that for four places of articulation we only need two features, so it would be unnecessary to have all of 'labial', 'alveolar', 'palato-alveolar' and 'velar' (the headings of the four main columns in (1) above). [+coronal] consonants are those like /t, d, s, z, θ, ð, r, l . . . / in English which are articulated with the front of the tongue; non-coronal or [−coronal] consonants are those like /p, b, m, k, g, h . . . / in English which are not so articulated. [+anterior] consonants are those like /p, t, m, f . . . / in English which are articulated in the front of the mouth; non-anterior or [−anterior] consonants are those like /tʃ, dʒ, k . . . / in English which are articulated relatively far back in the vocal tract. We accordingly have the four classes illustrated in (2):

2   [+coronal, +anterior] – e.g. t, d, s . . . i.e. dentals, alveolars
    [+coronal, −anterior] – e.g. tʃ, dʒ . . . i.e. palato-alveolars
    [−coronal, +anterior] – e.g. p, b, m . . . i.e. labials,
    [−coronal, −anterior] – e.g. k, g, h . . . i.e. velars, etc.

This arrangement should make it clear why /t/ and /d/, which are both [+coronal, +anterior], form a more natural class than /t/ and /p/ which differ in their specification for the feature [coronal]. To describe /t/ and /p/, while simultaneously excluding everything else, would necessitate postulating the unnatural class of 'either [+coronal . . .] or [−coronal . . .]'. In general, disjunctions of this kind are a sure sign that no generalization is being captured: either because there is no generalization, or because the theory is inadequate to capture it.

At last we have reached the problem. The fact that there are further places of articulation than the four accommodated here can be accounted for by exploiting other distinctive features, but as every sound has to be given a value for every feature, all the sounds of the language have to be categorized with respect to at least these two, and in some cases it is not at all clear what that characterization should be. In particular, what is 'Y'? The question may seem inconsequential, but if one is elaborating a theory which is supposed to provide a basis for a systematic and explanatory description of the world's languages, the assignment of sounds to categories must be rigorous, or the theory is not testable and hence not very interesting. It is uncontroversial that 'y' ([j] in the International Phonetic Alphabet) and other palatal consonants should be [−anterior]; the issue is whether they are [+coronal] or [−coronal]. Articulatorily, it is clear that the palatals are intermediate between the [+coronal] alveolars and palato-alveolars (/t, tʃ/ etc.) on the one hand and the [−coronal] velars (/k, g/ etc.) on the other. It would of course be possible to stipulate one way or the other that palatals should be ascribed to a particular class, but this would be to say that the matter was not empirical but purely definitional: that no data from any language could cause a revision in that assignment. However, it is possible to get evidence from languages to show that the choice is not arbitrary but should go in one particular direction, and more interestingly, in the same direction for all languages.

In their classic book *The Sound Pattern of English*, Chomsky and Halle categorized the palatals, including the /j/ at the beginning of English 'yes', as [−coronal]. This was a departure from the earliest work in distinctive features: in Jakobson, Fant and Halle's *Preliminaries to Speech Analysis* the palatals were described as [+coronal], but in neither case was any empirical phonological evidence given in support of the decision. I think there is good evidence that the earlier analysis was right and *The Sound Pattern of English* analysis wrong. The rest of this essay presents two radically different kinds of such evidence.

The first piece of evidence comes from language acquisition, specifically from the developing phonology of my elder son, Amahl, at the age of about two. One of the noticeable characteristics of his speech was a pervasive rule of consonant harmony, whereby alveolar and other consonants assimilated to the point of articulation of a following velar in the same word. Instead of saying 'duck', Amahl, like many other children, consistently said '*guck*', replacing the alveolar /d/ of the adult word with the velar 'g', so that both the consonants in the word had the same point of articulation for him: that is, they were in harmony. A wide range of other words were treated the same way, including such examples as those in (3):

3 dark   pronounced as *gark*   [gaːk]
   drink   "   *gick*   [gik]
   leg   "   *geck*   [gek]
   ring   "   *ging*   [giŋ]
   singing   "   *ginging* [giɲiŋ]
   thick   "   *gick*   [gik]
   jug   "   *guck*   [gʌk]
   snake   "   *ngake*   [ŋeːk]
   stuck   "   *guck*   [gʌk]
   taxi   "   *gaggy*   [gɛgiː]
   chocolate   "   *goggy*   [gɔgiː] (from 'chockie')

The other divergences from the adult form were regular and predictable, but are irrelevant to the current discussion. What is relevant is the precise set of consonants which underwent this process of consonant harmony. It was not the case that all consonants were harmonzied indiscriminately. For a number of words Amahl maintained the adult pronunciation for the relevant consonant or treated it quite differently, leaving it out altogether, for instance, so that we had the examples in (4), where the adult form again has a velar at the end of the word:

4 pig   pronounced as *bick*   [bik]
   bang   "   *bang*   [baŋ]
   back   "   *back*   [bak]
   fork   "   *walk*   [wɔːk]
   (all adult /f/s were pronounced as [w] at this time)
   Mike prounonced as *Mike* [maik]
   work   "   *work*   [wəːk]
   hook   "   *ook*   [uk]
   (all adult /h/s were left out at this time)

and so on. In terms of traditional phonetic labels, the classes which respectively did and did not harmonize were a pretty heterogeneous collection, but in terms of distinctive features, it was completely transparent that the relevant, and maximally

simple, characterization was in terms of [+coronal] as opposed to
[−coronal]. Every [+coronal] consonant which occurred before a
velar assimilated to that velar − without exception. Every
[−coronal] consonant which occurred before a velar failed to
assimilate − again without exception. What about 'y', the palatal
/j/? For Amahl there was no doubt: 'y' patterned with the
coronals, producing pronunciations like the following:

5   young pronounced as *gung*   [gʌŋ]
    yak   "   *gack*   [gak]
    yucca   "   *gugga* [gʌgə]

and so on.

The implication is clear. For the child, the consonants fall into
two complementary classes: those which harmonize in the
relevant environment and those which do not. The simplest
assumption one can make is that he identifies the two classes by
reference to some single simple property. (This is not necessary of
course, but good scientific practice demands that one takes the
simplest explanation compatible with the facts.) The only
property which is plausibly provided by current phonological
theory is the feature [coronal]. But if [coronal] is being used as
the crucial feature, then its definition must be such as to include
the palatals as well as the dentals, alveolars, palato-alveolars, etc.
The example is particularly cogent in that we can see the
language being manipulated before our eyes in a way which
would otherwise be opaque. It seems that Jakobson et al. were
right after all.

The second example is different in several respects: the
language is Ewe (a Kwa language of Ghana) rather than English;
it involves the adult language rather than language acquisition;
and the crucial process is not one in which coronal consonants
undergo some process, but one in which they constitute the
environment for some process.

It is well known that whereas English has a contrast between
/l/ and /r/, as seen in such pairs as 'law' and 'raw' or 'marrow'
and 'mallow', many languages do not: hence the usual weak jokes
about having a fright on Japanese Air Lines. Ewe is one language
which has no contrast between [l] and [r]. Though both sounds
occur, they are in 'complementary distribution': where one occurs

the other may not, and vice versa. In English 'clear' and 'dark' 'l'
are in complementary distribution, with clear [l] occurring before
a vowel and dark [ł] everywhere else. Thus although 'leaf' and
'feel' contain the same phonemes but in reverse order, the
pronunciation of the 'l' is different in the two cases. There is no
danger of misunderstanding if the two sounds are switched
because (as our spelling reflects) English has no contrast between
them, but the pronunciation would sound foreign.

In Ewe [l] occurs initially and after one set of consonants, as in
(6), while [r] occurs only after the other set of consonants, as in
(7),

6	ló	– crocodile
	gblɔ̀	– to talk
	kplé	– and
	blávè	– twenty
	klò	– knee
	mlɔ̀	– to sit
	flẽ	– to tear
	ɸle	– to buy
	gli	– wall
	ɣla	– to hide
	xlẽ	– to read
	ŋlɔ	– to write
	vlódodo	– contempt
7	sro	– horse
	tré	– calabash
	srɔ̃	– to learn
	adré	– seven
	dzre	– to fight
	tsró	– rind

The obvious generalization is that [r] occurs after a [+coronal]
consonant and [l] occurs everywhere else, including initially. This
time the interesting point is to discover what happens after a
palatal consonant. In fact Ewe has two palatal consonants: /j/
(like English 'y') and /ny/ (like French 'gn' in 'agneau' (lamb)),
both of which can occur in clusters of the relevant sort, giving
examples like those in (8):

8 yrá – to bless
   nyrẽ – to sharpen
   nyrã – to be wild

Again the implication is obvious: assuming that the distribution of
these sounds is determined as simply as possible, and exploiting
the distinctive features made available by the theory, we are
driven to the conclusion that [+coronal] must include rather than
exclude the palatals. That is, we have another piece of evidence
for the definition of one of the features from the universal set.

A couple of points need to be made to finish up. First, recent
theories of phonology have moved away from the classical theory
depicted in *The Sound Pattern of English* in a number of important
respects: in particular the reliance on binary distinctive features is
not as absolute as it used to be, and multi-dimensional statements
have replaced the simple linear ones described here. As far as I
can see, however, all current theories – autosegmental, dependency or whatever – all need a construct equivalent to the feature
[coronal], so the data presented here are still relevant to the
definition of its theoretical cousins. Secondly, the evidence given is
obviously not conclusive. It is perfectly conceivable that comparable arguments from the next twenty languages will all point in
the opposite direction, or in conflicting directions, with the
implication that the assumed simplicity of the processes described
was really chimerical. It may be that the child learning his first
language was using a more complex, list-like, basis for his
consonant harmony. It may be that speakers of Ewe have
internalized a grammar which needs a messy disjunction of
'either–or' statements to specify the distribution of [l] and [r]
correctly. In the absence of these other twenty pieces of evidence,
however, the hypothesis that the universal definition of coronal
should be such as to make it include the palatals is the best
available. These examples serve to show in microcosm how one
can construct an argument for a particular theoretical position,
which – in virtue of its role in theory construction – has universal
implications, on the basis of the detailed analysis of apparently
peripheral data.

Y is not as trivial as it looks.

Notes

p. 94   The discussion of universals and their role in theory construction is pervasive in Chomsky's work. For a summary, cf. Smith and Wilson (1979), esp. chap. 12.

p. 94   For the phonetic and phonological background presupposed here, cf. the Introduction, the Appendix and the Glossary in this book. The clearest introduction to phonology is Hawkins (1984).

p. 94   The best known click language is Xhosa (pronounced with an initial voiceless, aspirated lateral click). The languages with most phonemically distinctive clicks are the Khoisan languages, with up to 30 or more. Not unusually, the best first source for information on these languages is the *Encyclopaedia Britannica*, where the relevant part of the article on 'African Languages' is by the distinguished Africanist O. R. A. Köhler.

p. 94   On Chinese, cf. Newham (1971); on Cockney, cf. Wells (1982).

p. 96   On the presence of voiceless nasals in child speech, cf. Smith (1973) and essay 11, 'Lellow Lollies'. Amahl's pronunciation of his own surname was 'hmit' [m̥it]. On Burmese, cf. Ruhlen (1976).

p. 97   The distinctive features used here are those set out in Chomsky and Halle (1968).

p. 97   It is a slight simplification to say that all segments are specified for every distinctive feature. There are some features, [strident] for instance, which are irrelevant for vowels: it is physically impossible to have a strident vowel. However, all consonants are specified for the so-called 'major class' features [coronal] and [anterior].

p. 98   In Jakobson, Fant and Halle's book palatals were actually described as [−grave]. This corresponds exactly to [+coronal] in the Chomsky and Halle system.

p. 98   On Amahl's consonant harmony, cf. essay 4 'The Puzzle Puzzle'. For full details, cf. Smith (1973).

p. 100   On Ewe, cf. Smith (1968). The data are all from this article, from Ansre (1961), or from conversations with Gilbert Ansre, who patiently taught me some of his language.

p. 101   In the examples in (6) to (8), the following conventions apply:

′ an acute accent indicates a high tone
‵ a grave accent indicates a low tone
mid tones are unmarked
˜ indicates nasalization of the vowel over which it appears
'ɸ' is a voiceless bilabial fricative, in contrast with the labio-dental 'f'
'x' is a voiceless velar fricative

'ɤ' is a voiced velar fricative

'ŋ' has the same value as in English: a voiced velar nasal

'ɔ' is a half-open vowel, in contrast with 'o'

'kp' and 'gb' are phonemic units: voiceless and voiced coarticulated labio-velar plosives respectively

'ny', the palatal nasal, would be represented [ɲ] in the alphabet of the IPA.

On recent developments in phonology, especially of a non-linear kind, cf. van der Hulst and Smith (1982, 1985).

10

Time and Tense

What, then, is time? If no one asks me, I know: if I wish to explain
it to one that asketh, I know not . . .

St Augustine's puzzlement about the nature of time is more than
matched by the linguist's puzzlement about tense. Understand-
ably, because tense is supposed to 'indicate time', as the *Oxford
English Dictionary* puts it, but the indication is rarely unequivocal;
and to have an ambiguous hint about the inscrutable risks being
remarkably unhelpful. The problem resides in part in the
conceptual obscurity of time as a philosophical notion, but much
more in the fact that 'time' and 'tense' are both ambiguous and
tend to be used with unrivalled sloppiness.

At first sight there appears to be no problem: time is either
past, present or future, and languages have a 'tense' for each of
them. So we have the kind of contrast illustrated in (1):

1a The prime minister resign*ed*.
1b The people *are* happy.
1c There *will* be dancing in the streets.

where the morpheme '–ed' tagged onto *resign* shows that it is past,
'are' is the present form of the verb *be*, and 'will' marks futurity. If
the core of what you can expect from a theory of tense is that it
provide a means of determining for each utterance the time when
the event described in that utterance takes place, then we are not
doing too badly.

It is not always quite so straightforward. In (2):

2 Robyn *lectured* at four o'clock on Thursday.

we again have an apparent past tense 'lectured' identifying past
time. But in (3):

3   If Robyn *lectured* now I could sit back and relax.

the same item, 'lectured', seems to pick out the present or the immediate future, and in (4):

4   According to our original plans Robyn *lectured* next week.

the time indicated is unambiguously future.

Just as the single tense represented by 'lecture*d*' can refer to any of the three times – past, present and future, so can three different tenses all pick out the same time. For instance: in the last example '. . . Robyn lectured next week', the future is marked by 'lecture*d*', but we could equally well have the example in (5):

5   Robyn lectures next week.

with a 'present tense' verb, or (6):

6   Robyn *will* lecture next week.

with the 'normal' form for the future – the auxiliary 'will'. Clearly the adverbial 'next week' is responsible for our ability to construe these examples correctly, but comparable examples can be found without the helpful presence of such elements. In (7):

7   It's time we left.

the 'past' tense *left* is obligatory: it's unacceptable to say either 'It's time we leave' or 'it's time we shall leave', even though the time of leaving is clearly present or future. Similarly, in (8):

8   Jane tells me you're divorced.

the 'present' *tells* must be taken as referring to a past time. Even if this last example is interpreted as characterizing a habit of the egregious Jane ('Every time I see her, Jane tells me you're divorced') the telling must have been taking place in the past.

Some of the apparent difficulties are caused by the use of the same word 'tense' to refer either to a grammatical category or to a semantic category. As a grammatical term 'tense' is usually used to designate the set of endings you can add on to verbs: 'love, lov*es*, lov*ed*, lov*ing*' and so on. One of the roles of such endings is indeed to give some clue as to the time referred to in the sentences containing them – that is, to the semantic (or meaning) category of time, but they have a large number of other functions as well. We have glimpsed one of these already in the potentially habitual interpretation of 'Jane tells me you're divorced'. Habituality is one of a number of 'aspectual' distinctions most frequently associated with Russian and the other Slavonic languages, and more usually exemplified by the contrast between perfective (or completed) and imperfective (or ongoing) activity as in (9):

9a   Fred has eaten the banana.
9b   Fred is eating the banana.

The basic difference between tense and aspect (as categories of meaning) is that tense is 'deictic' whilst aspect is not. Deictic elements ('deictic' and its related noun 'deixis' come from the Greek for 'to show') are those like the personal pronouns, whose contribution to the meaning of a sentence is such that you need to know who the speaker is before you can evaluate its truth. So (10):

10   *I* am the president.

is true if uttered by George Bush and false if spoken by Jesse Jackson. Moreover, it is true if uttered in the United States of America, but false if uttered in the United States of Mexico, and is only true in the USA *now*. Person, time and place are thus linguistic categories which are sensitive to the context of utterance in a way that categories such as voice, aspect and mood are not. It makes no difference to the truth, as opposed to the style, of a sentence whether you couch it in the active or passive (the category of 'voice') as in (11):

11a   Fred was seduced by a mermaid.
11b   A mermaid seduced Fred.

Similarly, the claim in (12):

12   Thatcher treats her Cabinet colleagues like children.

is the same as the 'aspectually' different claim in (13):

13   Thatcher is treating her Cabinet colleagues like children.

in so far as it could be true or false independently of when, where or by whom it was said; and the palpable differences of 'mood' in (14a) and (14b):

14a   The queen demands that the princess leave.
14b   The queen demands that the princess leaves.

is in no way dependent on the speaker or the time or place of the speaking. (The latter suggests an element of habituality lacking in the former.) Each of these contrasts is carried in part by a difference in the endings on the verb, but only the use of these 'tense' endings to signal *time* differences is deictic.

Although it may be useful to separate out the genuinely temporal properties of 'tense' from other non-deictic properties, it hasn't really helped us very much with seeing how the form of a sentence enables us to identify the time of the event described, because we still have a many-to-many relation between inflectional endings and times to cope with. That is, given a 'past tense' form we may still find it indicates the future or the present, and a future interpretation may be compatible with any morphological tense. At this stage, the reaction may be irritation: given a sentence like (15):

15   Esme kissed me.

it is obviously possible to interpret it only as referring to the past; and given one like (16):

16   She loves me.

the only coherent construal is one in which the emotion obtains in the present. The somewhat perverse possibilities I constructed earlier were crucially dependent on the presence of other linguistic entities, in particular of temporal adverbials like 'tomorrow', 'next week', 'now', and so on. In fact each morphological 'tense' has what one might call a 'default' interpretation which holds unless it is overridden by the presence of some other stronger category, such as a deictic adverbial. What we need is then a specification of which other categories may override the default, and whether non-linguistic factors may also take precedence over the default interpretation associated with particular morphological forms.

We have already seen examples of the force of temporal adverbs like 'tomorrow' and 'yesterday'; of expressions like 'tell' or 'it's time', and of the effect of conditional clauses with *if*; but different temporal interpretations can be a function of the context in which a sentence is uttered as well as the form of the sentence itself. A simple example is provided by the choice between habitual and non-habitual interpretation. A sentence like (17):

17   Bill bullies his little sister.

is normally taken to be habitual, whereas another sentence with the same tense, such as (18):

18   Harpo admires Rembrandt.

is typically descriptive of a single state. The difference derives from the class of verb concerned: 'admire' is said to be 'stative' whereas 'bully' is 'dynamic' – a semantic contrast found in all languages and one which ultimately encodes a difference of temporal structure. As Lyons puts it in his classic work on semantics: a state

is conceived of as existing, rather than happening, and as being homogeneous, continuous and unchanging throughout its duration. A dynamic situation, on the other hand, is something that happens . . . [and] it may or may not be under the control of an agent.

Despite this universal contrast, virtually any sentence in English can have either a habitual or a non-habitual interpretation, dependent entirely on the context in which it is processed. It is sometimes difficult to dream up appropriate contexts, but the stage direction in *The Winter's Tale* – 'Antigonus leaves, pursued by a bear' is an example where a non-habitual reading is forced despite the usual interpretation of 'Antigonus leaves' as descriptive of a series of actions; and even 'Harpo admires Rembrandt' can be habitual, as witness the continuation 'whenever he thinks there is an appreciative audience'.

So far I have used 'time' exclusively to refer to the time at which the event described in the relevant sentence takes place. It is customary to distinguish this 'Event Time' (E) from the time of utterance of the sentence, usually referred to as 'Speech Time' (S), with past, present and future then being formally characterized as having E preceding S, being simultaneous with S, or following S respectively. Using a comma to indicate simultaneity, and left to right order to show temporal succession, we have the possibilities in (19):

19 Present: S, E   as in: John knows the answer.
    Past: E – S as in: John knew the answer yesterday.
    Future: S – E as in: John will know the answer tomorrow.

It was the insight of the distinguished philosopher Hans Reichenbach to realize as long ago as 1947 that the logic of temporal relations was so complex that a third notion of time was needed. He called this third notion of time 'Reference Time' (R), and used it to characterize what are traditionally referred to as the perfect tense, pluperfect tense, and so on. His system uses E, S and R, and the relations of simultaneity and succession to define thirteen possible 'tenses', supposedly sufficient to describe the tense systems of all the languages in the world. Some of the possible combinations can only be illustrated by slightly implausible sentences, but I think all the examples in (20) are both grammatical and acceptable:

20 E – R – S – He had eaten the pie.
    E, R – S – He ate the pie.
    R – E – S – He was going to eat the pie.
    R – S, E – Yesterday, he wanted to eat the pie now.
    R – S – E – Yesterday, he wanted to eat the pie tomorrow.
    E – S, R – He has eaten the pie.
    S, R, E   – He is eating the pie *or* He eats the pie.
    S, R – E – He's about to eat the pie.
    S – E – R – He will have eaten the pie by then.

S, E – R – Tomorrow it will be obvious that this is wrong.
E – S – R – Tomorrow he will have eaten the pie two days
     previously.
S – R, E – (Then) he will eat the pie.
S – R – E – He will be going to eat the pie.

The idea is that, in the first example for instance, the event of pie-eating took place not only before the time of utterance (Speech Time) but also before some reference point established either in the sentence or the context. Typically then this sentence would occur immediately after such a reference time had been fixed, as in (21):

21 When I caught up with him, he had eaten the pie.

R time is fixed by the clause 'When I caught up with him', which is itself *prior* to S time (as indicated by the past tense 'caught'), but *after* E time. All the other examples can be interpreted in a comparable fashion; it just takes a little patience to fit sentences to formulae. (It even takes a little patience to convince oneself that there really are only thirteen possibilities – work it out.)

Despite its ingenuity and the fact that for the first time Reichenbach provided a plausible analysis for sentences containing *have*, there are problems with this treatment. The formulae are supposed to provide a partial semantic representation for the corresponding sentences, with the probable implication that the truth conditions of the sentences could potentially differ if they are characterized by different formulae. However, if one takes pairs of sentences differing only by the position of R, they seem always to have the same truth-conditions. So 'E, R – S' and 'E – R, S', illustrated by 'he ate the pie' and 'he has eaten the pie' must in any situation be both true or both false. They might not, of course, both be appropriate or even grammatical. For most speakers of (British) English (22):

22 He ate the pie already.

is barely acceptable whilst (23):

23   He has eaten the pie already.

is fine; and for all speakers (24):

    24   He has eaten the pie yesterday.

is ungrammatical, whereas (25):

    25   He ate the pie yesterday.

is entirely normal. Despite the fact that the traditional equation of semantics with truth conditionality is no longer tenable, this suggests that the role of 'have' may be not so much semantic as pragmatic. In Reichenbachian terms 'have' marks R time as simultaneous with S time (for 'has') or before S time (for 'had'); in pragmatic terms it instructs the listener to access a *present* context. That is, the hearer is informed that to guarantee the optimal relevance of his interpretation, he must interpret an utterance containing 'have' in a context whose propositional content includes *now*. Recall that the context for the interpretation of an utterance is a set of propositions, marked among other things for time, and compare the two exchanges below between A and B in the context 'Anyone who writes a best-seller becomes extremely wealthy':

    26   A 'John wrote a best-seller (once).'
           B 'Yes, but that was ages ago; so it's irrelevant.'
    27   A 'John has written a best-seller (*once).'
           B 'Yes, but that was ages ago; so it's irrelevant'.

In the second exchange A could feel justifiably piqued at B's response, as it directly contradicts the current relevance of his remark, made explicit by the choice of 'has written' rather than 'wrote'.

A pragmatic theory (specifically the Theory of Relevance) can also account for the disambiguation of the (unexpectedly) ambiguous example (28):

    28   If John speaks he has lost.

where the times of the two events described: 'John's speaking' and

'John's losing' may occur in either order. This sentence could be used to inform your interlocutor indirectly of either of two distinct rules of a game, either 'If one speaks during a game one is therefore disqualified' or 'The loser of a game is the one who has to announce the result of that game to the adjudicator'. (Both of these rules are actually true of some forms of tournament chess). In the former case, John's speaking *causes* his disqualification and hence must precede his losing; in the latter case, John's speaking is *evidence* for his having already lost, and hence follows his losing.

Both 'John speaks' and 'he has lost' are morphologically present tense, and neither contains a deictic adverb or other marker of Reference Time that would force a particular sequential reading, so an interpretation in terms of either causation or evidence will be entirely determined by the Principle of Relevance. This in turn will operate differently in different contexts. If the game is manifestly over and hence the proposition that 'the game is over' is part of the context, then an evidential reading will be the only appropriate one, and hence the temporal sequence of events must be such that the losing precedes the speaking. If the game is manifestly still in progress and hence the proposition that 'the game is in progress' is part of the context, then only the causal reading will be accessible, and hence the sequence of events must be one where the speaking precedes the losing. In either situation, it may also be the case that the hearer interprets the utterance either habitually or non-habitually as well.

To work out when something you are told about happens, it is necessary to take account not only of the structure of the sentence: its morphologically marked tense, the presence of adverbials, the use of particular verbs, the deployment of conditional markers such as *if*, and so on, but also of the context in which that sentence is uttered, in particular, the immediately preceding utterance, and information provided by the physical environment. In other words the phenomena of time and tense are both linguistic and pragmatic.

It is not surprising that Augustine had a hard time with time: his theology was pretty advanced but his linguistic theory was minimal, and Pragmatic Theory hadn't even been invented.

Notes

p. 105   Some of the examples and discussion in this essay have been modified from Smith (1981b).

p. 105   Augustine's remark has been widely quoted: cf. e.g. Gale (1968: p. 40).

p. 107   On aspect, especially in the Slavonic languages, cf. Comrie (1976).

p. 107   The most systematic treatment of tense, aspect and mood is in Lyons (1977: vol. 2). The quotation on states and dynamic situations is from p. 483.

p. 110   Reichenbach's innovatory analysis appeared first in his (1947). It has been widely adopted and adapted since: cf. e.g. Smith, C. (1978), Hornstein (1977).

p. 111   On the status of truth conditions in semantic theory, cf. Ladusaw (1988: pp. 103f). More and more phenomena which used to be considered 'semantic' are yielding to pragmatic treatment.

p. 112   For discussion of the correct division of labour as between semantics and pragmatics, cf. Kempson (1988).

p. 112   On the context for interpretation, cf. Sperber and Wilson (1986a) especially ch. 3, and essay 7 above, 'Wilt Thou have this Man to thy wedded Wife?'.

p. 112   Example (28) is discussed in both Smith (1981b) and Smith (1983b).

11

Lellow Lollies

In linguistics as in politics, revolutions breed animosity as well as new ideas, with the partisans of each side indulging in hostilities against the enemy. While many linguists would dearly love to rid the earth of their rivals, less extreme measures are usually resorted to, with the combatants restricting themselves to vilification and verbal sniping. In attacks on theoretical rivals, one of the favoured strategies is to accuse one's opponent of being 'empirically irresponsible' or 'theoretically vacuous' (or both). Such attacks presuppose that there are standards available by reference to which one can judge the adequacy or inadequacy of a linguistic analysis, and, indirectly, the linguistic theory which has made that analysis possible.

What is thought to be an 'adequate' account of some domain will depend on the perceived satisfactoriness of the explanations that are provided for the data in that domain. Moreover, as people's perceptions differ, and as analyses become deeper with increasing insight, it is in principle impossible for anyone to achieve a final victory: yesterday's explanations, like yesterday's weapons systems, however sophisticated they seemed to be when they were invented, will always be seen as inadequate for tomorrow's battles. Furthermore, a device which is adequate for the solution of one problem may be useless when confronted by a different one.

As part of his attempt to seek explanations and go beyond the mere amassing of mountains of partially understood data, Chomsky introduced a hierarchy of three 'levels of adequacy' which grammars and theories should aim to achieve: 'observational, descriptive and explanatory adequacy'. A grammar is *observationally adequate* if it recapitulates the observed data explicitly: i.e. it is essentially a representation of facts. A grammar is *descriptively adequate* if it attains observational adequacy for a significant range of cases and gives a characterization of the data in psychologically valid terms. A theory is *explanatorily adequate* if it allows a reasoned choice among competing descriptively adequate grammars.

An intuitive feel for this progression can be derived from the consideration of so-called 'strong' and 'weak' forms of the kind in (1) to (3):

1a   I am the greatest.
1b   I'm the greatest.
2a   Cindy is sulking.
2b   Cindy's sulking.
3a   Fred *can* wiggle his ears.
3b   Fred can wiggle his ears.

where the second (b) form is in each case a 'weakened' form of the first (a) form. In the case of (1) and (2) the weak form is explicitly marked in English orthography by the use of the apostrophe to indicate the loss of the relevant vowel. In the case of (3) there is no orthographic reflex of the pronunciation difference, but in (3a) the vowel in 'can' is the same as that in 'hat'; in (3b) it is normally pronounced as a schwa, ([ə]), i.e. like the first vowel in 'above'.

Not all the words of English apparently eligible to participate in these changes show this kind of alternation between strong and weak forms – the 'can' in 'It was Nicolas Appert who taught the world how to *can* food' is unable to change – and a simple listing of the full range of possibilities, of the kind given in standard textbooks of pronunciation, achieves observational adequacy. This is not a trivial achievement. To compile such a list necessitates not only scouring a vast number of texts and checking the results with native speakers (including oneself, if one is a native speaker of the language in question), but also exploiting a sophisticated notational system to indicate the correct pronunciation, elaborating some notion of relatedness, so that 'am' is related to ''m' and 'is' to ''s' rather than the other way round, and perhaps giving some guidance as to when weak or strong forms should be used.

To proceed to descriptive adequacy it is necessary to give an explicit account of the distribution of weak forms. This turns out to be somewhat complicated for a number of reasons, of which the most serious is explaining why the weak form is sometimes impossible, as in (4):

4a John is planning to come at the same time as I am.
4b *John is planning to come at the same time as I'm.

It is perfectly acceptable to say either 'John is planning . . .' or 'John's planning . . .'; and if the sentence is continued, the result is again acceptable, as seen in (5):

5 John's planning to come at the same time as I'm planning
   to go

An obvious hypothesis to try out is that weak forms cannot occur at the end of the sentence: this would account for the contrast in (4) and (5) as well as a number of other examples, but it would fail with (6):

6a John is planning to come tomorrow at the same time as I
    am today.
6b *John is planning to come tomorrow at the same time as
    I'm today.

where the weak form is completely impossible even though it is not in final position. In fact the reason is both more complex and more interesting, requiring an analysis of the syntactic position in which the potentially weak form finds itself. The main difference between (5) and (6) is that in (5) the verb 'planning' is repeated in both halves of the sentence, whereas in (6) it is left implicit or understood. Within generative grammar this implicit verb is represented explicitly by an 'empty category', written 'e', which is present in the syntactic structure. It must in fact be present in the syntactic structure in order for the sentence to conform to a universal principle (the 'Projection Principle'), which insists that all information about lexical structure be explicitly represented. In this case the relevant information is the fact that the auxiliary 'be' (in the form *am*) has to be followed by a verb phrase. Thus the structure of (6b) would be represented in part as in (7):

7   John is planning to come tomorrow at the same time as I
    am e today.

where the 'e' stands in for the sequence 'planning (to come)'. The
reason why weak forms are impossible in (4b) or (6b) is that they
are excluded from appearing next to empty categories.

There is interesting corroboration of this analysis in the (non-)
occurrence of weak forms in indirect questions of the kind in (8):

8a   Tell me whether the party's tomorrow.
8b   Tell me where the party is tomorrow.
8c   *Tell me where the party's tomorrow.

There is a striking difference between the possibility of having a
weak form ' 's' for 'is' when the indirect question is introduced by
'whether' and the impossibility of that weak form when the
indirect question is introduced by 'where' (or 'when'). Standard
generative analyses of questions (both direct and indirect) involve
an analytic stage in which the temporal 'when' or locative 'where'
occurs immediately adjacent to the verb 'be': their structure is
comparable to that which shows up overtly in so-called 'echo-
questions', used to express incredulity or bewilderment, of the
kind in (9):

9a   The party's *where* tomorrow?
9b   The party's *when* tomorrow?

In (8), the item 'where' (similarly 'when') has been removed from
this position to the front of the embedded clause. That is, the
structure of (8b) would be as in (10):

10   Tell me where the party is e tomorrow.

with, again, an empty category adjacent to the 'is' blocking the
possibility of a weak form. Scepticism about this analysis might be
tempered by the observation that echo questions with 'whether' in
place of 'where' or 'when' are completely impossible:

11   *The party's whether tomorrow?

'Whether' is always in clause-initial position and never occurs after 'be' in the way that 'when' and 'where' do; correspondingly, there is no evidence for an empty category after 'is' in examples like (8a) or (11), and hence nothing to stop the appearance of the weak form in (8a).

There are other aspects to a complete treatment of the syntax and phonology of 'weak' forms, but it should be clear what kind of considerations need to be taken into account to achieve descriptive adequacy. We have gone beyond a phonological statement, taking cognizance (in this example) of syntactic conditions too; where, moreover, the productivity and independent motivation of these syntactic factors indicate that the analysis is psychologically real – a correct reflection of our mentally represented grammar.

To progress to explanatory adequacy is harder still; in particular, because only general *theories* rather than individual *grammars* can attain this level anyway. We should be encouraged in our pursuit, however, by the failure of the hypothesis that it was occurrence in sentence-final position that blocked the appearance of weak forms. We have seen elsewhere that grammatical rules are typically structure-dependent. Empty categories are part of the structure of a sentence in a way that 'final position' is not, so an account which depends crucially on empty categories is more likely to derive from an explanatorily adequate theory than an account which depends on notions like 'final'. To get a little closer to explanatory adequacy, it is helpful to consider a further property of the preceding explanation for the distribution of the examples in (6) to (11) – its 'directionality'.

When we speak, we start with some kind of thought which, mediated by the syntax, gets converted into a stream of sounds. When we listen, we start with the stream of speech sounds and interpret them as a sentence which then serves as the basis for inferring what the speaker intended us to understand. These procedures are clearly *not* reflected in the structure of the (competence) grammar, which is *neutral* as between speaker and hearer. There is nevertheless a sense in which certain components of this competence grammar have precedence over others: specifically, the statement of some rules and principles requires access to information from other components of the grammar, whereas the reverse is not the case. For instance, the principle of subjacency illustrated in essay 3, 'Grammar and Gravity' above, can only be formulated if one already has some idea of Phrase Structure, whereas one can develop a great deal of Phrase Structure without making any reference to subjacency. The 'directionality' in such cases is logical rather than temporal; it belongs to competence rather than performance. In the same way, syntactic rules and principles have logical precedence over phonological ones. That is, the theory of grammar makes the strong, falsifiable, claim that in the grammar of no language will it turn out to be desirable or necessary to formulate the rules of the syntax so that they refer to phonological information, but it will repeatedly be the case that the rules of the phonology need to refer to syntactic information.

In the current case, the phonological rule relating the forms 'am' to ''m', 'is' to ''s', and so on, (a rule usually referred to as vowel reduction) has to make use of syntactic information, the location of an empty category, in order to account optimally for the facts. By contrast, it would be impossible to formulate a rule of the syntax to take account of phonological information. For instance, it is not just an accident that neither English nor any other language constrains the operation of passivization so that only words beginning with 'p' can be moved: such a rule would be logically possible but is excluded by the form of the theory.

When account is taken both of the structure dependence of the statement of the distribution of weak forms, and of the crucial exploitation of the 'priority' of syntax, we can hope that our theory is beginning to achieve a level of explanatory adequacy which makes possible the choice of a descriptively adequate grammar which can handle these facts. Real explanation only comes when our theory enables us to explain how it is that native speakers come to concur in their rather subtle judgements of such examples as (6): presumably few parents coach their offspring on such matters, and the direct evidence is both hard to hear and infrequently come across. We have then a classic example of the 'poverty of the stimulus': the child ends up knowing more than he or she has obviously been able to learn. 'Explanatory adequacy' is accordingly often referred to as 'acquisitional adequacy': that is, the theory needs to be able to explain how children are able to acquire their first language on the basis of minimal evidence.

Equivalently, how does the child (or the theory) select the correct
grammar out of the myriad grammars compatible with the facts?

Solving this 'logical problem of language acquisition' is taken to
be the ultimate task of linguistic theory, and as a second example
of the kind of progression illustrated for weak forms, I would like
to revisit 'The Puzzle Puzzle' (see essay 4 above) and try to show
the same kind of gradation using developmental data.

Recall that at the age of two or so Amahl, like many young
children, had the following divergences from the adult pronunciation of the words he was learning: (the adult form is given
on the left, and to the right of the arrow is given Amahl's
pronunciation in both English orthography and in the alphabet of
the International Phonetic Association):

12a	duck	→ *guck*	=	[gʌk]
	drink	→ *gick*	=	[gik]
	ring	→ *ging*	=	[giŋ]
	snake	→ *ngake*	=	[ŋeːk]
	zebra	→ *weeber*	=	[wiːbə]
	knife	→ *mipe*	=	[maip]
	nipple	→ *mibbu*	=	[mibu]
	stop	→ *bop*	=	[bɔp]
12b	broken	→ *boogoo*	=	[buguː]
	open	→ *ooboo*	=	[ubuː]
12c	green	→ *geen*	=	[giːn]
	blue	→ *boo*	=	[buː]
	brush	→ *but*	=	[bʌt]
	new	→ *noo*	=	[nuː]
	bump	→ *bup*	=	[bʌp]
	tent	→ *dent*	=	[det]
	Smith	→ *mit*	=	[mit]
	bird	→ *beebeep*	=	[biːbiːp]
12d	mash	→ *mat*	=	[mat]
	mat	→ *mat*	=	[mat]
	match	→ *mat*	=	[mat]
	mass	→ *mat*	=	[mat]
12e	eye	→ *eye*	=	[ai]
	eyes	→ *eye*	=	[ai]
	cheese	→ *dee*	=	[diː]
12f	lorry	→ *lolly*	=	[lɔliː]

yellow → *lellow* = [lelo]
hello → *'ellu* = [elu:]

Again, an exhaustive listing of all the child's deviations from the adult norm would attain observational adequacy. Again, even this is not a trivial achievement, as it presupposes meticulous data collection and a considerable amount of phonetic and phonological analysis to establish precisely what range of sounds and contrasts the child has mastered.

To proceed to descriptive adequacy it is necessary to exploit the rule-governed nature of the relationships between the adult and child forms so that one can make predictive statements about how the child will pronounce new words he has never heard before. To do this entails formulating all the rules that the child gives evidence of using productively and constituting them into a kind of grammar of phonological development. The examples in (12a) involve the regular assimilation of a coronal consonant to a following velar ('duck, drink, ring, snake') or labial ('zebra, knife, nipple, stop'); those in (12b) involve the harmonization of the two vowels; (12c) gets rid of the second of two consecutive consonants ('l' in 'blue', 'r' in 'green' and 'brush', 'y' in 'new', 'w' in 'bird' (what he was trying to say was really 'tweet-tweet'!), or the first of two consecutive consonants ('n' in 'tent', 'm' in 'bump', 's' in 'Smith'). The examples in (12d) involve a rule merging several different consonants in the adult language; those in (12e) one losing final /z/; that in (12f) a rule changing 'r' and 'y' (but not 'h') to 'l'.

Constructing such a grammar takes even more work, but it is still too simplistic. One of the major lessons of the linguistics of the past decade has been that multiplying rules is only a means to an end, it is not an end in itself. The end is to explain how and why it is those particular rules the child appears to use; to discover what kind of rules are possible universally; and ideally to eliminate them in favour of general principles.

One step towards the achievement of explanatory adequacy is taken by reducing the plethora of rules in the previous paragraph to the status of incidental side-effects of universal principles. As spelt out in 'The Puzzle Puzzle', all the rules listed here (and all the rest) were instantiations of such principles: a tendency to maximize vowel and consonant harmony; a tendency to reduce clusters of consonants to a single item; a tendency to simplify the overall system by merging contrasts of the adult language; and a tendency to reflect grammatical simplification. The last of these is another instance of where the explanation for a phonological fact comes from a different sub-theory of the grammar. Amahl's failure to pronounce the final consonant in 'eyes' was nothing directly to do with his phonological system, but a function of his lack of a singular/plural distinction in the syntax. The pronunciation of 'cheese' without the /z/ was a result of his assumption that 'cheese' was really a plural too.

A second step in the same direction can be taken by showing that superficially unexpected changes in the child's pronunciation over time are a natural consequence of formal properties of the grammar attributed to him. Theories differ in the details of the technical apparatus they provide (in their weaponry, if we extend the analogy to war that we started with). Transformational grammar uses Phrase Structure rules and Transformations; Generalized Phrase Structure Grammar uses Phrase Structure rules but no Transformations; Word Grammar uses neither. Generative Phonology uses a rather complex array of feature-changing rules which can be exemplified in the present case by the account provided for the child's merging of words like 'pit' and 'bit' as [bit]. This absence of a voicing contrast in his speech (he had voiced sounds – like [b, d, g] at the beginning of words and voiceless ones – like [p, t, k] at the end) was most easily described by formulating the rule in (13):

13   [+consonantal] → [+voiced]

that is, all consonantal segments in the adult language, whether voiced or voiceless, are voiced as far as the child's phonology is concerned. (The difference between initial and final consonants is described by a separate rule which I ignore here.)

One particular aspect of the development of Amahl's pronunciation looked initially somewhat complex and surprising, but on inspection turned out to be a natural consequence of the formal *simplification* of a rule like (13). The phenomenon involved is the gradual mastery of the voicing contrast over a period of about nine months, and can be best elucidated by listing Amahl's pronunciations for the same group of words at three different times, as shown in (14):

14	T_1		T_2		T_3	
pit	→	[bit]	pit	→	[pit]	pit	→	[pit]
bit	→	[bit]	bit	→	[bit]	bit	→	[bit]
spit	→	[bit]	spit	→	[pit]	spit	→	[pit]
Smith	→	[mit]	Smith	→	[mit]	Smith	→	[m̥it]
snake	→	[ŋeːk]	snake	→	[neik]	snake	→	[ŋ̊eik]
			slug	→	[lʌg]	slug	→	[ɬʌg]

His pronunciation at T_1 is accounted for (in the relevant respects) by a rule deleting adult /s/ before a consonant, and by the rule in (13). The pronunciation at T_2 is accounted for in part by the same rule deleting /s/ and the *loss* of rule (13): that is, he now distinguishes 'pit' and 'bit' just as the adults around him do. This still ignores one aspect of his pronunciation: the fact that he equates 'spit' with 'pit' rather than with 'bit'. Phonetically the 'p' in 'spit' is half-way between the /p/ in 'pit' and the /b/ in 'bit', but there was no doubt that at T_2 it was identified with /p/ rather than /b/. To accommodate this fact, it was necessary to postulate another rule, (15):

15   [+consonantal, −sonorant] → [−voiced] /#s ——

which makes non-sonorant consonants after initial /s/ voiceless. The specification '[−sonorant]' is necessary to ensure that examples like 'Smith, snake' and 'slug', with a 'sonorant' consonant after the /s/, were excluded from the purview of the rule, as they remained voiced.

It was at T_3 that there appeared a number of unexpected pronunciations. Amahl started at this stage to produce words like 'slug' and 'slip' with the voiceless lateral sound found in the Welsh pronunciation of 'Llanelli': a sound he could never have heard in any of the English words uttered around him. Moreover, he simultaneously produced words like 'Smith' and 'snake' with voiceless nasals: again sounds not found in English though they occur frequently enough in Burmese and Nahuatl (the language of the Aztecs). This apparently bizarre development (one in fact not uncommon in child language) is accounted for by the formal simplification of rule (15): specifically, the omission of the feature specification [−sonorant] from (15) will ensure that the rule applies to 'Smith' and 'snake' just as it did to 'spit'. In other words an apparent complication in the child's development is seen to be the result of a simplification, given the kind of rule system provided by the theory. To the extent that such phenomena can be multiplied and validated they indicate that our theory is approaching explanatory adequacy.

Unfortunately, the Generative Phonological armamentarium is not always so acquisitionally adequate. On the one hand the system is so rich that it can describe innumerable phenomena that in fact never occur: simply reversing the plusses and minuses in all the rules mentioned would give a depressingly convincing example; on the other hand there are common processes which the formalism is incapable of describing simply, and hence cannot hope to *explain* at all.

An example of this last type has been emphasized by Spencer in an interesting attempt to use a reanalysis of Amahl's data to argue for the greater adequacy of an Autosegmental Theory *vis-à-vis* traditional Generative Phonology.

Autosegmental Phonology started from the observation that some processes – especially 'suprasegmental' phenomena of stress and intonation – were 'autonomous' (hence the name) of the sequences of vowels and consonants they were associated with. One can specify a falling or rising intonation independently of the string of segments it ranges over and, more importantly, the changes that such tones undergo may in many instances be unaffected by the nature of those segments. Accordingly, in Autosegmental Theory statements about stress and pitch are given on an 'autosegmental tier' independent of the tier on which statements about consonants and vowels are made. Precisely which properties of the total phonological description are autonomous in this way is an interesting empirical question, which is the subject of considerable research.

Spencer suggested that to account for the kind of 'lateral harmony' found in (12f) above (i.e. where all the consonants in the child's pronunciation are the lateral /l/), it is desirable to separate off 'laterality' from the other consonantal features. One advantage of this treatment is that it avoids the imposition of a left-to-right order on the process involved: in 'yellow' (pronounced as [lelo]), the harmony 'spreads' from the right to the left, in 'lorry' (pronounced as [lɔli:]) the harmony spreads from left to right. In traditional Generative Phonology this could only be described by using two different rules, but the process is clearly a unitary one that should be described by a single rule. Separating off laterality autosegmentally and associating it with all the consonants involved at one fell swoop neatly captured this unitariness.

The same idea also solved a further problem. One of the less common and more puzzling of Amahl's pronunciations was illustrated by the words in (16):

16   queen   → *geem* = [giːm]
     twice   → *dife* = [daif]
     quick   → *gip* = [gip]
     squeeze → *geep* = [giːp]

where the final consonant of the adult word ends up as a labial ([m], [f] or [p]) in the child's speech, presumably because of the /w/ following the *initial* consonant in the input. Intuitively this is another case of consonant harmony, though as the post-consonantal /w/ disappeared in Amahl's speech, this is not immediately obvious. By detaching 'labiality' from the sequence of segments and giving it its own autosegmental tier, Spencer was able to simplify the statement of the process. More interestingly, this separation predicted correctly that the child's ability to produce consonant clusters involving a /w/ should emerge at the same time as the disappearance of the pronunciations in (16). Under the original description this simultaneity was simply an accident.

These facts and their analyses may seem esoteric and the theoretical differences they have prompted arcane; but just as the arms race advances by each side making minor improvements to the strength of its armour or the power of its missiles, so does the war between theories progress by first one side and then the other proving itself more adequate at providing explanations for common problems, by building more sophisticated devices which can achieve the same (or better) results with a lower expenditure of effort. Since the technical innovations of the 1950s and 1960s in both syntax and phonology, everyone has been able to describe the facts somehow or other, just as on the world stage we have all been able to destroy each other. Progress in theory construction involves deepening our understanding by devising new or improved explanations, or by having recourse to new domains of evidence.

How to account precisely for why a two-year-old says 'lolly' for 'lorry' may seem an odd point of departure for new theoretical insight, and it's a pity that much of the abusive argumentation in linguistics is also at the two-year-old level, but at least these nursery wars stimulate intellectual progress rather than mutual annihilation.

Notes

p. 115 For a good account of one particular series of hostilities cf. Newmeyer (1980). His chapter documenting the downfall of 'Generative Semantics' is in fact entitled 'The Linguistic Wars'.

p. 115 Both the accusations quoted are from Givón (1979: p. 44): a particularly vitriolic attack.

p. 115 Chomsky introduced the idea of 'levels of adequacy' in his (1964b). Cf. also his (1965) and Smith and Wilson (1979) esp. chap. 11.

p. 116 For 'schwa' and the other technical vocabulary used in this essay, cf. the Appendix.

p. 116 A good traditional survey of weak forms is given in Gimson (1962: pp. 239-43).

p. 117 The first person to relate the possible occurrence of weak forms with the presence of empty categories (or 'deletion sites' in the terminology of the day) was King (1970).

p. 117 For empty categories in current theory, cf. Chomsky (1986).

p. 119 'Whether' may occur immediately after 'be', as in 'It could be whether he's going to be invited to the party'. Even in such a sentence 'whether' is the initial element of its own clause and not the complement of 'be'.

p. 119 For structure dependence, cf. Chomsky (1972), and essay 6 'The Oats have eaten the Horses'.

p. 120 For subjacency, cf. essay 3, 'Grammar and Gravity' and references therein.

p. 120 For the passive, cf. essay 18, 'Linguistics as a Religion'.

p. 121 'The logical problem of language acquisition' is the subtitle of Hornstein and Lightfoot (1981), *Explanation in Linguistics*.

p. 121 It is perhaps surprising that developmental data are no more relevant to the logical problem of language acquisition than data drawn from adult language. There is no *a priori* weighting of different types of evidence here or elsewhere: cf. Chomsky (1980a) for discussion. It is none the less clear that developmental or 'acquisitional' data are no less relevant than other kinds.

p. 121 For further discussion of the data in (12), cf. essays 4 'The Puzzle Puzzle' and 9 'Y'. All the data come originally from Smith (1973).

p. 122 On rules vs principles, cf. Chomsky (1986), Smith, N. (1988).

p. 123 'Generalized Phrase Structure Grammar' eschews all transformations but deploys a wider range of categories and features than 'Transformational' Grammar. The standard reference is Gazdar et al. (1985).

p. 123 'Word Grammar' is a form of Dependency Grammar which makes minimal use of the notion 'constituency'. The standard reference is Hudson (1984).

p. 124 The progression shown in (14) is taken from Smith (1973: pp. 156f). 'Slug' was not attested at T_1.

p. 124 With regard to the voiceless laterals, it is perhaps relevant to point out that Amahl heard only English and Hindi in his early years. Neither contains such sounds. For details of his linguistic background, cf. Smith (1973: pp. 7–8).

p. 125 On the richness of the descriptive system, it is important to stress the need for limiting the power of the theory. The aim is to characterize the notion 'possible human grammar', so it is essential not only that all possible grammatical rules and principles can be described, but also that no impossible ones can be. To pursue the military analogy, it would be excessive to use tactical nuclear weapons to quell an inner city riot. It would doubtless be successful, but something a little more subtle would be preferable.

p. 125 Spencer's reanalysis is the subject of his (1986).

p. 125 For Autosegmental Phonology in general, cf. van der Hulst and Smith (1982, 1985), Goldsmith (1979).

p. 126 Spencer's suggestions are clearly still not the last word: there are many problems with his account, not least the status of the rule associating 'labiality' with the appropriate consonant. The arms race continues.

12

Data, Evidence and Theory Change

According to Mr Gradgrind, 'facts alone are wanted in life', and there is a common belief that the heart of science involves amassing a large collection of facts and accounting for them by postulating general laws. If, however, one is asked 'What is a fact?' the answer will depend to a large extent not only on the domain of interest but on one's theory about that domain. Gregory gives the example of an archaeological dig, where decisions about whether holes located on the site are to be catalogued as 'post-holes' made in the building of prehistoric huts, or simply as rabbit-holes, dips in the ground or whatever, are determined to a considerable extent by the hypotheses the archaeologist makes about the nature of early houses. The assumption that all huts were round as opposed to rectangular will lead to different conclusions about what the data are: i.e. what are post-holes and what are not. We do not start with a set of facts labelled 'post-holes' and simply have to account for them; we start with a jumble which will yield data only as the result of making hypotheses derived in turn from a theory.

In linguistics there is a comparable problem in deciding what constitute the facts. There are of course some elementary facts that (nearly) everyone can agree on: that (1):

1   Mice talk.

even though implausible, is grammatical; that (2):

2   Both John and Bill are similar in liking caviare.

is redundant; that (3):

3   My son has grown another foot.

is multiply ambiguous, and so on. But more interesting cases (more interesting because they are sufficiently complex to cause disagreement and hence differentiate among approaches) are not so clear-cut. In early work on the formal (mathematical) properties of grammars, it was claimed that there was a contrast between pairs of sentences such as those in (4):

4a   The table is as long as the door is wide.
4b   The table is as long as the door is long.

where, because of the repetition of 'long', (4b) was judged to be unacceptable and putatively ungrammatical, whereas (4a) was uncontroversially unobjectionable. A few years later the same examples were both deemed to be fully acceptable, thereby altering the responsibility of the grammar, and in fact simplifying the formal properties of the theory, as it was no longer necessary to specify the (non-)identity of the adjectives 'long' and 'wide'.

I want to look in a little bit more detail at one particular example of how generative theory has changed over the years and how the range and treatment of data have changed with it: as data become relevant as evidence for some particular theoretical position and are accordingly taken up or dropped.

When interviewing prospective linguistics students, many of whom have no clear idea at all as to what they would be letting themselves in for if they were accepted, we often ask them to work out on their feet an account of the difference between reflexive and non-reflexive pronouns illustrated in (5):

5a   John betrayed himself.
5b   John betrayed him.

To make the task manageable in a stressful situation, we usually ask how they would correct a foreign learner of English who made such mistakes as 'John betrayed myself' and 'I betrayed me'. Most candidates do reasonably well and come up with something like the suggestion that you use the reflexive forms ('himself', 'myself', and so on) if the subject and the object refer to the same person, and the 'ordinary' form otherwise. This prompts us to give the further example in (6):

6   John told Mary about herself.

in which the subject (John) is not involved at all. The expected answer is that you can simplify the previous account by omitting mention of 'subject' and 'object' and just say that you use the reflexive form when you refer to the same person for a second time. This in turn elicits a problem example of the kind illustrated by (7):

(7) John wanted me to shave himself.

which seems to meet the relevant criteria but is blatantly impossible in English. Again most students manage to point out that what is crucially different in such an example is the existence of the extra clause, marked by the additional verb 'wanted', and that the generalization they have struggled to come up with has to be restricted by some such statement as 'within a single clause'. There are many further twists by reference to which we can prolong the torture: sufficient to make it reasonably easy for the candidate to come up with at least one or two correct generalizations, and for us to get an idea if he or she is likely to take to the subject. Anyone who comes up immediately with all the right answers is likely to do well at linguistics, provided it also gives them some intellectual satisfaction. (Failure is not final: it merely provokes us to turn to a different subject.)

Frequently, an intelligent student will join in enthusiastically and try to demonstrate that the account we have so far jointly provided is inadequate, and hence that we are wrong. For instance, after the first stage, when it looks as if a statement in terms of 'subject' and 'object' is all that is required, a candidate will often suggest that the sentences in (8):

8a   I came myself.
8b   I myself came.

are counter-examples, in that *come* doesn't have an object but it looks as if it has a reflexive pronoun following it. The response is to point out, or persuade the student to discover, that there are two classes of 'reflexive' pronoun: those where it is an argument (subject or object) of the verb, and those where it is merely an emphatic reinforcement for such an argument. Only the former of these is relevant for the problem under discussion. This suggestion is usually met with outraged incredulity until further slightly more convincing examples are adduced. First, with some verbs you can get a contrast between the two kinds of 'himself', so (9):

9   He followed himself.

could be the equivalent of either 'He had two successive turns' or of 'He himself had the next turn', and though stylistically scarcely felicitous, it is possible to have both of them in one sentence, as in (10):

10a   He followed himself himself.
10b   He himself followed himself.

Second, the emphatic variety can occur in places where the other cannot, so (11a) is fine, but (11b) is suspect:

11a   As for myself, I view this argument with suspicion.
11b   ?As for me, I view this argument with suspicion.

and so on. The point is that until we have some explicit hypothesis about what a reflexive is and where it can occur, it is not possible to decide even whether 'I came myself' is or is not part of the domain of discussion. It can be made to be part of the domain by fiat: 'every form containing "self" must be accounted for', but because of the insistence on treating the surface phonological form as sacrosanct, this risks missing generalizations of a more interesting kind.

How does a grammar account for the differences between reflexive and non-reflexive pronouns? In early work on trans-formational grammar, up to and including the 'Standard Theory', it was argued that both ordinary and reflexive pronouns were derived from full Noun Phrases by means of transformations, so a sentence like (5a), 'John betrayed himself', was derived transformationally from a structure of the form 'John betrayed John' by replacing the second occurrence of 'John' by the 'appropriate' (i.e. agreeing in person, number and gender) reflexive pronoun. This analysis accounted automatically for the complementary distribution of pronouns like 'me' and 'myself' in (12):

12a   I like myself.
12b   He likes me.
12c   *I like me.
12d   *He likes myself.

With some additional, independently motivated assumptions, it also accounted for the *meaning* of many examples containing reflexives; and it was in tune with the tendency to account for any phenomenon whatever by means of transformations.

Moreover, most of the arguments in the literature about the interaction of transformations crucially involved reflexivization, which was thus at the centre of theoretical developments, and as well-established as it was possible to be. Indeed, one of the great successes of the treatment was that it extended automatically to the behaviour of imperatives such as (13):

13   Wash yourself.

The reflexive here apparently has no antecedent at all; but given the unacceptability of examples like 'Wash himself' or 'Wash myself' and the interpretation of such sentences as being addressed to a second person singular interlocutor, the assumption was made that a 'you' in subject position was present at Deep-Structure level, was present therefore to trigger the rule of reflexivization and was later deleted. The deletion was in fact optional: further support for the analysis was derived from the possibility of having an equivalent slightly 'emphatic' sentence like (14):

14   You wash yourself.

where the subject actually showed up. Examples of real 'emphatic' reflexives (such as (15)):

15   Wash yourself yourself!

were simply considered irrelevant, and were generally not treated as data.

There were, of course, problems. The standard account failed to accommodate so-called 'snake' sentences of the kind exemplified in (16):

16a   John saw a snake near him.
16b   ?John saw a snake near himself.

where (16a) with 'him' is perfectly acceptable, but (16b) with the expected form 'himself' is only marginally acceptable. It failed to account for so-called 'picture-noun' reflexives of the kind illustrated in (17):

17   John realized that a picture of himself had been found.

where the usual constraint that the reflexive has to be in the same clause as its antecedent appears to have been violated: compare the standard ungrammatical example in (18):

18   *John realized that Mary liked himself

It made the wrong syntactic and semantic predictions about examples containing quantifiers like 'every' and 'none'. Thus, (19a):

19a   Everyone likes everyone.
19b   Everyone likes himself.

was predicted to be ill-formed, because the subject and object are the same but the latter has not been replaced by 'himself' (or 'themselves'), and even if the rule is made optional, it is clearly not the case that (19a) means the same as (19b).

In the Standard Theory, it was assumed that the meaning of a sentence was determined by the Deep Structure alone, that transformations had no role to play and that Surface Structure was hence irrelevant to semantics. The pair of examples in (19) cast doubt on this position and, as the difficulties of accounting exhaustively for the distribution and meaning of reflexives mounted, the transformational account was gradually abandoned in favour of an 'interpretive' account which simply generated reflexive pronouns *in situ* by means of Phrase Structure rules and left their correct construal to rules of semantic interpretation.

To some extent this interpretive theory suffered from many of the same defects as the 'transformational' one. Both theories had such great descriptive power that it was hard to find phenomena that argued decisively for one or the other. Nevertheless, the newer theory had certain advantages of both a theoretical and a descriptive kind. (Meta-)theoretically, it constrained the power of transformations by removing a class of cases where these referred to referential – semantic – information, and replaced them by interpretive rules: a class of rules which needed access to such information anyway. Further, an interpretive rule generalized easily to account for phrases which involved *non*-co-reference such as 'someone else' or 'another', data which had not even been considered relevant to the earlier analyses; and it avoided completely the difficulty of 'recursive' sentences like (20):

20   The man who deserves it will get the prize he wants.

which represented a horrendous problem for a replacement analysis, because the pronouns 'it' and 'he' – supposedly replacements for the co-referential Noun Phrases 'the prize' and 'the man' respectively – are actually co-referential with the Noun Phrases 'the prize *he* wants' and 'the man who deserves *it*': structures which already contain pronouns. If these contained pronouns were in turn to be derived transformationally from full Noun Phrases, one would be trapped in an infinite regress.

However, the very considerable complexity of the 'interpretive' analysis made it likely that both theories were inadequate: after all, children learn to control these constructions with little difficulty in a few years; and there were apparent generalizations that neither theory captured. For instance, there are parallels between sentences involving passivization and sentences involving reflexivization which are not accommodated, or even considered, by either treatment. Example (18) provides evidence that a reflexive cannot be too far away from its antecedent (it has to be in the same clause). Similarly, (21):

21   *John was believed that Mary liked.

shows that the subject of a passive cannot move too far from its
original object position. 'John', as the object of 'liked', cannot turn
up as the subject of 'believed' in a different clause. It was not until
1979–80 with the advent of 'Government and Binding' Theory
that a more satisfactory treatment of both reflexives and a wide
range of other constructions was found.

At the core of the new theory is the idea of modularity. The
grammar is now taken to consist of a number of relatively
autonomous sub-theories for each of which grammatical statements of maximum generality are given, the complex distribution
of data that we see on the surface being a function of their
interaction. The previously all-important transformational component of the grammar is now reduced to a single schema: 'Move-
Alpha' (hereafter Move-x) which permits the movement of any
constituent anywhere, subject on the one hand to universal
constraints and on the other to idiosyncratic, lexical, conditions
imposed by the individual language. The best developed of these
sub-theories is known as Binding Theory, which deals with
possible relations between different kinds of Noun Phrases and
their antecedents, specifying the distribution of reflexives like
'himself' and other 'anaphors' such as 'each other', of full Noun
Phrases like 'John', and of pronouns such as 'him' and certain
phonetically null elements (known as empty categories) which are
postulated to fill the holes left by moved constituents.

The theoretical vocabulary of the rest of the model has also
changed. As is implicit in the name of the latest instar of the
theory, the central notion is Government, intuitively in the
traditional sense – as when a preposition governs the accusative –
but with a rigorous formal definition. Binding, which is
represented by co-indexing to indicate referential dependency,
takes place under government: essentially within some specified
'domain', a constituent such as NP or S, known as the 'Governing
Category'. The statement of the distribution of pronouns,
reflexives and full Noun Phrases then reduces to the simple set of
principles in (22):

22a   An anaphor must be bound in its governing category.
22b   A pronominal must be free in its governing category.

22c   Referring expressions must be free.

'Anaphor' includes both reflexives and reciprocals like 'each other'; pronominals are transparently entities like 'him'; 'referring expressions' are other Noun Phrases excepting dummies like 'it' and 'there'. Apart from the typology of expressions, the crucial notion is clearly that of 'governing category' (a concept previously unavailable in the theory). In the examples in (23) and (24), the governing category is delimited by [. . .] and the expression and its antecedent are in italics.

23a   [*John* saw *himself* in the mirror.]
23b   **John* saw [*himself* was wrong].
23c   [*John* believed *himself* to be wrong.]

In (23a) the governing category is the finite sentence and 'himself' is correctly bound by John within that sentence and so the result is grammatical. In (23b) 'John' is not in the same finite clause as 'himself' and so the result is ungrammatical. In (23c) the embedded clause is non-finite, and therefore not a potential governing category. Accordingly, the two items 'John' and 'himself' occur in the same governing category and the result is again acceptable.

24a   [*John* saw *him* in the mirror.]
24b   John saw [*he* was wrong].
24c   [*John* believed *him* to be wrong.]

We have here the same governing categories as before, but the possibility of interpreting the pronoun as the same as the antecedent 'John' is precisely inverted. In (24a) and (24c) 'him' must refer to someone other than 'John' – it must be 'free' (= not bound) in the governing category indicated by [. . .]. In (24b) 'John' and 'he' *can* be co-referential because they occur on either side of the '[' which marks the boundary of the governing category. If the pronoun in these last examples is replaced by the full Noun Phrase 'John', the result is that the two occurrences of 'John' in each sentence must be interpreted as non-co-referential, irrespective of the governing category boundaries, i.e. the NP must always be free. On the assumption that the empty category left by movement rules has the properties of an anaphor, the same principles account for the ungrammaticality of the passive sentences in (21), whose structure in the relevant respects is given in (25):

25   *John* was believed [that Mary liked e].

'John' and its trace, the empty category indicated by 'e', are in different clauses and so the trace is not properly bound: hence the sentence is ungrammatical.

This sophistication of the theory, superficially complex though it may appear, allows an elegant simplification and generalization of (part of) the grammar. The motivation for the kind of formulation of Binding Theory given above is to maximize the generality and universality of the statements in the grammar by postulating deeper and deeper abstract principles governing the distribution of items in individual languages. The symmetry in the treatment of the different kinds of Noun Phrase types and the coverage of previously unconsidered constructions are good indications (apart of course from its empirical adequacy) that the analysis is correct.

Recent developments, however, have indicated that the attainment of this symmetry is at the cost of sacrificing symmetry elsewhere. The statements involving 'governing category' of the kind given in (22) are reminiscent of the locality constraint of 'subjacency' discussed briefly in essay 3, 'Grammar and Gravity', and in recent work Chomsky has replaced his earlier formulation 'An anaphor must be bound in its governing category' (= 22a) by 'An anaphor must be bound in a local domain'. The same point has been emphasized by Koster who has attempted to unify this 'Principle A' with subjacency. The theoretical development arose from taking into account a set of data (from Dutch and German) which had previously been largley ignored, and has the advantage of finally accommodating the 'snake' sentences illustrated in (16), which were still unaccounted for. There is, as always, a cost to be paid: Koster's treatment of snakes involves an *ad hoc* rule deleting '–self' after certain prepositions, and the parallelism between anaphors and pronominals is now less explicit.

On the other hand, part of Koster's reanalysis relegates

Principle C to pragmatic, non-grammatical, status. In isolation, such a development is neutral with regard to the relative merits of rival accounts of pronouns and anaphors. A certain measure of support accrues to it, however, from the deafening silence over the last generation about imperatives. The demise of the transformational account left us with no satisfactory grammatical treatment of examples like (13) – 'Wash yourself'. But imperatives in general lend themselves to a pragmatic account, in which the subject, and the antecedent of any reflexive contained in the imperative, are identified from the context, and not by grammatical rule.

It may be then that Koster's desirable unification does not have too severe a cost after all. As usual, the range of data covered by the new theory will depend on their ability to constitute evidence for some plausible set of hypotheses. The new theory will not need to accommodate all the data of its predecessors; it may give up apparently insightful analyses of some constructions, if the alternative is sufficiently elegant. We may even find that what were once considered central grammatical data are no longer included within the grammar.

I started by noting, with Gregory, that 'facts' are not independent of the theories that generate them. I would like to finish by noting, with Feyerabend, that new theories will always contain elements of the *ad hoc*, but that *provided* these new theories are fruitful and interesting, this is not something that should be held against them.

Feyerabend describes how Galileo defends the view that the earth moves, against the Aristotelians' 'Tower argument' by developing both a relativistic theory of motion and an *ad hoc* hypothesis: the principle of circular inertia. Far from being reprehensible, such *ad hoc* hypotheses 'have a positive function; they give new theories a breathing space, and they indicate the direction of future research'. Mr Gradgrind would be aghast.

Notes

p. 129   Mr Gradgrind, the 'hero' of Dickens' novel *Hard Times*, is obsessed with demonstrable facts.

p. 129   The example of 'post-holes' is from Gregory (1973: p. 83).

p. 129 On acceptability vs grammaticality, cf. essay 5 'Quails and Oysters'.

p. 130 The examples in (4) were first discussed in Chomsky (1963), and subsequently in his (1977: p. 122), where they are deemed to be grammatical. The historical change in their status is documented in Pullum and Gazdar (1982) esp. pp. 476-7.

p. 130 A clear introduction to the properties of reflexives is given in Radford (1988), chap. 1.

p. 132 The 'Standard Theory' is that of Chomsky (1965).

p. 133 The first attempt to deal reasonably comprehensively with the differences between pronouns and reflexives in English was Lees and Klima (1963). They dismiss 'emphatic' reflexives as follows: 'We shall not attempt to study or analyse the so-called "emphatic" constructions in –self, as in *John did it himself*' (p. 17). They have been discussed extensively more recently: cf. Edmondson and Plank (1978) and Verheijen (1986).

p. 134 'Snake' sentences were first discussed in Lakoff (1968). More recent discussions appear in Chomsky (1981a), Reinhart (1983), Carden (1986) and Koster (1987).

p. 135 'Interpretive Semantics' – a family of theories in which semantic representations were derived from Surface Structure – is best exemplified by Jackendoff (1972), which gives detailed analyses of reflexive and other sentence types. For the history of the conflict between 'Interpretive Semantics' and 'Generative Semantics', cf. Newmeyer (1980).

p. 135 On the infinite regress produced by examples like (20), cf. Bach (1970).

p. 135 On the 'adequacy' of theories, cf. essay 11, 'Lellow Lollies'.

p. 136 Government and Binding theory grew out of the Pisa Lectures, published as Chomsky (1981a).

p. 136 For the idea of 'modularity' cf. Chomsky (1986) and, in a somewhat different sense, Fodor (1983). There is an elementary discussion in the Introduction above.

p. 136 Empty categories have been of central importance in much recent work: cf. Chomsky (1981a, 1981b, 1986, 1988a). For an elementary example of their utility in accounting for the distribution of 'weak forms', cf. essay 11, 'Lellow Lollies'.

p. 136 'Government' has received a number of slightly different technical definitions. The core notion is in each case that a head govern its complements. '(Cf. essay 6 'The Oats have eaten the Horses', and the Appendix.)

p. 136 'Co-indexing' (to indicate co-reference or referential dependency) is usually represented by subscripting the relevant categories. I have indicated it here by putting the appropriate items in italics.

p. 136   The Principles of the Binding Theory given in (22) are taken from Chomsky (1981a: p. 188).

p. 137   'Finite' sentences are those marked for the contrast between present and past (in English). Cf. essay 10 'Time and Tense'.

p. 137   Sentences like 'John believed John was wrong' are normally taken to refer to two different people called 'John'. In cases of so-called 'accidental coreference' these two people may turn out to be one and the same person – hence the 'normally' in the text. For discussion, cf. Evans (1982).

p. 138   Chomsky's more recent formulation of Principle A of the Binding Theory is taken from his (1986: p. 166).

p. 138   Koster develops his ideas *in extenso* in his (1987), cf. especially chap. 6. The rule of *self* deletion is on p. 343.

p. 139   For a pragmatic treatment of imperatives, cf. Downes (1977).

p. 139   Feyerabend's discussion of Galileo is in his classic (1975). The quotation is from p. 93.

p. 139   The possibility of having theory change at all is discussed interestingly in Field (1973).

13

Annie's Botty-wotty

Babies are disruptive. They force a radical reorganization not only of their care-takers' life-style but also, it would seem of their thought processes and their language. All but the most austere modify their speech when talking to (or even about) small children: dogs and rabbits become doggies and bunnies; pronouns are replaced by names, so that 'I'll get it for you' is replaced by 'Daddy get the book for Timmy'; and a host of apparent simplifications to the sounds and the syntax appear to impose themselves willy-nilly. This kind of 'baby-talk' is most characteristic of mothers, hence the label 'motherese' usually attached to it, but fathers, caretakers, older siblings and virtually everyone else indulges. In a letter to his wife Darwin somewhat embarrassingly talks about how 'I long to kiss Annie's botty-wotty'; hardly the style normally associated with the author of *On the Origin of Species*.

Attitudes to motherese have been as diverse as its users. Most commentators have ignored it; some have condemned it as a pernicious obstacle to the child's learning of the proper forms of the language; some view it as a valuable teaching aid, and it has even been suggested that the systematic modifications people make in speaking to children are sufficient to undermine Chomskyan appeals to innatist explanations for language acquisition. It is this last claim that makes motherese a topic of current interest, but before investigating the details of the claim, it is worth looking more closely at the factual basis of the assumption that motherese really is simpler than 'normal' speech.

Consideration of 'doggies', 'botty-wotties' and similar examples in baby-talk mode might make one dubious about any claims for simplicity. Why should 'doggy' with two syllables be easier to use, perceive, remember or pronounce than 'dog' with one? Is the reduplication in 'botty-wotty' really a simplification in any sense of the word? Moreover, a glance at other languages does nothing to alter the view that phonological simplicity is not a major force: the Berber baby form for 'dates' is [b:ʕu] (where 'ʕ' is a voiced pharyngal fricative and the ':' indicates a lengthened 'b';, and for 'nasty' it is [xxishtt]. One could respond that these forms may be markedly simpler than their adult equivalents, but the problem is that there is no absolute notion of simplicity to which one can appeal, and although certain phonological processes are common in motherese forms around the world, they do not leave us with any clearly simpler forms to pronounce, and sometimes the result of these processes is more complex by the standard criteria than the original. For instance, [ch] (as in 'church') is generally held to be more complex than [s], but in Hindi baby-talk adult 's' is replaced by 'ch' so that 'Sona' (both a name and the verb 'to sleep') is pronounced [Chona].

If the phonology provides little comfort to those who believe that motherese is simple, maybe the syntax – which anyway provides the real challenge to language acquisition, because of its acknowledged much greater complexity – really is simplified. Again, the problem we are confronted with is one of defining 'simplicity'. Mathematically it is extremely simple to invert a series of terms: to convert 1–7–9 to 9–7–1, for instance. Inversion occurs in the grammars of human languages too, but it is inversion of a different kind in being always structure-dependent. For instance, 'I will' can be converted to 'will I' to form a question corresponding to the original statement, but the process is correctly viewed not as a simple inversion or reversal of the words but as an operation which takes the auxiliary verb and places it before the subject. 'My friend will come' yields 'Will my friend come?' not 'Come will friend my?'. Indeed, the most meticulous investigation of the syntactic properties of motherese came to the conclusion that as regards word-order, incidence of construction types, change over time and so on motherese was 'more complicated than normal speech'.

Despite this inauspicious start, the claim that we have no agreed metric of simplicity cuts both ways: the near universality of motherese and the equally near universality of the belief that it is used as a teaching aid may indicate that our (mothers') instincts

are right: motherese *is* simpler, we just don't know how to
quantify that claim yet. Assuming that this is indeed the case,
what are the implications for linguistic theory, in particular
Chomsky's innatist arguments based on that theory?

One of the major reasons for the philosophical importance of
Chomsky's work in linguistics is the conclusion that our
knowledge of language must be to a considerable degree innate
rather than learned, thereby lending support to a rationalist,
Cartesian, view of the mind rather than an empiricist one. The
central plank in this argument for innateness is the 'poverty of the
stimulus': mature speakers know demonstrably more about their
language than it is rational to assume that they have been taught
or have learned. Every speaker of English agrees that the
examples in (1):

   1a John told the joke to the policeman.
   1b John told the policeman the joke.
   1c John reported the accident to the policeman.

are acceptable, whereas that in (2):

   2 *John reported the policeman the accident.

is not merely infelicitous but ungrammatical. It is entirely
comprehensible but it is not English. It is scarcely plausible that
everyone who shares this intuition has been given explicit
instruction to the effect that such examples are wrong (what
precisely would you tell someone who made such mistakes to do?);
it is unlikely that everyone has heard the first three examples and
uniformly leaped to the conclusion that the last (unheard) one is
therefore impossible; and the implication seems to be that our
knowledge about (2) must be due at least in part to properties of
the mind that are independent of experience, i.e. must be innate
or genetically determined. An intelligent Martian given (1a) and
(1b) would probably make the analogy between (1c) and (2) with
unerring ease. Why don't we? At least part of the answer has been
that only some 'analogies' are possible, and that this is not one of
them.

A further, if subsidiary, part of the innatist argument has often
been that the speech children are exposed to is 'degraded', so that

'the child's conclusions about the rules of sentence formation must be based on evidence that consists, to a large extent, of utterances that break rules, since a good deal of normal speech consists of false starts, disconnected phrases, and other deviations from idealized competence'.

It was of this particular claim that motherese was claimed to be a refutation. Speech to young children tends *not* to be 'degraded' in this way: sentences addressed to them are usually short, well-formed and intonationally marked so as to be identifiably aimed at them. This possible removal of one of the premises in the innatist argument, allied with the 'obvious' role of the putative simplifications present in baby talk as an aid in language acquisition – even indeed their role as a teaching device – led to the conclusion that the existence of motherese invalidated the poverty of the stimulus argument, and hence undermined the claims of innateness partially based upon that argument.

The ubiquity of motherese – it is found in almost every culture that people have looked for it – and the uniformity of speakers' impressions that it is a teaching device may make it plausible that motherese is functional, and a recent textbook in psycholinguistics comes to the conclusion that 'young children hear organized, simplified and redundant sentences which provide an ideal basis for language learning'. However, even if motherese has a function it is not established that that function is the seemingly obvious one of helping the child to learn the grammar of his or her language. There is a tendency in the literature to confound several things that need to be kept separate: language and communication, linguistic form and linguistic function, length and complexity, data structures and the rules that make those structures possible, and (especially) learning and development.

The first confusion has a long history which can be traced back to the 'use' theories of meaning associated with the Speech Act analyses of Austin and Searle, but has its most recent incarnation within the acquisition domain in the work of those like Wells who view 'language as interaction'. It becomes clear that Wells is using this title provocatively as short-hand for something like 'the importance of interaction in the acquisition of language and of language in the acquisition of communication skills', but there is a widespread tendency to assume that the pre-eminent or even only function of language is communication, and that mastery of the ability to communicate implies mastery of language. In fact communication can take place with or without language, and language can be used for purposes other than communicating (thinking for instance). It is quite plausible that motherese facilitates communication (via whatever language has already been learned) and also of course provides some of the input without which no language acquisition at all could take place. It does not follow that it is causally involved in the acquisition process itself, still less that motherese or any specifically modified form of input is necessary to language acquisition. Young children are better prepared to master their mother tongue than one might suppose: certainly better prepared than Halliday suggests when he goes so far as to claim that 'in the very first instance he [the child] is learning that there is such a thing as language at all'. But to have a message to communicate entails the existence of some system of mental representation in which that message can be framed – a Fodorian 'Language of Thought' – and learning a language involves both a mapping of the structures of the Language of Thought onto the structures of the language being acquired, and a second-order ability to manipulate these structures appropriately in communication.

Given their partial independence, it is not surprising that these two aspects of 'language acquisition' may be dissociated in some cases of pathology. The classic example is of 'John' who 'showed a marked schism between these two areas', with his syntactic–semantic system intact but his use of language for communication being 'almost totally ineffective'. That is, he could produce well-formed sentences of some complexity, but was unable to use them appropriately in context. If command of syntax can be separated off from its appropriate use in this way then it is clearly possible that motherese may be effective in one domain but not in the other.

The second confusion alluded to, the form/function contrast, refers to the relation between a particular linguistic structure – e.g. a word order in which the (auxiliary) verb precedes the subject, as in 'had the children come' – and the use typically made of that form – e.g. to ask a question. The distinction is obvious enough, but the relation between particular forms and functions is many to many (the example given above could be part of a counterfactual conditional 'had the children come I should have seen them' or a negative statement 'scarcely had the children come than I saw them'; and a question could be asked without the word-order given here 'the children had come?') so that learning one does not entail learning the other. Discussions of motherese which simply list percentages of 'questions' or 'statements' are therefore unrevealing of the details of syntax that the child to whom the speech is addressed is exposed.

The rules of grammar, unlike the processes of arithmetic never make use of mathematical concepts like 'third' or 'reverse the order', so it is mildly surprising to see the preoccupation among workers in motherese (and language acquisition more generally) with counting. The standard measure of complexity is the Mean Length of Utterance (MLU), to which is frequently added the percentage of 'long' utterances, the average number of morphemes occurring before the main verb, and so on. Unfortunately, simplicity of analysis is not the same as brevity of data. One can argue convincingly that the analytic simplicity of a construction should be reflected in the succinctness of the rules needed to generate that construction, but this need have no implications for length, because even simple rules can be recursive: that is, they can reapply to produce indefinitely long structures. In fact children of all ages take great delight in nursery rhymes like 'The Court of King Caractacus' precisely because of the pleasure and power derivable from simple repetition of a single pattern. In the final line, given in (3):

3 'If you want to take some pictures of the fascinating witches who put the scintillating stitches in the breeches of the boys who put the powder on the noses of the faces of the ladies of the harem of the court of King Caractacus, you're too late, because they've just passed by.'

much of the effect is achieved by repeatedly exploiting the rule that allows a Noun Phrase to be made up of a Noun Phrase and a following Prepositional Phrase, where this Prepositional Phrase is itself composed of a Preposition and a Noun Phrase: potentially *ad infinitum*, definitely *ad nauseam*.

For reasons of limitations in their powers of concentration, short-term memory and attention span, it may none the less be plausible to assume that a child's mental development should be

reflected in increasing length of utterance; it is not at all plausible
to think that the absence of specific grammatical indicators typical
of early speech in or to the child should be beneficial to him in
developing his linguistic system. In general, the richer and more
varied the input data the easier the overall task of language
acquisition for the child. A language can be generated by any one
of an indefinitely large number of grammars, and any particular
structure grossly underdetermines the rules that describe it. The
more evidence the child receives in the form of different
construction types, the smaller the set of grammars he has to
choose among. We have already seen that rules and structures are
not in a one-to-one correspondence and that except in cases of
severe pathology children do not learn most of their sentences
verbatim but rather construct them afresh on the basis of the rules
they have acquired. It follows that even a complete catalogue of
the constructions used by care-taker and child would fail to
determine what the rules of the grammar internalized by the child
were.

Consider a simple example. We started with the observation
that typical cases of motherese consist in the replacement of
pronouns by full Noun Phrases as in (4) rather than (5):

4   Daddy get the book for Timmy.
5   I'll get it for you.

This seems to obviate for the child part of the problem of
determining the referent of items like 'me' and 'you' which shift
from occasion to occasion, by replacing them with names which
(at least as far as the child is concerned) are likely to have unique
referents. Simultaneously, however, it removes some of the crucial
evidence the child will need to fix the properties of his grammar,
specifically the module of his grammar devoted to Case.

Case theory accounts for a wide range of phenomena depending
on the contrast between 'nominative' (subject) and 'objective'
case: the difference between 'he' and 'him' in 'he saw him', and
including the contrast between the acceptable (6) and the
ungrammatical (7):

6   For me to go there is impossible.
7   *Me to go there is impossible.

where (7) is ungrammatical because the subject of an infinitive like 'to go' has to have case assigned to it by some element such as the 'for' in (6) or the verb 'want' in 'I want him to go'.

All languages have Case in the syntactic sense it is used here; some languages mark these case differences explicitly in the morphology – Latin is the classic example, other languages have no morphological case at all – Chinese, for instance; and some, like English, mark it in the pronominal system but not elsewhere. In those languages that do have morphological case, it provides useful evidence of the syntactic structure of the sentence involved, so that in the limiting case one can even have minimal pairs differentiated exclusively by the (morphological) case difference, as in (8):

8a   The man who knew *he* was going left.
8b   The man who knew *him* was going left.

If the pronoun he/him is replaced by a full Noun Phrase, such as 'John', the resulting sentence is ambiguous with one interpretation corresponding to each of the examples in (8), as can be seen in (9):

9   The man who knew John was going left.

This ambiguity indicates that (9) has two different structures in one of which (corresponding to (8a)) 'John' is the subject of 'was going', in one of which (corresponding to (8b)) 'John' is the object of 'know'.

Examples like (8) are perhaps extreme, and cause some initial processing difficulty because they are superficially so similar but structurally so different. The point of the example is, however, that the only surface clue to that difference – the (morphological) case difference – is eliminated in motherese type examples of the kind in (4). Far from helping the child one is making his/her task ultimately harder by withholding relevant information. As Gleitman and Wanner put it in an elegant discussion of the subject 'the narrower the range of data, the more hypotheses can describe them'.

The obvious response at this stage is to protest that such examples as (8) are way beyond the abilities of children at an age at which motherese is likely to be used. This just postpones the problem. A child exposed only to utterances in which overt Case differences were suppressed would come to the conclusion that he or she was learning a language like Chinese, which has no overt Case markers, and would then have to unlearn that part of the grammar when he or she finally did receive the appropriate input. Alternatively, if the universality of Case is construed as evidence for its innateness (which is possible and plausible, though not necessary) then the avoidance of morphological Case contrasts in motherese is simply postponing the availability of evidence for the language-specific shape taken by a category the child already has. The only thing he or she really has to learn is the phonological and morphological shape of the forms that instantiate universal categories, and the consistent use of motherese might postpone this task until the child has progressed beyond a stage when such tasks as lexical identification are likely to be a problem. In fact, transcriptions of parent/child interactions indicate that children receive a refreshingly varied and inconsistent input, not even mothers can speak motherese all the time.

Much of the discussion of the potential effects of the mother's input to the young child has been predicated on the assumption that children learn their first language in the same way that they learn to read or play chess. It has even been assumed that care-takers actively *teach* children to speak: hence motherese is a 'teaching aid'. As hinted above, this story is implausible if only because of the current impossibility of specifying what is to be taught: the distribution of pronouns and reflexives has pre-occupied some of the best minds in the world for years, so it is unlikely that *every* child who ends up speaking English appro-priately has been given the relevant instruction. This truism is obscured by the concentration in the literature on the very early stages of linguistic development. When attention is restricted to utterances of the complexity of 'kiss Mummy' it is easy to forget that what the child ends up knowing is something inordinately more complex – e.g. that (9) is ambiguous. It is not impossible to teach chimpanzees sentences consisting simply of a verb and a noun; it is impossible, by orders of magnitude, to teach them the syntax necessary to disambiguate (9). Motherese might be good for chimps; our own linguistic abilities are somewhat superior.

One of Chomsky's more radical observations is that not only is it implausible to assume that we *teach* our children to speak, it is also implausible to think that they *learn* to speak, if by learning is meant the kind of process whereby we master reading or chess. He points out that we don't speak about children learning to achieve puberty or to grow arms rather than wings, and suggests that the acquisition of language is more like physical (maturational) development than learning, or even like the metamorphosis of a tadpole into a frog.

Language development is overwhelmingly robust, appearing to be independent of physical limitations such as sight, intelligence or even hearing, in a way quite distinct from truly *learned* capabilities. We have already seen the example of John whose grammatical and pragmatic abilities were so vastly different, but other pathological examples give an even clearer insight into the modular autonomy of the linguistic system and its ability to emerge against seemingly overwhelming odds.

Let us take three representative examples. Yamada describes the case of Marta who was so severely retarded at the age of 18 years that she had difficulty remembering unstructured three-item sequences, but could produce sentences up to twenty words in length, as in (10):

10   She does paintings, this really good friend of the kids who I went to school with last year, and really loved.

Gleitman describes the linguistic development of blind children who use terms like 'look' and 'see' correctly despite their having no appropriate non-linguistic experience, and makes the further interesting point that the 'onset time [of language] is predictable as time since conception (neurological development) not time since birth (exposure time)'. Finally Dodd and Hermelin have described the acquisition of phonology by deaf children, some of whom by using visual information from lip-reading develop linguistic abilities entirely comparable to those of hearing subjects, even to the extent of being able to identify rhymes.

What can one conclude from these striking achievements? Far from needing motherese to ensure the normal development of language, that development needs merely to be 'triggered' by some minimal appropriate exposure to linguistic data in a normal environment. The innate linguistic system is so rich that even very little such exposure is sufficient to 'fix the parameters' of permissible variation. If we take the specific case of pronouns, a fairly basic part of our grammar and one which has figured widely in discussion both of linguistic theory and of motherese, it looks as if categories such as 'pronominal', including *he, me* and so on, 'anaphor', including *himself, myself* and so on, and 'names' including *Timmy, the dog* and so forth, are antecedently available to the child: he is born provided with such categories. All he needs to learn are the phonological shapes associated with each of these in the language he is exposed to, and relatively minor details of the kind which separate say Japanese from English. In Japanese a reflexive anaphor equivalent to 'himself' has a different range of possible syntactic positions than in English: it can occur further from its antecedent than can 'himself', but that antecedent must be a subject. Accordingly, using English examples to illustrate both Japanese and English sentences, we have the distribution given in (11):

11a   John washed himself.
11b   *John asked Mary to wash himself.

where (11a) is grammatical in both languages, but (11b) is grammatical only in Japanese, and in (12):

12   John told Bill about himself.

which is ambiguous in English, with 'himself' co-referential with eitehr 'John' or 'Bill', but is unambiguous in Japanese, with himself coreferential only with 'John'.

Evidence for the differences between such examples is available in relatively simple sentences, provided, for instance, that the developing child has acquired examples of pronouns distinct from names. Motherese – if it were consistently used – would obscure that evidence. Indeed, as far as the learner is concerned, the apparent structural complexity of language may in reality be a help not a hindrance, because the mind comes already attuned to the kind of structures language presents.

We do not need to come to the conclusion that motherese is pernicious; it is too sporadic and ephemeral for that. Moreover, its universality indicates that using it may well be psychologically beneficial: the empathy with the child that it reflects is probably conducive to feelings of well-being on both sides. We can certainly conclude, however, that it is linguistically unnecessary, and hence irrelevant to the hypothesis that a large part of our linguistic competence is genetically determined. The main function of motherese is probably to make babies psychologically tolerable rather than linguistically proficient.

Notes

p. 142 The quotation from Darwin's letter is from Burkhardt and Smith (1986: p. 319).

p. 142 The best collection of papers in this area is Snow and Ferguson (1977). The attitudes mentioned can all be found in this volume, cf. esp. Cross.

p. 143 The Berber data are taken from Bynon (1977: pp. 221, 225). Pharyngal fricatives, made with a constriction in the pharynx, are rare in the languages of the world, but occur phonemically distinctively in Arabic, Berber, and a number of related languages. The double 'x' in the transcription of the word for 'nasty' represents a lengthened voiceless velar fricative.

p. 143 The 'simplicity' of 's' ([s]) *vis-à-vis* 'ch' ([tʃ]) is standardly captured by the greater markedness of the latter. For details, cf. Chomsky and Halle (1968).

p. 143 The most meticulous investigation of motherese syntax is Newport, Gleitman and Gleitman (1977). The quotation is from p. 122.

p. 144 Chomsky has frequently spelt out his position on innateness (cf. e.g. 1972, 1975c, 1986). On the Cartesian background, cf. Chomsky (1966). The 'poverty of the stimulus' is discussed in his 1986 under the heading 'Plato's Problem'.

p. 144 Evidence from Martians is hard to come by, but foreign learners of English, whose acquisition of the language is based on intelligent strategies of analogical formation as well as on their purely linguistic ability, make comparable mistakes.

p. 144 The best discussion of 'possible analogies' is Pinker (forthcoming).

p. 145 The quotation about the speech children are exposed to being degraded is from Chomsky (1967: p. 441 n.40).

p. 145 Whether motherese is found in *all* cultures depends on how you define it. Schieffelin (1979) suggests that baby talk is not used among the Kaluli of New Guinea, but Fernald (1984), who includes differences of voice quality and pitch range in her discussion, claims that it is universal.

p. 145   The quotation about motherese being 'an ideal basis' is from Harris and Coltheart (1986: p. 45).

p. 145   The classical references for Speech Act theory are Austin (1962), and Searle (1969). The view that meaning could be reduced to usage is now defunct.

p. 145   The expression 'language as interaction' is the title of chap. 1 of Wells (1981).

p. 146   The quotation from Halliday is from his 1973: p. 10.

p. 146   On Fodor's Language of Thought, see his 1975, and essays 6, 'The Oats have eaten the Horses', and 17 'Useless Grammar'.

p. 146   The case of John is from Blank et al. (1978).

p. 147   Calculations of the Mean Length of Utterance were pervasive in the language acquisition studies of the 1960s and 1970s. The examples here are from Cross (1977).

p. 148   Modern Case theory originated with Jean-Roger Vergnaud: cf. Rouveret and Vergnaud (1980). It is discussed extensively in Chomsky (1981a, 1986). The example in (7) is ruled out by the so-called 'Case filter' which ensures that all overt Noun Phrases are assigned Case.

p. 149   The examples in (8) are from Winograd (1983: p. 370).

p. 149   The quotation from Gleitman and Wanner is from their 1982: p. 40.

p. 150   Typical exponents of the view that motherese is a teaching aid are Bynon (1977), and in a somewhat modified form, Ferguson (1977).

p. 150   On the abilities of chimpanzees, cf. Premack (1986), and esp. Carston (1987).

p. 150   Chomsky's radical views on language 'learning' can be found in several places e.g. his 1986.

p. 151   The analogy of language acquisition to metamorphosis is due to Gleitman (1981: p. 110).

p. 151   The case of Marta is from Yamada (1988). The example in (10) is from p. 197. The same example, differently transcribed, is quoted by Curtiss on p. 95 of the same book.

p. 151   The quotation about the linguistic development of blind children is from Gleitman (1981: p. 111). A much fuller discussion apears in Landau and Gleitman (1985).

p. 151   The remarkable abilities of deaf children have been documented in a number of papers by Dodd: cf. in particular Dodd and Hermelin (1977). Further case-studies of lip-reading can be found in Dodd and Campbell (1987).

p. 152   On parametric variation and parameter fixing, cf. Chomsky

(1981c), Roeper and Williams (1987), Smith, A. (1988), Smith, N. V. (1988), and essay 6, 'The Oats have eaten the Horses'.

p. 152   On Japanese, cf. Kuno (1973). For details of the Binding Theory which accounts for the distribution of pronouns and anaphors, cf. Chomsky (1981a, 1986), and essay 12 'Data, Evidence and Theory Change'.

14

In my Language we SHOUT

Human languages provide a remarkable number of different ways of saying the same thing. One can report the sighting of a pyknic pachyderm by uttering any of the sentences given in (1) (where bold face indicates greater stress):

1a   I saw a hippopotamus.
1b   I saw a **hippopotamus.**
1c   It was a hippopotamus that I saw.
1d   What I saw was a hippopotamus.
1e   A hippopotamus is what I saw.
1f   I **did** see a hippopotamus.
1g   **I** saw a hippopotamus.

and so on, *ad* almost *infinitum*.

Although one can usually get somewhat grudging agreement that any of the above would be true in the same situation, people have a strong intuition that the various examples do not really say quite the same thing but present different emphases and attitudes to a situation that might indeed evoke any of them. So much is common ground. Specifying in more detail what precisely 'emphasis' means, or even whether it is the appropriate conceptual category is not so easy. At the School of Oriental and African Studies in the mid-1960s we devoted a series of departmental seminars to the subject of 'Emphasis', concentrating on the different syntactic and phonological devices that different African languages deployed in the translation of examples like (1). It was mildly interesting in an anecdotal way, but rapidly became irritating as we came to no useful conclusions; and, after listening for some time to a plethora of suggestions about how you could convey emphasis by fronting the relevant constituent, by adding special markers to it, by reversing the usual word-order, and so on, an (Akan-speaking) Ghanaian colleague exploded in exasperation and said 'In my language we SHOUT'.

His impatience was understandable. What he wanted was a principled account of how and *why* variations like those in (1) occurred, and what he was getting was an unprincipled taxonomy restricted to the 'how'. Given the state of linguistic theory at the time, there was little hope of providing substantially more than a list of sentence types with descriptive labels attached. However, the history of how such constructions have been treated in linguistics in the years since then offers a good example of the rise and fall of particular analyses and concepts as greater understanding is achieved. Ultimately it also provides an example of how particular data are held to fall inside or outside the scope of a theory: how the resposibility of a theory to the facts changes as those facts fall under different kinds of generalization. In the present case, the rise of a theory of performance, which could provide at least a partial explanation for the examples concerned, relieved the competence theory of the need to contort itself to handle recalcitrant facts which were in principle beyond it.

In early transformational grammar, examples like (1f) were handled by incorporating an abstract marker 'Emph' (for emphasis) into the Phrase Structure rules. The presence of this element was then supposed to trigger the insertion of the auxiliary 'did', predict the contrastive stress which occurs on 'did' and the impossibility of having such stress on the following verb, and provide a basis for whatever the semantic function of such (stressed) auxiliaries is. Similar suggestions were made for incorporating 'topic' and 'focus' into the grammar with somewhat different effects.

This analysis displayed a certain ingenuity in assimilating the occurrence of 'did' in examples like (1f) to its occurrence in a wider range of constructions, but it suffered from a number of defects, of which the most worrying was the apparently arbitrary choice of the constituent 'Emph' as a purely syntactic matter, unconstrained by considerations of language use. That is, not only did this treatment ignore the contextual determinants of 'emphatic' sentences, but postulated a constituent which, in being neither phrasal nor lexical, was syntactically anomalous and *ad hoc*.

.   Even at the grammatical level, the analysis is scarcely illuminating: the phonological facts of stress are not dependent solely on the non-phonological category emphasis, as even semantically empty elements may be stressed for reasons of parallelism as can be seen in (2):

2   John wanted to do something, but he didn't know what *to* do.

where the infinitive marker 'to' has no meaning of its own but still occurs stressed. Moreover, semantically emphasized items need not be phonetically stressed, as can be seen in the variant of (1c) given in (3):

3   It **was** a hippopotamus that I saw.

where the important part of the message may not be the past time encoded in 'was' but the fact that a hippopotamus was the animal seen. Syntactically, the appearance of 'do' is neither necessary nor sufficient for emphasis, and semantically it is not clear that there is anything to say, precisely because of the doubt about the status, semantic or non-semantic of the category involved.

One of the many determinants of a choice among the examples in (1) is the difference between which information contained in the utterance is presupposed by the speaker to be knowledge shared by him and his interlocutor, and which information is not so shared. Accordingly, such examples are standardly said to have different 'presuppositional effects', which are then treated with any or all of a complex array of technical terms and formal devices. In addition to the original 'presupposed' versus 'asserted', these include 'focus' and contrasting pairs such as 'given' versus 'new', 'theme' versus 'rheme', and 'topic' versus 'comment'. All of these purport to provide an account of some of the differences, but they seem rather simply to multiply *ad hoc* labels whose justification is at best intuitive and at worst arbitrary, and whose relation to the rules of the grammar is anyway obscure.

The contrast between 'given' and 'new' is supposed to be a reflection of what the speaker thinks the hearer knows. The speaker of (1b) or (1c) assumes that his hearer already knows he has seen something: this is 'given' or 'old' information, and highlights the 'new' information about the hippopotamus by stressing it or 'clefting' it (i.e. putting it at the front of the sentence after 'it was'). The relation of 'given' and 'new' to the contrast between 'theme' and 'rheme' is somewhat obscure: the rheme of a sentence is usually said to be that which adds most new information, whereas the theme is the 'first' constituent of a sentence. In an example like (4):

4   Linguistics I find puzzling.

uttered in a general discussion of the subject, 'linguistics' would be both given and theme, whilst my finding it puzzling would be new and rheme. Puzzling too (though consistent with at least parts of the literature) are the definitions in Collins *Dictionary* which say that the rheme is 'usually, but not always, associated with the subject' whereas the theme is 'usually but not necessarily the subject'.

The 'topic-comment' distinction is somewhat similar to the preceding dichotomies, especially in its murkiness. According to the *Encyclopaedic Dictionary of the Sciences of Language* (generally a very reliable, if somewhat dated compilation), 'The topic . . . of an act of enunciation is what the speaker is talking about, the object of discourse . . . the *psychological subject*; the comment . . . is the information that the speaker means to convey relative to the topic . . . the *psychological predicate*.' We are further assured that 'emphasized' or equivalently, 'focused' elements do 'not necessarily represent the comment', a category later described as 'arbitrary'. Focus refers to the word or constituent with the greatest emphasis, which – according to another standard text – 'always conveys the new information'. The notion of presupposition itself – perhaps the least unsuccessful, and certainly the most rigorously defined, of the various ideas invoked to describe the kind of differences manifest in (1) – is supposed preeminently to account for the different status of the pair of examples in (5):

5a   I saw a hippopotamus which was smothered in treacle.
5b   The hippopotamus I saw was smothered in treacle.

In (5b) it is presupposed or taken for granted that I had seen a hippopotamus, and it is asserted merely that it was treacly, whereas in (5a) both these propositions are asserted.

There is clearly a considerable overlap between what is presupposed and what is given, between what is given and what is topic, between what is topic and what is theme, and so on; without it being obvious whether any of these terms should be eliminated in favour of any (or all) the others.

It should be becoming apparent that my Akan colleague's frustration was caused by our failure to provide a consistent theoretical account of the inherently interesting phenomena we had observed, and by the arbitrariness of the assignments we *were* able to give. For instance, in (1b) 'a hippopotamus' is held to be new information, in (1e) it is given, so we would typically expect to find exchanges like those in (6) or (7):

6   A 'What did you see?'
    B 'I saw a *hippopotamus.*'
7   A 'You can't really expect me to believe you saw a hippopotamus.'
    B 'A hippopotamus is what I saw – I don't care whether you believe me or not.'

But one can interchange B's responses to A's utterances and still have coherent dialogues, as witness (8) and (9):

8   A 'What did you see?'
    B A hippopotamus is what I saw – I don't care whether you believe me or not.'
9   A 'You can't really expect me to believe you saw a hippopotamus.'
    B 'I saw a hippopotamus.'

The fact that one could construct scenarios or provide pronunciations in which the initial assignment of some constituent to 'given' or 'new' was reversed, was accommodated by invoking different contrasts, such as that between theme and rheme, or presupposition and assertion. But this just provided a set of labels rather than the required theoretical explanation; in this case moreover, an explanation which could derive its force from a combination of competence and performance factors. That is, we need not simply an account of the grammatical possibilities, though this is clearly a necessary prerequisite to a full treatment, but also an account of the circumstances where each of these constructions is appropriate. Recent work by Sperber and Wilson in Relevance Theory provides the possibility of just such an explanation.

Their theory of relevance includes as a proper sub-part a theory of utterance interpretation which is compatible with, indeed presupposes, an explicit grammatical theory of a Chomskyan kind. Given this grammatical background and the Principle of Relevance, which is central to their theory, they claim that nothing else is necessary to account for the range of interpretations arrived at for the sentences in (1) and elsewhere. Instead of postulating any of the notions 'given', 'new', and so on, to mediate the relations between the syntactic structure of sentences and their presuppositional effects, they defend the view that the 'syntactic and phonological organization of an utterance may directly affect the way it is processed and understood' with the implication that *indirect* treatments of the kind of phenomena discussed here are needlessly complex.

Many of the details of their analyses are neutral with respect to the fine details of the syntactic theory exploited, but they crucially need to refer to a 'focal scale' which is phrase-structurally defined. The (somewhat simplified) syntactic structure of 'I saw a hippopotamus' is given in (10):

10

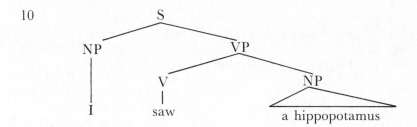

and they suggest that its logical form, which will be recovered as the hearer processes the sentence, is essentially isomorphic to this, as displayed in (11):

11
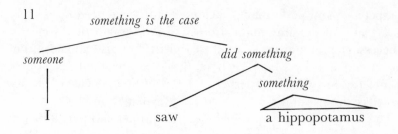

In (11) the node labels are variables over conceptual representations. Understanding a sentence then involves making a series of anticipatory hypotheses, both syntactic and conceptual, on the basis of what has already been processed. You start with the unconscious assumption that what your interlocutor says will describe some situation or event (the sentence 'S', corresponding to 'something is the case'); on hearing 'I', you assign it to the category (subject) NP, and hypothesize that it will be followed by a VP suggesting that your interlocutor 'did something'. The next word processed, 'saw', both confirms this hypothesis and provides the basis for the next stage in the process. 'See' is transitive – it requires an object – and so the hearer will make the anticipatory hypothesis that 'I saw something'. By the end of the sentence all the provisional assumptions made by the hearer should have been confirmed, as the speaker is presumed to be optimizing the relevance of what he is saying by providing maximal information at minimal processing cost to his interlocutor.

The sequence of anticipatory hypotheses in (12):

12a I did something.
12b I saw something.
12c I saw a hippopotamus.

forms a scale, on which each representation entails the one immediately preceding. This hierarchy, allied with the placement of stress, defines a 'focal scale' which guides the interpretation of the utterance: different stress assignments inducing different focal scales. With the stress on the final element, as given in (1b), the focal scale is as in (12); with stress on the initial element, as illustrated in (1g), the focal scale is as in (13):

13a   Someone saw a hippopotamus.
13b   I saw a hippopotamus.

That is, the initial stress of (1g) has the effect of alerting the listener to the fact that this constituent ('I') is filling in as the argument for a predicate the hearer should already be able to predict. It is this anticipation that explains the tacit implication that the utterance is a response to a question like 'Who saw a hippopotamus?' rather than 'What did you see?' or 'What happened?'. Thus the focal scale, using stress as a processing guide for the hearer, allows a reconstruction of the difference between 'given' and 'new', without the need to incorporate those concepts explicitly into the descriptive framework.

Even the apparently gradient character of the given–new distinction can be captured in the theory. The fact that an utterance may answer one question while simultaneously raising another is accounted for by the contrast between 'foreground' and 'background' implication. For instance, (1b) with the focal scale in (12) might derive the major part of its relevance from (12b): if, say, my eyesight had been seriously impaired. In this case, (12b) would be a foreground implication of (1b), whereas if the major part of the utterance's relevance accrued crucially to (12c), then (12b) would be only a background implication. Where the cut-off point between background and foreground comes will depend on the context the hearer constructs to interpret the utterance in. As this context is itself partly dependent on the hearer's encyclopaedic knowledge, the utterance may be partly 'new' and partly 'given', in any proportion.

The presence or absence of different elements on the focal scale also provides the basis for an account of the presuppositional difference between (5a) and (5b). Both of these imply that 'I saw a hippopotamus', but in (5a) this is actually on the focal scale – it is a development of the preceding hypothesis 'I saw something', and corresponds to the question 'What did you see?' – whereas in (5b) this implication is *not* on the focal scale, and the appropriate corresponding question would be something like 'What did the hippopotamus you see do?' or 'What happened to the hippopotamus you saw?'

Similar remarks pertain to the examples in (1c) and (1d): 'It was a hippopotamus that I saw' and 'What I saw was a hippopotamus'. In neither of these does 'I saw a hippopotamus' figure on the focal scale, in both of them 'my seeing something' is already given and the 'hippopotamus' fills the variable slot. These 'clefted' and 'pseudo-clefted' examples illustrate the further possibility the speaker can exploit of making differentially available the encyclopaedic information associated with different lexical entries. Speech necessarily occurs ordered in time, and speakers exploit this to give priority to certain aspects of contextual information over others. By putting 'saw' before 'hippopotamus' or 'hippopotamus' before 'saw', the speaker forces the listener to access one lexical item before another. Accessing that lexical item involves not only retrieving the purely linguistic aspects of our knowledge about it, but also the idiosyncratic knowledge of an encyclopaedic kind that we have acquired.

With examples as simple as the ones so far looked at, it is hard to illustrate this, but if we take slightly more complex ones, the difference should become clearer, and with it, the possibilities of characterizing the notion 'topic'. Consider the minimally different pair in (14):

14a   The male hippopotamus is identified with *Seth*, the God of storms.
14b   Seth, the God of storms, is identified with the male *hippopotamus*.

Intuitively (14a) has the male hippo as its topic while (14b) has Seth as its topic. In each case, the topic is relatively unstressed and occurs early in the sentence. In each case it serves to activate the lexical entry, encyclopaedic information from which will be relevant for the processing of the rest of the sentence. Little more needs to be said.

It is not uncommon to draw a distinction between 'sentence-topics' of this kind and 'discourse-topics': the primary subject matter of a whole story, conversation or other 'discourse'. Within Relevance Theory, however, it is not necessary to make special provision for a 'discourse-topic' extending beyond the confines of a sentence. Utterances can be relevant whether or not they are about the discourse-topic as normally conceived. Just because a paragraph about Seth includes a sentence about Thoth, it does not thereby cease to be relevant. That is, the notion of discourse-topic is superfluous, and the notion of sentence-topic can be captured without special provision needing to be made, given that one independently needs the notions of syntactic structure, temporal ordering, and stress.

A quarter of a century on, we can begin to do something to alleviate my colleague's frustration. Discussion of stylistic effects of the kind illustrated here is fruitless in a theoretical vacuum. So much was already partly apparent at the seminars, hence the attempt to couch the discussion within the theoretical framework of generative grammar. This framework at least gave us the possibility of describing reasonably adequately the facts that were in need of explanation. Blatantly, however, there was no possibility of achieving such an explanation solely within the confines of that theory. The reaction of some was simply to reject the theory of generative grammar on the grounds that it had failed. The correct response came with the appreciation that the formal grammatical aspects of the problem were only half the story and that we needed a theory of language-use into which they could be embedded. Such a theory of language-use has only emerged in the past decade. It is instructive to note that this has not simply replaced the grammatical theory, but is complementary to it. What has changed is the perception of the nature of the problems involved. 'Topic', 'given', 'presupposition' and so on are not themselves grammatical concepts but refer to phenomena which can only be described against a grammatical backcloth. The Chomskyan distinction between competence and performance has been justified almost exclusively within linguistics by concentrating on the competence side at the expense of performance. Relevance Theory has finally rehabilitated the study of performance.

My Akan friend doesn't need to shout any more.

Notes

p. 156   A good survey of the kind of stylistic effects discussed in this essay, though from a quite different viewpoint, can be found in Prince (1988).

p. 156   On the notion of truth in linguistic description, cf. Kempson (1988).

p. 157   For Akan, specifically Twi, cf. the dated, but still unsurpassed, Christaller (1875).

p. 157   The early transformational treatment referred to is that of Katz and Postal (1964). The insertion of the auxiliary 'do' was first proposed in Chomsky (1957).

p. 158   The *ad hoc* is not necessarily always pernicious: cf. essay 12 'Data, Evidence and Theory Change'.

p. 158   For the literature on 'presuppositional effects', cf. Sperber and Wilson (1986a) and references both there and in: Halliday (1967–8), Clark and Clark (1977), Reinhart (1981), Taglicht (1984) and Prince (1988).

p. 158   On shared and mutual knowledge, cf. the papers in Smith (1982a).

p. 159   The *Encyclopaedic Dictionary* is Ducrot and Todorov (1981). The quotation is from p. 271. The quotation about 'new information' is from Clark and Clark (1977: p. 32).

p. 161   The quotation about 'syntactic and phonological organization' is from Sperber and Wilson (1986a: p. 204). The Principle of Relevance is discussed in essay 7, 'Wilt Thou have this Man to thy wedded Wife?'

p. 161   (10) and (11) are not completely isomorphic because of the extra 'V' node in (10). Nothing in the argument depends on this asymmetry. I have drawn heavily on Sperber and Wilson (1986a) chap. 4, section 5 for the discussion here.

p. 162   For entailment, cf. the Introduction above.

p. 164   For discourse-topic, cf. Keenan and Schieffelin (1976) and Brown and Yule (1983), esp. chap. 3.3.

15

Clive

I first met Clive in Oxford when he was nine years' old: animated, mischievous and almost totally speechless. He clearly understood a considerable amount of what was said to him, as he could correctly carry out complex instructions of the kind 'put your hand at the back of your head, stand on one foot, and shut your eyes', but his spoken output was limited to 'yes' and 'no', sounds akin to mewing and bleating to indicate cats and sheep, and a variety of explosive noises in imitation of guns going off. Prospects were not bright.

Clive's history provided no adequate explanation for his inarticulateness. He had been admitted to hospital briefly at the age of six after drinking a considerable quantity of his father's whisky, and again at the age of seven after an overdose of Tofranil – a drug which had been prescribed for 'over-activity', but psychological and neurological tests showed nothing that would account for the severity of his deficit.

I saw Clive again when he was ten and eleven, and there were some hopeful signs of improvement in his speech. He was still extremely limited in his use of language, but he now produced sufficient speech to make it clear that some of his deviations from the adult norm were typical of normal children acquiring their first language and not exclusively pathological.

When young children are acquiring their first language they typically mispronounce the words they are learning in predictable ways. Sequences of consonants are often reduced to a single item, so 'blue' and 'green' might be pronounced 'boo' ([bu:]) and 'geen' ([gi:n]); consonants with different places of articulation in the adult language are made to 'harmonize' in the child's speech, so that 'duck' and 'top' might be pronounced '*guck*' ([gʌk]) and '*bop*' ([bɔp]); and contrasts in the adult language like those differentiating 'mat, mass, match' and 'mash' might all be neutralized to '*mat*' ([mat]). All these normal processes were illustrated in Clive's speech, though he also gave evidence of an even greater number of abnormal characteristics. Examples that one could justifiably consider normal, albeit for a much younger child, were the pronunciations shown in (1):

1   Freda   pronounced as   *Feda*   [viːdə]
     three   "   *fee*   [fiː]
     lorry   "   *lolly*   [lɔliː]
     cheese   "   *tease*   [tiːz]

What still kept his speech markedly deviant was both the grossness of his neutralizations – virtually all vowels ended up as schwa ([ə]) and the inconsistency of his performance: that he pronounced 'lorry' as '*lolly*' on one occasion was no guarantee that he would pronounce it that way the next time, and indeed he came up with '*rara*' ([rərə]) and a number of other variants. Moreover he seemed not to generalize the distinctions he had learned: his phonological acquisition seemed to proceed piecemeal word by word, with his correct pronunciation of the 'ou' in 'house' apparently being of no assistance to him in learning to say the same sound in 'mouse'. Most strikingly, he segmented every utterance into discrete units separated off by glottal stops, giving his speech a disjointed and staccato rhythm. Despite the progress, his phonology was still so limited that it was impossible to establish whether he had any productive mastery of syntax at all. His ability to obey instructions showed that he had some, but most of that could be explained on the basis of his knowing the meaning of individual words, with no need for syntactic links between them.

The last time I saw him in this period Clive's linguistic system seemed to be static, though there were one or two signs that he might be developing some rudimentary syntactic ability: he contrasted 'I'm dead', 'you're dead' and 'they're dead' in his gun games; he had a few appropriate commands like 'help me'; and most encouragingly, he extended his correct use of 'up' (and 'down') to include the technically incorrect but developmentally normal 'upper' for 'higher'. The best evidence we have that children learning their first language do so by constructing their own rules (rather than learning by simple imitation of their adult models) is provided by the over-generalization of these rules. Clive's use of 'upper' for 'more up' or 'higher' was the clearest indication we had had that he was doing more than imitate.

I didn't see Clive again for fifteen years. The son of an English mother and an American father, he had already spent a considerable time on each side of the Atlantic when I first met him, and he now returned unexpectedly to the States. Then in 1987 we re-established contact and had the opportunity to visit him for a week in Cape Cod, Massachusetts. Before our stay on the Cape we had learnt that Clive had progressed so much that he now held down two jobs and was looking forward greatly to seeing us again. We were as excited and apprehensive about the reunion as he was. How would he have changed and developed in the intervening years? Would the hopeful signs of normal linguistic maturation shown when we last saw him have been translated into genuine progress? Most importantly, would we learn enough from his long drawn out case to be in a position to help other people in his position by better diagnosis and therapy?

Clive greeted me warmly with 'Hi, Dr Smith' in a voice which was normal except for the glottalization that I remembered from before, and he proceeded to display an impressive range of grammatical structures way beyond what could have been predicted from his earlier lack of fluency. It was clear how he was now able to work for his living, even if it was still necessary to concentrate extremely hard to filter out the effects of his phonology, and even if his abilities were still dramatically impoverished in comparison with the average for his age, now 26 years.

In the course of the next few days we talked at great length with Clive, and administered large numbers of psychological and linguistic tests, all of which he attempted with cheerful avidity and most of which he completed with a concentration and effort that would put most people to shame. Some of the tests he even did (correctly) faster than I could: the inability to express oneself is not necessarily an indication that there is nothing to express, and the attempts of an outmoded school of psychology to give everyone a single undifferentiated 'Intelligence Quotient' would be laughable were they not so pernicious.

In displaying his abilities for us Clive answered a number of our theoretical questions, but confronted us with even harder ones. Although he communicated reasonably freely, at least with those who knew him, and appeared to control a wide range of syntactic structures, his receptive knowledge of grammar, when tested so that contextual effects were no longer available to offset his linguistic disabilities, was dramatically impoverished. As a linguist I was interested in discovering the nature of the *grammatical* knowledge that Clive disposed of: his productive performance indicated that, while not 'normal', it was extremely well-developed and at any rate remarkably better than when I had seen him previously; his receptive performance indicated that it was virtually non-existent. How was he compensating for the deficit we appeared to have found?

There was no doubt of his productive ability. In spontaneous speech he used simple clauses containing: (i) overt subjects, (ii) direct objects, (iii) indirect objects, (iv) prepositional phrases, (v) adverbials, etc. He appeared to have command of: (vi) simple sentence word-order, (vii) sentences with topicalized constituents, (viii) expletive *there*, (ix) comparatives , (x) impersonal *you*, (xi) negatives, (xii) *yes/no* and (xiii) WH questions, (xiv) some conditionals, (xv) temporal and (xvi) locative adverbs, (xvii) reflexives, (xviii) some quantifiers, (xix) part of the tense-aspect system, (xx) the singular/plural contrast, (xxi) purposives, (xxii) co-ordination, (xxiii) some relative clauses, and so on. The examples in (2), chosen to illustrate each of the (underlined) categories mentioned, give a flavour of his output.

2 (i)   *lines* go different ways
   (ii)   the boy has *the brush*
   (iii)   they do it *all the kids*
   (iv)   she live a street *in Boston*
   (v)   the water drips out the faucet *sometime*
   (vi)   *the bug fly with wings, the tree does not fly*
   (vii)   *last night* I got it
   (viii) *there*'s a parking lot there
   (ix)   fence *better*
   (x)   *you* get clams
   (xi)   the lady *not* looking

(xii)   *is it a boat?*
(xiii)   *why* he is happy?
(xiv)   *if you want some coffee, I'll get it* (coached)
(xv)   cold *in the winter*
(xvi)   they move me out of *there*
(xvii)   he shot *hisself*
(xviii)   *both* ears
(xix)   last night I *got* it/so they *get* married
(xx)   need an aid in the *ear*/he is missing his *ears*
(xxi)   he go down the clock – *tell the time*
(xxii)   *you button the coat and you zipper the coat*
(xxiii)   a car *who flies* (Chitty-Chitty-Bang-Bang)

Despite this impressive array of examples at his productive disposal, when Clive was tested on a comparable range of constructions for his understanding, his performance was close to random on some, and good only on prepositional phrases. To test his comprehension in the absence of contextual clues, we used a battery of tests of which the best-known were TROG (Test of Reception Of Grammar) and the Birkbeck Test for Comprehension of Reversible Sentences. In each of these the format is to show the subject a set of four pictures, read him a sentence which is an appropriate description of only one of them, and ask him to point to the correct picture. A typical sentence is 'the horse is chased by the man' for which the subject is confronted by: a picture of a man chasing a horse; a picture of a horse chasing a man (that is, the 'reverse' of the correct version), a picture of a man sitting on a horse, and a picture of a dog chasing a horse. The last two are 'lexical distractors' designed to check that the subject knows the meaning of the relevant words; the important one is the second (reversed) sentence, called a 'grammatical distractor', as it is designed to test whether the subject can cope with the difference between different grammatical constructions. In this case the difference is one between active and passive sentences, and the hypothesis is that if the subject doesn't control this distinction, he will be as likely to point to the picture of a horse chasing a man as to the (correct) picture of a man chasing a horse. This is particularly likely given that men and horses are in the real world equally likely to chase each other, and that the word order of the passive is the opposite – in relevant respects – of the active.

In both tests Clive performed at chance level on 'reversible' actives and passives. In fact his performance was virtually random on all constructions except those involving prepositional phrases as in 'the box is in the basket', for which the relevant illustrations included both a box in a basket and a basket in a box. On these he performed almost flawlessly. In the Birkbeck Test he appeared at first to be doing rather well, even on the reversible actives and passives: he got 12 out of 14 correct. On the second version of the test, however, he got 8 out of 14 wrong, and an analysis of the individual words involved showed completely arbitrary results.

Clive is a willing, co-operative and intelligent subject, so we tried to elicit from him judgements on the acceptability of sentences we had devised to contain various different sorts of mistake (a notoriously difficult exercise for anyone). His responses were remarkable and at times endearing. He reacted equally happily to 'John is very tall' and 'John is tall very', to 'John is tall enough' and 'John is enough tall'. Where the word order makes no difference to the meaning in the standard language he appeared not to care which was used: if he was having to communicate despite having a defective grammar, such examples would be the least important. In his spontaneous speech, he used a number of reflexives appropriately, so we tried to check out his command of the Binding Theory – that bit of current syntactic theory that accounts (among other things) for the difference between ordinary pronouns like 'him' and reflexive ones like 'himself'. His response to being asked to explain what 'John shot him' means was: 'he shot hisself'. Being then asked to explain what 'John shot himself' means he replied 'he did shot hisself'. Hoping to find some evidence of grammatical awareness, I plied him with the ungrammatical 'John shot myself'. His reaction was instantaneous: 'bad' – but his judgement was not linguistic – he immediately continued 'not right to shot hisself'!

As a final test we presented him with various violations of 'sub-categorization' restrictions. The verb 'put' has to be followed by both a Noun Phrase and a Prepositional Phrase, so it is grammatical to say 'John put the car in the garage' but neither 'John put in the garage' nor 'John put the car' is possible. Similarly, 'find' has to be followed by an object, whereas 'come' cannot be: in traditional terms they are transitive and intransitive verbs respectively. Clive failed to react directly to ungrammatical sentences designed to illustrate such restrictions, but his responses indicated that he did at least have as part of his lexical knowledge the fact that 'put' and 'find' do require objects. For instance, his reaction to 'she put in the garage' was 'the car'; to 'the boy came the fish' was 'he eat it'; to 'John found the' was 'found something on the ground', and so on.

How can we explain the disparities between Clive's productive and perceptive behaviour? First, it is clear that his vocabulary is excellent. He knows words such as 'exasperate', 'vicar' and 'germinate', and except for the most esoteric items performed faultlessly in identifying pictures from words and retrieving words for pictures. Moreover, there is good evidence that his lexical entries (the totality of information – phonological, morphological, syntactic, semantic and encyclopaedic – associated with any word) extended beyond the ability to pair sounds with concepts. Apart from the evidence already mentioned that he 'knew' that certain verbs need an object, he made some interesting mis-readings. He read 'could' as 'can', 'were' as 'was' and, remarkably, 'limes are sour' as 'lemons are sweet'. Significantly, he did not read 'can' as 'were' or any other logical possibility, indicating that, as in the standard language, 'can' and 'could' shared a lexical entry, but that 'can' and 'were' did not.

What is most striking about his linguistic behaviour is his exploitation of contextual cues to facilitate communication in the absence of perfect control of the grammar: what we might call 'compensatory pragmatics'. I was given a striking instance of this soon after arriving in Massachusetts. It became apparent that Clive was a fan of the Boston Red Sox (baseball team) and that this was therefore a good topic of conversation. Having lived in Boston some twenty years previously I dredged up from my memory the name of the then hero 'Yastrzemski'. Instantly Clive replied 'coach now'. His answer lacked a subject, a verb and an article, but communicatively it was all that was necessary.

All communication exploits the Principle of Relevance, the pragmatic principle that leads you to maximize contextual effects at minimal processing cost – to get the most cognitive reward for the least effort. In some sense, Clive's reply satisfied the spirit of the Principle, despite the effort for the listener involved in decoding a strictly ungrammatical sentence. The level of relevance he achieved was comparable to that achieved by anyone else.

More cogently, another assumption of Relevance Theory provides a partial explanation for other aspects of Clive's verbal behaviour. In interpreting any utterance one uses the immediately preceding utterance as part of the context, and a sentence is 'relevant' if you can use it, together with the context, to deduce conclusions that wouldn't follow from either of them alone. In ordinary English this allows us to leave out information that it would be redundant to specify. In elementary language classes one has exchanges like those in (3):

3   'Where are you going?'– 'I am going to school.'
    'What are you doing?' – 'I am eating a banana.'

In real life one has exchanges like those in (4):

4   'Where are you going?– 'School.'
    'What are you doing? – 'Eating a banana.'

where the ellipsed subject is easily reconstructible from the immediately preceding question. In standard English there are grammatical constraints on precisely when the subject (and other elements) can be ellipsed, but in Clive's English no such constraints exist: his grammar fails to make the distinctions. Pragmatically this doesn't matter: thus, when asked 'Why do we pay taxes?' he replied (with some perspicacity) 'to pay Reagan' – an answer which is both appropriate and grammatical. When asked 'Would you like to fly?' he answered 'need some clothes to do that', and when showing us a picture of his work place he pointed to one area and said 'long time ago was my classroom'. Each utterance was completely appropriate, informative and relevant, but the last two were ungrammatical. We would have said: '*I'd* need some clothes to do that' and 'a long time ago *this* was my classroom': not because these forms are pragmatically superior, but because they are grammatically necessary.

For Clive, it is clear that all the examples were of a kind: in each case his command of contextually controlled ellipsis leads him to omit the subject (and other elements) irrespective of the grammatical repercussions of this strategy. In view of this memory-saving pragmatic strategy it is important to bear in mind that, when analysing the speech of any speaker, the presence or absence of a subject may be grammatically felicitous or not, and may be pragmatically appropriate or not. Different patients have different deficits, and knowing only that someone has produced a sentence without a subject tells one nothing of interest unless one knows the context in which that sentence occurred.

Current views of language acquisition exploit the 'principles and parameters' approach of Government–Binding theory. By postulating a set of universal, innately determined principles which allow a certain amount of 'parametric variation', the logical problem of explaining how children can learn their first language so fast and on the basis of such poor evidence is partially solved. If one takes the 'Head-first/Head-last' parameter, for instance, all the child needs for the parameter to be appropriately fixed is one piece of triggering data from a wide range of possible construc-tions. One does not need to learn both that verbs precede their objects and that prepositions precede their complements (in English), or that verbs follow their objects and 'prepositions' (actually 'postpositions') follow their complements (in Japanese): learning either fact should suffice to fix the parameter as 'Head-first' for English or 'Head-last' for Japanese, with concomitant saving for the language-acquiring child.

In the case of Clive, it looks as if he failed to set the parameters of his grammar. Whichever module of his grammar one looks at: Binding theory (dealing with pronouns and reflexives), thematic theory (dealing with the arguments – subject and objects – required by different verbs), it is either lacking or incomplete. Rather than the 'triggering' process typical of the language acquisition of normal children, it looks as if for Clive language learning really is *learning* and, given the poverty of the stimulus, that learning is necessarily partial. To be a little more specific, his learning of syntax, like his earlier learning of phonology, appears to have proceeded piecemeal; learnt contrasts were not general-ized; strategies are applied inconsistently; and every utterance is either the result of verbatim learning or the product of inserting items into one of a set of learnt syntactic frames, rather than the output of a set of generative rules. His pragmatic ability is largely intact, enabling him to decode simple inputs on the basis of a more than respectable lexicon; and a number of syntactic schemata or frames enable him to produce something which approximates to normality.

Clive is a fighter and works extremely hard to overcome a disability we can barely understand. Sadly there are many like him who are not able to work and do not benefit from the incredibly supportive home environment that he does. Moreover, every person with a language disability is different from every other, so that the lessons learnt with Clive may not be relevant to the next person one sees. Gradually, however, one can see patterns and adopt techniques to maximize the abilities that any particular patient does dispose of. In Clive's case we have strong evidence for the desirability of trying to develop pragmatic abilities even in the absence of a properly functioning grammar. More importantly, given his total early inarticulateness and subsequent development, we have evidence that no-one should be 'written off'. Clive was written off by a number of people, and even those who helped him learn to speak appear to have done so in an inhuman manner. He spent some time in an institution where the punishment for any misdemeanour was being chained to the banisters, or being thrown into cold water. A typical example of Clive's spontaneous speech revealed a great deal, despite its linguistic imperfections:

'They mean. Cold bath – ice in it. They do it all the kids.'

No one deserves treatment like that. Clive's progress despite lack of appropriate schooling and intermittent institutional cruelty provides an example we can all learn from.

Notes

p. 167   All my work with Clive has been done in conjunction with the distinguished neuropsychologist Freda Newcombe, who originally introduced me to him. I am extremely grateful to her for continued help and guidance. We hope to produce a more detailed and technical analysis of his psychological and linguistic abilities in due course. 'Clive' is not his real name.

p. 168   A preliminary analysis of some aspects of Clive's language appears in Smith (1975).

p. 168   For normal early language development, cf. essays 4, 'The Puzzle Puzzle', and 9, 'Y'.

p. 168   'Schwa' ([ə]) is the sound of the unstressed vowel at the beginning of *above*. A glottal stop ([?]) is the sound used in a number of dialects of English, most notably Cockney, to replace the 't' in *butter*.

p. 169   On the inadequacies of 'IQ', cf. e.g. Gould (1983).

p. 171   TROG is elaborated in Bishop (1977, 1982). Clive scored at about the five-year-old level. The Birkbeck Test is still in the process of being developed. I am extremely grateful to my colleague Maria Black for both providing me with a prototype version and explaining it to me.

p. 172   For Binding Theory, cf. Chomsky (1981a, 1986), and essay 12 'Data, Evidence and Theory Change'.

p. 172   The clearest treatment of sub-categorization is in Radford (1988).

p. 173   For the Principle of Relevance, cf. Sperber and Wilson (1986a), and essay 7, 'Wilt Thou have this Man to thy wedded Wife?'

p. 175   For 'principles and parameters', cf. Chomsky (1981c). For the Head-first/Head-last parameter, cf. Chomsky (1986, 1988a) and essay 6, 'The Oats have eaten the Horses'.

p. 175   What precisely constitutes a 'pragmatic pathology' is still an open question. Clive provides an interesting contrast with the case of 'John' in Blank et al. (1978): cf. essay 13 'Annie's Botty-wotty'.

16

The Numbers Game

To the layman the hall-mark of the scientist is the ability to measure and quantify, to give his (or her) statements the respectability of numerical justification. D'Arcy Thompson encapsulates this view at the beginning of his monumental classic *On Growth and Form* with the words 'numerical precision is the very soul of science', and, in the hard sciences, progress has often gone hand in hand with refinements of mathematical or statistical technique. Indeed, modern statistics arose in part as the result of such early mathematicians as Gauss attempting to refine the accuracy of physical measurements; and the question of molecular reality (whether atoms and molecules are real, physical entities or mere abstractions) was settled only when reliable ways were devised to count them.

It is clear that without mathematics, modern science and technology would be impossible. Neither the benefits of laser surgery nor the horrors of star-wars, neither the delights of hi-fi nor the misery of noise pollution would have arisen in the absence of a mathematically based scientific technology. Does it follow that any science must have a mathematical basis? Before addressing this question it is necessary to make a distinction between the axiomatization of a discipline in terms of a mathematical system and the quantification of the observations made in that discipline. The former seems to be straightforwardly desirable and the extent to which it is possible for any subject provides a reasonable rough guide to the scientific rigour of that subject, whereas the latter is more circumscribed in its relevance. Ideally, an axiomatized system will generate theorems which can then function as hypotheses to be tested by techniques involving quantificational (statistical) analysis. Positive outcomes from such tests reinforce the validity of the system, negative ones should induce changes in the overall theory or, more probably, changes in the experimental technique which led to the result, in the hope that subsequent tests are more favourable.

Let us look at a typical example of the use of quantificational data in linguistics. I choose an example almost at random from a recent paper entitled 'A Text-based Analysis of Non-narrative Texts'. The author ran experiments to check readers' intuitions as to what constituted an appropriate discourse-topic: roughly the subject matter of a text which gives it its cohesion *as* a text. After reading a text, subjects were presented with four sentences, described as: (1) a prototypical proposition; (2) a statement of specific information; (3) a highly generalized proposition; and (4) one with a general predicate but a specific argument. They were then asked to choose the one 'which best represents the discourse so that it could be interpreted as the proposition the discourse is about'. The results were given as: (1) 66 per cent; (2) 0 per cent; (3) 9 per cent; and (4) 22 per cent. Sadly these figures are meaningless. Apart from the mysterious loss of 3 per cent and the complete lack of any statement of the statistical significance of these results, there is a worse problem of how the results bear on the initial hypothesis. Are we to assume that discourse-topics are identifiable by only two-thirds of speakers? That it is an optional extra that may or may not occur? Or what? Two points are salient: first the notion of discourse-topic is anyway otiose. The phenomena of connectivity and cohesion that Giora wishes to characterize can be described more perspicuously in terms of the optimization of relevance. Moreover the different results found can then be attributed to differences in the accessibility of the context that individuals postulate to interpret the text in. Secondly, even if the notion were viable theoretically, there is no way that voting of the kind illustrated here would either validate or invalidate it, because there is no causal chain specified between the existence of the topic, the content and structure of the test sentences and the judgements of the subjects.

This example might seem unfair, so let us consider three further simple instances of the use of statistics in language study: in sociolinguistics, in typology, and in language acquisition.

In sociolinguistics the main use of quantitative data has been to correlate the use of different linguistic variables, such as the presence or absence of an /r/ in the pronunciation of words like 'car' and 'card'; the use of 'done' versus 'did' as the past tense of 'do'; and the inclusion of 'what' in sentences like 'John is bigger than (what) Bill is', with such socially defined parameters as age, sex, education, race, occupation and provenance. As none of these linguistic variables is in a one-to-one correspondence with any of the social variables, but equally none is random, statistical data are used to illuminate which social variables determine which linguistic ones in what kind of hierarchical order. For instance, the presence or absence of an /h/ in one's pronunciation depends in part on the particular word involved: some people pronounce /h/ in both 'house' and 'apple', some only in 'house', some in neither. In part, however, it depends on a range of other factors: the speaker's age and sex, the formality of the situation, and so on. It is a truism in sociolinguistics that, as Hudson puts it, such 'facts call for a quantitative treatment of the data', which moreover seems 'particularly relevant to theoretical linguistics because [it] involve[s] precisely those aspects of language – sounds, word-forms and constructions – which theoretical linguists consider central'.

It is perhaps worth clearing up the misapprehension in that last remark first. To be of interest to a linguistic theorist it is not sufficient that the talk be of words and such like, rather the talk has to have implications of some kind for the theory concerned, by supporting or contradicting one of the claims derivable from it. In the present case it is not clear how this could be done. It is obvious that different communities exhibit variation in their speech: people in Paris speak French while those in Washington speak English and those in Montreal cope with both; it is equally clear that children don't speak the same way as their grand-parents, that males and females are not necessarily identical in their linguistic abilities, and so on. In short, any social parameter whatsoever may be the locus for some linguistic difference. Unfortunately nothing of interest to linguistic theory follows from this, so quantifying the difference is irrelevant to linguistics even though it may be of interest to the sociologist if it gives him or her a recognition criterion for some socially relevant variable.

The classic example of a quantificational sociolinguistic study is provided by Labov's investigation of the determinants (age, class and casualness) of New Yorkers' pronunciation of /r/, pre-consonantally and finally, in words like 'fourth' and 'floor'. His hypotheses: that the pronunciation with /r/ would be more common among the young, among the high-class and in less casual situations, appeared to be only partially borne out: the age factor was decidedly more complex than this. But for present purposes two points are of more relevance. First, he provided no tests of statistical significance, so his interpretation of the figures is anyway suspect. Secondly, even if he had, they would have had no implications for linguistic theory, as they failed to address any linguistic issue. That is, he started from the observation that variation occurred and proceeded to discover the bases for that variation along parameters all of which were socially defined.

It is often suggested that variation of the kind described is a refutation of the generative paradigm, in that it contradicts the idealization to homogeneity made in Chomsky's *Aspects*. This again betrays a misunderstanding of the kind of enterprise linguists are involved in: the claim of a generative grammarian is that one's grammar is a mentally represented psychological construct which can *ipso facto* differ from person to person. The idealization is the claim that the unquestioned empirical non-homogeneity of any community (or even of any individual on different occasions) is irrelevant to a characterization of possible grammars and hence possible states of the mind. It is logically possible that the heterogeneity of actual dialectal, stylistic and idiosyncratic variation is necessary for first-language acquisition, but no evidence for this has ever been presented, and it seems unlikely in principle that a homogeneous input would make language learning impossible.

It is not inconceivable that quantificational sociolinguistic studies might have implications of a kind which would interest the theoretical linguist. It is an open and interesting question what the nature of the mentally represented grammar(s) of a bilingual is. Does he or she manipulate two quite separate systems? Is there a single system? Or is some intermediate position correct? Given that bilingualism and bidialectalism are two points on a continuum, it should be possible to investigate this issue on the basis of what is known as 'accommodation' between dialects: that is, the modification to his system that a speaker uses when conversing with a speaker of a different dialect. In his book

Dialects in Contact, Trudgill has investigated precisely this matter. Even here, the role of quantification is secondary. The most interesting conclusions are derivable from the observation of which linguistic features are subject to change, whether in the direction of convergence or divergence, as opposed to those which are impermeable to modification, and it is only rarely that a decision about this will necessitate statistical techniques of any complexity. How one relates these results (quantified or not) to questions about the mental representation of rules and lexical items is an unsolved problem. It is unsolved because we lack a theory of metalinguistic awareness which will enable us to make predictions correlating our use of linguistic rules with our consciousness of those rules; and we are still in need of a theory of bilingualism which is sufficiently explicit to make testable hypotheses over a quantified data base. We don't lack numbers, we lack insights.

Work in language typology is full of statements of the kind: 'languages with dominant word-order S–O–V tend to have postpositions', 'with greater than chance frequency . . .', and so on. Unless we have some specific content to add to 'tend' and 'greater than chance', these claims amount to no more than the assertion of an intuitive feeling or prejudice, predicated on the fact that some languages have property X and some languages do not. Scarcely a very interesting observation, as any replacement for X which does not express a strong universal (i.e. one actually evidenced in every language) will leave it true. Building on the work of Greenberg and others, Hawkins has now quantified such statements, finding for instance, that 92.19 per cent of S–O–V languages have postpositions and only 7.81 per cent have prepositions. Further, these probabilities are combined with those of other variables, such as the relative order of adjective and noun, to make possible a statistically based notion of 'harmonic' (or 'consistent') language; that is, one where constructions conform to the statistical norm, with a concomitant prediction that languages will be rarer the less consistent they are. This prediction appears to be largely confirmed on a wider scrutiny of the world's languages. Here then we seem to have a numerically based system making testable hypotheses which turn out to be confirmed by the data. What could possibly be more scientific than that?

Unfortunately, all that this demonstrates is that the choice of the initial sample was well made (or less optimistically, that the larger sample still suffers from the same defects). The claim that languages will be more numerous the more closely they approximate to a harmonic type is hardly surprising when the harmony they reflect is set up on the basis of the relative frequency of the relevant types in the initial sample.

It is a commonplace of work in language acquisition that children do not pronounce the words of the language they are learning in the same way as their putative adult models, nor indeed in the same way as their peers. Thus 'duck' may be rendered '*du*' ([dʌ]) by one child, '*guck*' ([gʌk]) by another and '*dut*' ([dʌt]) by a third. Despite these differences, the child's pronunciation is not random – no child pronounces 'duck' as 'daffodil' – and for any particular child it is usually possible to predict his or her pronunciation for any arbitrary word of the adult language: i.e. the behaviour is rule-governed. Armed with this knowledge and distinctive feature theory, Irwin and Wong produced a book full of tables itemizing the mispronunciations of a representative set of normal children at various ages in terms of which sound or distinctive feature was replaced by which other sound, how many times it was so replaced, and what the probability of such replacement was. The aim was to provide statistical norms by reference to which the abnormal development of children with developmental dysphasia could be measured and appropriate treatment initiated.

A typical example of their results is that at age two /m/ is produced correctly 97 per cent of the time, /d/ 64 per cent of the time and /r/ 20 per cent of the time. By implication, any child whose performance deviates markedly from this would be a *prima facie* candidate for speech-therapeutic investigation and intervention. Again we have a quantitative analysis making possible the statement of clinical norms with apparent direct application.

Again, however, what we really have is a radical misapprehension. Norms for correct pronunciation in language acquisition are useful only when the figures approach 100 per cent. If a three-year-old is investigated and is found not to conform to the expected percentages, nothing of any use or interest follows, unless and until a detailed analysis of his production and perception is performed. For instance, he may pronounce 'duck' as '*guck*' ([gʌk]), failing to produce a /d/ because of a consonant harmony process which is normal for his age, while producing /d/ correctly in 'Daddy'. If he pronounces 'duck' correctly and mispronounces 'Daddy' as '*Gaddy*' ([gadi:]), on the other hand, something probably is wrong, but the figures Irwin and Wong provide don't discriminate between the two situations.

All three of the examples discussed seemed, on the basis of techniques of numerical quantification, to provide a valid basis for predicting new phenomena. None the less I think that none of them in fact provides any insight into, or explanation of, the nature of the human language faculty, and only marginally of language use. To see why, it is useful to distinguish *explanation* and *prediction*. One can predict the time of sunrise, the occurrence of eclipses, or the inheritance of particular characteristics, without being able to explain these phenomena in terms of the rotation of the earth, the occultation of the sun's light and the principles of molecular genetics respectively.

The predictions made in each of the above examples amount simply to confident assertions to the effect that things will continue the same as they have been before. Moreover, in all three cases we are potentially misled because of the confusion of group data and individual data. Individual speakers' grammars differ from each other in a wide variety of ways, most obviously in the vocabulary, but also in details of pronunciation, of grammatical rules and so on. Despite their differences, each of a number of grammars may be perfectly normal even if it contains rules incompatible with those in another. In no case were explanations of the phenomena provided, because in no case were the mentally represented rule systems of individual speakers taken into account.

The lesson one should carry away from examples such as the above is that quantification is of value only if it is to be used to test an explicit hypothesis which arises from the predictions of a particular theory. It should also go without saying that it is worth doing only if the hypothesis has some interest. Elaborate exercises to establish truisms, such that people speak differently in different communities and environments are not really worth it. Equally importantly, the domain of interest of the hypothesis needs to be made clear: it is conceivably (though improbably) of vital social importance to know whether the old or the young, the black or the white, use a particular linguistic form (consider the importance of the 'shibboleth'). It does not follow that it is of linguistic interest. The grammar of German is not affected by the fact that German was Einstein's and Hitler's native language; linguistic theory is not affected by the fact that its subject matter can also be of interest to others: the hydrologist's theories are not affected by spitting.

There are areas in the language sciences where quantificational studies have a role to play. An obvious example is the setting of norms for developmental progression of the sort exemplified by Irwin and Wong's work. Here too though it is necessary to take cognizance of the fact that quantification needs to be used insightfully: using group data rather than individual data in such a case obscures rather than enlightens. More importantly, the quantification is parasitic on the results of linguistic theory, it is not determinative of them. In general the numbers game is irrelevant to the linguist both because the nature of his hypotheses do not usually lend themselves to quantitative testing in virtue of being a mental/psychological rather than a physical discipline, and more soberingly because we are still a long way from the explicitness of the physicists for whom quantification is a *sine qua non*. Lem describes statistics as 'the rationalist's substitute for demonology': we need to exorcise our demons.

Notes

p. 178   The quotation from D'Arcy Thompson is from p. 2 of his 1942.

p. 178   The examples from the development of modern statistics are from Pais (1982). Three of the methods for counting molecules are found in Einstein's work of 1905 (Pais, 1982: pp. 18-19).

p. 179   The 'Text-based Analysis' is Giora (1985). The quotation is from p. 127.

p. 179   On the relevance of Relevance to connectivity and cohesion, cf. Blass (1985), and essay 7, 'Wilt Thou have this Man to thy wedded Wife?'.

p. 180   The quotations from Hudson are from pp. 143 and 138 of his (1980).

p. 180   Labov's classic investigation is presented in his (1972).

p. 181   The idealization to homogeneity of the speech community was first put forward explicitly in Chomsky (1965). For discussion of a number of reactions to it, cf. Chomsky (1986: chap. 2), and D'Agostino (1986: chap. 1).

p. 181   For the competence of bilinguals, cf. Sridhar and Sridhar (1980).

p. 182   The reference to Trudgill is to his (1986). 'Convergence' and 'divergence' refer respectively to the increase and decrease in similarity of one's speech to that of the dialect of one's interlocutor.

p. 182   The statements on language typology are derived from Greenberg's seminal (1963) article.

p. 182   The statistical examples from Hawkins' work are taken from his (1980). It is worth emphasizing that this recent work, especially his (1988a, 1988b) are achieving real explanatory power.

p. 183   On the pronunciation of children learning their first language, cf. Smith (1973), and essay 4 'The Puzzle Puzzle'. The book by Irwin and Wong is their (1982). For further discussion, cf. Smith (1983d).

p. 183   For distinctive feature theory, cf. the Appendix, and essay 9 'Y'.

p. 184   For consonant harmony, cf. essay 4 'The Puzzle Puzzle'.

p. 184   On individual differences in people's grammars, cf. Smith and Wilson (1979: chap. 1).

p. 185   The importance of practical phonetics, or at least of being able to pronounce 'shibboleth', is clear from Jephthah's use of it in Judges 12 (*The New English Bible*, p. 286):

The Gileadites seized the fords of the Jordan and held them against Ephraim. When any Ephraimite who had escaped begged leave to cross, the men of Gilead asked him, 'Are you an Ephraimite?', and if he said, 'No', they would retort, 'Say Shibboleth.' He would say 'Sibboleth', and because he could not pronounce the word properly, they seized him and killed him at the fords of the Jordan. At that time forty-two thousand men of Ephraim lost their lives.

p. 185   The quotation from Lem is from his (1968: p. 10).

17

Useless Grammar

In one of his characteristically vitriolic pieces George Bernard Shaw recommended his readers to 'discard useless grammar', which he described as a 'devastating plague', and to 'spell phonetically'. Goldsmith had much the same attitude in his sardonic lines:

> Let schoolmasters puzzle their brain.
> With grammar, and nonsense, and learning,
> Good liquor, I stoutly maintain,
> Gives genius a better discerning.

This sentiment will doubtless appeal to anyone who has struggled to master the intricacies of the French gender system, the complexities of German irregular verbs, or even the idiosyncrasies of English spelling that were Shaw's perennial preoccupation. There is a worthy motive underlying Shaw's self-serving rhetoric, but like many of his ideas, the assumption that grammar either could or should be manipulated in the way that spelling might be was not thought through.

There is an implicit presupposition in Shaw that redundancy and irregularity in language are inherently bad. Redundancy is, by hypothesis, not useful and the term is faintly pejorative at best; so we should clearly welcome anything that did away with useless spellings of the kind seen in 'debt'; or with the repetition of the mark of the plural differentiating (1a) from its singular equivalent (1b):

1a   These child*ren are* Eskimos.

1b   This child *is an* Eskimo.

or with the double negatives characteristic of standard Spanish in
(2a) and non-standard English in (2b):

2a   *No vi nadie.*
2b   I didn't see no-one.

This kind of grammatical over-kill is ubiquitous: *all* languages
display redundancy in the information-theoretic sense, and do so
in roughly the same amount. Of more interest for the linguist is
the   inter-play   between   over-determination   and   under-
determination in the grammatical systems of languages. On the
one hand, sentences only partially determine the content of the
thought they are designed to give rise to. Thus, someone who
utters (3):

3   It's good enough.

leaves his interlocutor to work out the referent of 'it' on the basis
of the context, and leaves him to determine the parameter along
which 'it' is good to context and the imagination. On the other
hand, the message carried by the utterance of any particular
sentence is over-determined by the spoken or written form of that
sentence. For instance, the spelling of the word 'message' could be
simplified to 'mesage' with no loss of information because there is
no other word in English with which it could be confused. In
contrast, the distinction between 'pus' and 'puss' is carried
precisely by the difference between 's' and 'ss', so the extra 's'
conveys information.

Once one looks at whole sentences rather than the spelling of
individual words, the redundancy increases because choices of
lexical and grammatical item are mutually constraining. I can
write the previous sentence totally without vowels yet its
grammatical structure and meaning are still reconstructible, as
witness (4):

4   th rdndncy ncrss bcs chcs f lxcl nd grmmtcl tm r mtlly
     cnstrnng

For Shaw such redundancy was anathema. But even if one restricts attention to the orthographic system that he tended to confuse with the language it represents, it is not clear that redundancy of this kind is really pernicious. He makes a great fuss about the extra time it took him to write his articles and prepare them for publication because of the 'superfluous' letters in the English spelling system. However, one stage in that process involves proof-reading what one has written, and proof-reading a redundancy-free manuscript is a pain compared to proof-reading a redundancy-containing one. Consider the difference between 'The winning name is "Massachusetts"' and 'The winning number is "9747163284495"'.

Redundancy in the spelling system is a trivial matter, and even irregularity may not be entirely pernicious, as we shall see below. The situation is more interesting once one gets to the grammatical system. The kind of redundancy illustrated by the plural agreement in (1a) is characteristic of all natural languages. Not all languages have agreement, but all languages have redundancy of a comparable kind in some part of their grammatical system. This universality makes it unlikely that redundancy is an accident, and in fact it serves the useful function of facilitating communication in non-ideal conditions: e.g. in situations where one is a long way from one's interlocutor or surrounded by noise. If a particular grammatical contrast such as that between singular and plural is indicated several times, then it doesn't matter if one of the words marking it is lost in transmission because of a cough, a slip of the tongue, or a lion's roar.

Even this kind of redundancy is not of particularly great interest: it is a characteristic of all languages, and it is one which serves a function which makes it unlikely to be eliminable. Apparent redundancy of a semantic or stylistic kind is more intriguing and one which Shaw himself exploited in his literary writing. The simplest possible kind of example is provided by the repetition in the lines from *Androcles and the Lion* cited in (5):

5   *Lavinia*: Androcles, Androcles: whats the matter?
    Androcles: Oh dont ask me, dont ask me.

What can we glean from an example of this kind of redundancy? First, it is grammatically conditioned in that such repetition is not totally free: if I repeat 'totally' in the immediately preceding sentence to give (6a), the effect is of rhetorical emphasis; if I repeat 'is' to give (6b), the effect is of a hesitation or slip of the tongue rather than of a rhetorical flourish:

6a   Such repetition is not totally totally free.
6b   Such repetition is is not totally free.

Second, it is clear that the repetition in (6a) does have a rhetorical effect, however weak or trite in such a contrived example, indicating that the transmission of true information does not exhaust the role of the sentence concerned, as the truth value of a sentence with and without the repetition is presumably the same. In such cases the repetition forces a reappraisal of the *relevance* of the utterance concerned, conveying to the listener that the sequence involved is worth more attention and more processing effort than he might otherwise have suspected.

Stylistic effects more generally trade on what might appear to be redundancies in the grammar. From a purely logical point of view, the existence of a wide variety of truth-conditionally equivalent but syntactically and phonologically disparate constructions seems unnecessary. Rhetorically, it is a boon. The propositional content of (7):

7   Shaw stigmatized the redundancy of English grammar.

is the same as that of each of the examples in (8):

8a   What Shaw stigmatized was the redundancy of English grammar.
8b   The redundancy of English grammar was stigmatized by Shaw.

but their appropriate contexts and hence their stylistic effects are very far from the same. One of the achievements of Sperber and Wilson's theory of relevance is that it begins to provide the basis for an explicit way of describing and explaining the differences among such constructions with a characterization of how it is they achieve the effects they do. Their presupposition of a syntactic theory of a Chomskyan kind as a necessary explicit prerequisite to their notion of a 'focal scale' allows an initial explanation of why (8a) would be appropriate as a response to (9a), and (8b) to (9b) though not vice versa.

9a It's not really true to say that the author of *Pygmalion* condemned the verbosity of English writers —— [8a]
9b Whereas the idiocies of the English spelling system have been a bane to many —— [8b]

It seems that redundancy, at whatever level it is treated, is useful rather than useless. Perhaps Shaw was on safer ground with his strictures against irregularity. It is certainly true that the kind of regularization that two-year-olds go in for, making 'brought' '*brang*', or 'came' '*comed*', gives rise to no problem of interpretation and, if accepted by everyone, would save the misery of countless foreign learners of English. Nevertheless, irregularity is not an unmitigated evil. Even in the domain of spelling where Shaw was most acerbic, the irregularities of English can be useful. Our orthography distinguishes homophones that could otherwise be confused: if *you* wish to write about a *ewe* grazing under a *yew*, it's helpful to keep the [ju:]s distinct. The argument that context will usually tell you which one is meant – one is unlikely to confuse 'cleft' and 'klepht' after all – is not relevant to someone who is not sure whether the /gərila/ mentioned on the news is animal or human.

The odd spelling of many words can often give us a clue as to their provenance: 'ph' usually marks a word as being of Greek origin with the pronunciation of 'f' – leading various people to talk about Clafam Common. Not very important in English, this kind of etymological spelling can be a useful cultural index in the spelling system of other languages. In Hindi, words spelt with (their equivalents of) 'j' and 'z' are often pronounced identically; but the spelling with 'z' is a clear indication that the word concerned is a loan from Urdu or Persian and hence appropriately used in a different, usually more formal, context than one spelt with 'j'. More usefully, the phonetic irregularity of our spelling allows us to maintain a modicum of morphological regularity, preserving the relatedness of sets of words like 'telephone – telephonic – telephony', in which the orthographic 'o' is pronounced three different ways, and giving us clues as to the pronunciation and even meaning of words we are unfamiliar with.

Turning from the relatively manipulable domain of the orthography to the grammar proper, irregularity is as universal a feature as redundancy, but without the apparent functional utility of the latter. Even in Esperanto, a language invented to be without irregularity, the exceptionless nature of the grammar is only a function of its inventor Zamenhof's failure to specify many of the details of its syntax, so that many speakers are just not sure what is correct in some cases, and model their performance on that in one of their other languages. For instance, English and French differ from German and Russian in allowing what is known as 'unbounded movement'. In English, a Noun Phrase that is the target of a question can be moved to the front of the sentence, giving us the kind of example in (10):

10a   John suborned *the witness.*
10b   *Which witness* did John suborn?

This process can take place irrespective of the complexity of the sentences involved, so we can have the comparable pair of examples in (11):

11a   The barrister suggested that the policeman had per-
       suaded the defendant to get John to suborn *the witness.*
11b   *Which witness* did the barrister suggest that the policeman
       had persuaded the defendant to get John to suborn?

Parallel examples in French are prefectly acceptable, but if one translates (11b) literally into German, the result is totally ungrammatical. In German, the movement of a phrase like 'which witness' is 'bounded'. Such subtleties of grammar were ignored in Zamenhof's codification of Esperanto, with the result that people speaking the language will impose the pattern of their first language, whatever that happens to be. The fact that there are no irregularities in Esperanto then is just a function of the incompleteness of the descriptions of its grammar.

In fact, irregularity can be grist to the linguist's mill rather than chaff to be rejected as useless. Before exemplifying how, it is worth pointing out that no irregularity is likely to be really pernicious because historical change would eliminate it if it became too severe; the capacity of the human memory is so vast that memorizing the few hundred (or even thousand) morphological irregularities of the most complex grammar is only a slight burden, except for those coming to the task in later life. Most irregularity involves the morphology rather than the syntax – i.e. the finite inventory of forms and not the really productive processes of the grammar, and even here it is usually restricted to the most frequently occurring words in the vocabulary. The equivalent of 'to be' is irregular in most languages that have a word for it, but 'to love' is irregular in none of the first twenty-five languages I checked it out in: this despite the title of a popular West End production a few years ago entitled 'The irregular verb to love'.

There is one notable exception to this generalization: the Chinese writing system, mastering whose complexities may indeed represent an educational handicap, because of the time needed to spend on that rather than other subjects. When one considers the possible advantages of our orthography, the problems presented by English spelling pale into insignificance in comparison. Even the case of Chinese is peripheral, inasmuch as the complexity is a property of the orthography and not of the language itself. Here, deviation from perfect regularity can be helpful.

Irregularity provides us with evidence of the *rule-governed* nature of language. It implies the existence of regularity, which in turn implies the existence of something determining that regularity. This becomes clearest in the over-generalizations indulged in by young children. A child who says 'mine car' for 'my car' has regularized a pattern exemplified by (12):

12   The car is his – it's his car.

to the inappropriate example in (13):

13   The car is mine – it's mine car.

This is done not on the basis of direct imitation (adults and older siblings do not normally indulge in this sort of change), but by inducing a rule on the basis of perceived regularities in the input as filtered through the child's genetically determined language faculty. The alternation in form between 'my' and 'mine' is irregular *vis-à-vis* the identity of 'his', but it is precisely the regularization of this pattern which indicates that what the child is doing in learning his first language is not simply parroting what goes on around him, but devising his own set of grammatical, in this case morphological, rules.

Examples of this type could be multiplied endlessly: 'I comed', 'two sheeps', 'no go there', and a host of others all provide evidence of the child's nascent rule-inducing capabilities. It is a little more interesting to look somewhat more closely at those areas where either irregularity does not appear or those where despite its appearance, children do not regularize. An example of the second is provided by the majority of syntactic domains. There is a well-known asymmetry in the distribution of 'likely' and 'probable', two words that appear to be virtually perfect synonyms and which share some of their syntactic environments. Thus one cay say (14a) or (14b):

    14a   It is probable that Iran will invade Burkina Faso.
    14b   It is likely that Iran will invade Burkina Faso.

with no discernible difference in either syntax or meaning. However, although one can say (15a), (15b) is impossible:

    15a   Iran is likely to invade Burkina Faso.
    15b   *Iran is probable to invade Burkina Faso.

More surprisingly, children do not over-generalize to produce examples of this last kind, despite the fact that any traditional notion of analogy would make it extremely likely that they would do so. The reason is perhaps that whereas the morphological patterns of the language have to be learnt piecemeal, so that any item is liable to be moulded to a common pattern, the syntactic patterns are generally reflexes of universally determined principles, which apply to any item for which positive evidence of its relevance has been provided. That is, the child will only use a particular word (such as 'likely' or 'probable') in such a construction (in this case a construction involving movement of the NP 'Iran') if it has heard other examples of that particular item in that construction. That is, syntactic patterns (of some kinds at least) are resistant to regularization in a way morphological ones are not. If it is appropriate to say that a large part of the syntax develops as a result of the fixing of parameters, rather than being the result of the kind of learning needed to account for the growth of vocabulary and the completely idiosyncratic and unpredictable forms of morphological variation, then we could speculate that regularization is possible only in the latter domain.

The final question is whether there are any parts of language which show no irregularities. If over-generalization provides evidence for the rules that children induce and, by hypothesis, mentally represent, it prompts the question of what the properties of the other mentally represented system – the Language of Thought – are. The simplest assumption is that the language of thought is the same as or at least isomorphic to Natural Language. But Natural Language grammars deploy a number of different levels of representation: Phonetic Form, Deep Structure, Surface Structure, and Logical Form in Chomsky's current framework, not all of which are presumably relevant to thinking. The null hypothesis would then be that the language of thought was distinct from natural languages in restricting itself to the level of Logical Form: it is obvious that the concept 'pig' is entirely independent of its spelling or pronunciation; it is reasonably clear that the irregularity of the plural form of 'sheep' is irrelevant to its meaning, and so on.

Indeed it looks as if the Language of Thought should be entirely free of both redundancy and irregularity. The reason for the development of redundancy in Natural Languages is presumably to facilitate communication despite the existence of noisy channels; the reasons for the existence of irregularity are manifold but include most noticeably the effects of (simplifying) grammatical change in one part of the system bringing about complication in other parts. (For instance the massive simplification in the phonology of Li-Jiang Chinese has effected considerable complication in its morphological structure, leading to the development of large numbers of compounds of the 'funny-peculiar' – 'funny-haha' type.) But just as there is no need for the language of thought to have redundancy as it is a vehicle for thinking not communicating, so is there no likelihood of its having any irregularity, as the prime causes – borrowing from other linguistic systems, historical change, misperceptions and so on – are again irrelevant. It is an open question what the exact relationship between natural languages and the language(s) of thought is, but it looks as if it is only in the latter that Shaw's desiderata could be met. Most grammar is essential to our thinking and communicating; even the 'useless' bits are quite handy for the latter function, and it is only in the mind that Shaw's desire to purge language of its redundancies and irregularities could be met.

Notes

p. 187   The expression 'useless grammar' and the other quotations from Shaw are from p. 17 of his Preface to Wilson (Shaw, 1941).

p. 187   The Goldsmith quotation is from his comedy *She Stoops to Conquer*, Act I, scene 1.

p. 188   Information-theory aims to discover mathematical laws governing systems designed to communicate information. For an informal overview, cf. Gallager (1975), who estimates the redundancy of English spelling at 80%.

p. 188   The simplified spelling of 'message' as 'mesage' might be misleading as regards pronunciation. I ignore this aspect here.

p. 189   The quotation in (5) is from Shaw (1962: p. 123). The (lack of) punctuation is his.

p. 190   For Relevance Theory, cf. Sperber and Wilson (1986a). Examples similar to that in (6) are discussed on pp. 219ff. For a brief introduction to the theory, cf. essay 7, 'Wilt Thou have this Man to thy wedded Wife?'

p. 191   For the focal scale, cf. Sperber and Wilson (1986a: chap. 4.5) and essays 7 'Wilt thou have this Man to thy wedded Wife?', and 14, 'In my Language we SHOUT'.

p. 191   For homophony, cf. essay 8 'Must and the Randy Pachyderm'.

p. 191   For Hindi pronunciation, cf. McGregor (1972).

p. 192   For unbounded movement, cf. Chomsky (1977), and the discussion of 'subjacency' in essay 3, 'Grammar and Gravity', and Essay 18, 'Linguistics as a Religion'. Movement of this kind is not restricted to questions, but occurs in a wide range of constructions.

I am grateful to my colleague Professor John Wells for discussing the facts of Esperanto with me.

p. 193   I have been unable to trace any reference to 'The irregular verb "to love"', but I'm sure I didn't invent it. Any details would be gratefully received.

p. 194   For dicussion of the (lack of) over-generalization by children acquiring their first language, cf. Pinker (forthcoming). The example of 'probable' and 'likely' was first given prominence in Hudson (1972). For an alternative account of why children don't make this particular analogy, cf. Bloom et al. (1984).

p. 195   For parametric variation, cf. essay 13, 'Annie's Botty-wotty', and references therein.

p. 195   For the Language of Thought, cf. Fodor (1975), and essay 6 'The Oats have eaten the Horses'.

p. 195   Chomsky's current framework is best set out in his (1986).

p. 195   The system of Li-Jiang Chinese is discussed in Klima (1975: pp. 262-7).

p. 196   On the relation between Natural languages and the Language of Thought, cf. Smith (1983a).

p. 196   The Language of Thought may be used for communication between different sub-parts of the central system, but it is clearly not a communicative system in the way a Natural Language is.

18

Linguistics as a Religion

Linguists working within Generative Grammar are often accused
of subscribing to a dogma, as though their commitment to theory
were comparable to faith in a revealed religion. There are certain
obvious parallels between practising Christianity or Islam and
practising linguistics or surgery. In both cases the community
provides a framework of orthodox ideas which are explicitly
taught as correct and which determine the nature of the activities
that are carried out; in both cases appeal is regularly made to the
wisdom and authority of charismatic leaders like Moses or
Chomsky; in both cases the argumentation has the vitriolic
flavour of the *odium theologorum* which so distressed that early
linguist Melanchthon, who published a grammar of Greek when
he was 21 and spent the rest of his life supporting Luther. Most
strikingly of all, having a theory is a little like being in a state of
Grace: everywhere one looks one sees evidence for the validity of
one's belief; everything is interpreted in terms of the categories
and claims of the system of ideas involved, usually to the
bewilderment and incomprehension of outsiders.

Despite all these parallels, the resemblance is only superficial,
and understanding why may serve to give a little understanding of
what a theory is and how it works. Although there are linguists
who simply accept a theoretical framework unquestioningly
because it provides them with a useful descriptive tool, they are
not the theoreticians who either develop that framework, nor
usually are they the ones accused of dogmatism. Similarly, while
many linguists revere Chomsky because of his innovative genius
in both theory and description; as well, perhaps, for his radical
politics and outspoken attacks on the more mindless barbarisms of

government, all except an equally mindless minority are prepared to argue against him, and only accept his suggestions *if* they cast light on problems or issues preoccupying them, and not because they come from Chomsky. One is typically more cautious arguing against Chomsky than other linguists, but that is simply because experience has told one that he usually wins the argument, not because of any fear of anathema. Indeed, attacking Chomsky has often been a short-cut to an at least transitory fame! The aggressive and sometimes abrasive tone of some of the arguments between rival theoreticians is simply a reflection of basic human characteristics which show up equally indiscriminately in religion, linguistics, and a playground brawl – though the protagonists in the first two ought to know better.

To make the contrast clear, consider how the theory of generative grammar has changed over the last thirty years or so. In particular consider the rise and fall of the Generative Semantics movement, and the different treatments of that most popular construction the passive.

The success of Chomsky's epoch-making first book *Syntactic Structures* was due both to its redefinition of the field of linguistics as one where theory construction and evaluation along lines familiar from the hard sciences became possible, and more immediately to the intellectual appeal of its analyses of tradition-ally intractable problems within the grammar of English. Foremost among these was the ingenious treatment of the auxiliary system and the relation of active to passive sentences by means of a transformation. The essence of the 'Passive Trans-formation' was the inversion of the subject and object, with the concomitant introduction of *by* and *be*, and a change in the morphology of the verb from active to passive. This converted the structure in (1a) into the structure in (1b):

1a NP_1 V NP_2
1b NP_2 *be* V *-ed by* NP_1

optionally relating any of an indefinitely large number of transitive sentences of the kind exemplified by (2a) to those of a kind exemplified by (2b):

2a   Fido ate the bone.

2b   The bone was eaten by Fido.

Appealing though it was, there were several problems with this early analysis of passives (and even worse ones with more complex sentences involving more than one clause, or negatives), including in particular what structure to give the sequence 'by NP_1'. It is apparently a Prepositional Phrase, like the one in (3):

3   The doll was lying *by Fido*.

but to capture this fact was strictly beyond the power of the grammar, because transformations could insert items like *by* but were supposed not to introduce new category labels like 'PP': they could not 'build structure'. The *Syntactic Structures* analysis, which applied only to sentences containing transitive verbs, also failed to account adequately for 'pseudo-passives' of the kind seen in (4):

4   The proposal was talked about incessantly.

where non-transitive verbs like 'talk' were involved, and it provided no account of the claimed restriction on the occurrence of the passive to those verbs which could appear with manner adverbs. This (actually somewhat dubious) restriction was intended to explain the oddity of (5a) by relating it to the comparably odd (5b):

5a   Maud resembled her uncle Silas gracefully.
5b   Her uncle Silas was resembled by Maud.

As a result of a plethora of empirical and theoretical problems of this kind, the analysis of the passive given in Chomsky's *Aspects of the Theory of Syntax* exhibited a number of differences: the *by*-phrase was now introduced by Phrase Structure rule rather than by transformation, and the transformation itself was now obligatory – triggered off by the presence of an abstract passive morpheme – rather than optional. This tied in happily with the major innovation of the 'Standard Theory' as the position developed in *Aspects* became known, namely, that all aspects of meaning were determined at Deep Structure, the level defined as the output of Phrase Structure rules, and that transformations could not 'change meaning'. That is, it was not an accident that active and passive sentences were generally synonymous, but a desirable spin-off from the mode of their syntactic analysis.

The claim that transformations were meaning-preserving entailed that all sentences with the same Deep Structure must have the same meaning. From this it was but a short step to the claim that all sentences with the same meaning must have the same Deep Structure. It was a step taken enthusiastically by a group of linguists who inaugurated what became known as 'Generative Semantics', a movement that dominated the field in the late 1960s and early 1970s, but subsequently collapsed. The Generative Semanticists assumed that the meaning (or semantic representation) of a sentence was identical to its representation at Deep Structure, and hence argued that Deep Structure itself was superfluous. As part of this reductivist programme, they proposed that the various transformations which had been postulated were responsible not only for relating synonymous sentences, but also for generating structures which were subsequently converted into lexical items. Thus an example like (6a) was derived via the passive transformation from the same structure as that underlying (6b):

6a   The book is readable.
6b   One is able to read the book.

and even examples like 'under surveillance' were supposed, because their meaning includes the idea of 'being watched', to involve passivization in their derivational history: this despite the fact that there is no related verb 'to surveill'. The resulting system allowed processes of such power that the theory was threatened with vacuity. It was as though a saint were to use miracles to cure headaches as well as to raise people from the dead: an effective technique no doubt, but one that seems a little excessive when less drastic measures would be adequate. In fact, however, it was not initially the incipient unfalsifiability of the theory which caused its downfall, but its apparent falsification by simple examples. In particular, active and passive sentence pairs, like those in (7), which involve more than one quantifier (items like 'few' and 'many'):

7a   Many men read few books.
7b   Few books are read by many men.

seemed *prima facie* counter-examples to the core hypothesis of
meaning preservation. That is, (7a) suggests that many people are
of a type who read just one or two books (different books for each
person), whereas (7b) suggests that there is only a small set of
books (the same in each case) which are good enough to have
many readers. If the two sentences really differ in this way, and if
they are correctly related by means of the passive transformation,
then the rule does bring about a change in meaning and the
Generative Semantics position is untenable.

At the same time as the Generative Semanticists were
expanding the domain and power of transformational rules,
Chomsky was suggesting stringent constraints on any rule of
grammar, with the result that all previous formulations of the
passive were disallowed. Two aspects of the complex structural
changes exhibited in (1), where one NP moves to the left while
another moves to the right, and there is a simultaneous change in
morphological structure, were excluded on principled grounds.
One of the instigations for this development was the observation
that lexical processes of the sort linking 'read' and 'readable' were
typically sporadic, unpredictable and subject to idiosyncratic
exceptions. We have an apparently regular relationship between
'read' and 'readable', but there is no adjective in '–able'
corresponding to 'resent', no verb at all corresponding to
'malleable', and no hint of 'passive meaning' in 'capable'.
Transformations were supposed to capture *generalizations* and
using them to describe lexical structure was a misuse of their
power. Moreover, there was reason to believe that the traditional
sub-components of the passive – the movement of the object NP to
the left and the postposing of the agent NP to the right – were
needed independently of each other in examples like those in (8):

8a   John is easy to please.
8b   The destruction of the city by the enemy.
8c   The city's destruction by the enemy.

In (8a), the surface subject 'John' has been moved from the object
position to the right of 'please' – contrast: 'It is easy to please

John'; and in (8b) and (8c), 'the enemy' in the *by*-phrase has been moved from the initial subject position – contrast: 'The enemy's destruction of the city'. The implication of such examples and innumerable others was that particular processes, such as that moving a Noun Phrase, shuld be 'factored out' and stated independently of individual constructions like the passive.

The clearest manifestation of this development is in the range of constructions like questions, relative clauses and clefts which involve 'unbounded movement', the phenomenon whereby a constituent can be moved indefinitely far from its original position as in the set of sentences in (9):

9a John persuaded the police to get the judge to sentence the *thief*.

9b *Which thief* did John persuade the police to get the judge to sentence?

9c *The thief* that John persuaded the police to get the judge to sentence was an acrobat.

9d It was *the thief* that John persuaded the police to get the judge to sentence.

In all three examples (9b, 9c, 9d) it is hypothesized that the same unbounded rule has applied: that is, we have not separate processes of question formation, relative clause formation and cleft formation, but a single rule with three different instantiations. The result was a theory in which there are *no* construction-specific rules at all. All movement is reduced to a single statement 'Move-α', where α is shorthand for any of a number of different categories: Noun Phrase, Prepositional Phrase and so on, and limitations on where different constituents can move to is itself a function of other universal constraints, subject to 'Parametric Variation'. The passive rule, that archetype of the transformationalists' repertoire, has disappeared and the passive itself is reduced to the status of epiphenomenon, a by-product of the interplay of other conditions and constraints.

This time the change of analysis was motivated not so much by overt counter-example of the kind that led to the demise of Generative Semantics, but by the desire to capture more, and more abstract, generalizations. The situation is reminiscent of particle physics where the advances of the theoreticians tend to be made by increasing the deductive structure of the theory, deriving generalizations from ever more abstract principles. The Provost of my college once asked me if there were still a few transformations left to discover. The answer was that the interesting task was to undiscover those we already had. The cataloguing of individual rules is a useful taxonomic exercise, but it is of limited theoretical interest. We are now beginning to understand why we had the rules that were postulated and hence how we can get rid of them by subsuming them under deeper statements. It is obviously not the case that the passive construction has ceased to exist or that the problematic data which occasioned changes in the theory in earlier years have been swept under the carpet; rather we now have a theory of sufficient complexity to enable us to explain why it is that the passive and its companions no longer need to be elevated to their pristine status.

Even now of course the story is incomplete. The abstract account of the passive hinted at presupposes a theory which defines a number of levels of representation: Deep Structure, Surface Structure and so on; a substantial number of 'sub-theories' accounting for movement, for binding relations, for case and suchlike; as well as universal principles like subjacency limiting how far a constituent can move. But while the development of an abstract theory has broadened the generalizations that can be made, it has made the justification for any particular construct of the theory more indirect and further removed from the data. When there were fifty different transformations each one accounting for a particular construction it was easy to see the relation between the rules of the grammar and the data they were accounting for. When any one sentence is now the product of the interaction of a dozen abstract and complex constraints, it is harder to relate the theory to the data; it is easier to manipulate one part of the theory to accommodate apparent counter-examples because no-one is going to be able immediately to point to the side-effects of the change without a vast amount of work. Superficially, it returns us to a situation where the argumentation looks casuistical and adherents of a theory stick to it religiously in defiance of empirical evidence.

This impression is understandable but wrong. The complexity of the theory (a complexity which derives from its success) means that much of the argumentation is 'theory-internal'. For instance, in all recent versions of the current theory, a moved constituent leaves behind a 'trace' of its previous location in the form of an empty category 'e'. For instance, if a typical passive sentence like (10):

10   John was seduced by a mermaid.

involves movement of 'John' via 'Move-α' from a position immediately after 'seduced', the analysis of the sentence would involve the two stages in (11), with a deep structure like (11a) and a surface structure like (11b):

11a   [np was seduced John by a mermaid]
11b   [John was seduced e by a mermaid]

where the 'e' is a record of the original position held by 'John'. The pair 'John, e' is then referred to as a 'chain' which is created in the transition from Deep Structure to Surface Structure.

This development has given rise to a debate within Government–Binding theory about whether the notion Deep Structure is a necessary primitive, from which it is possible to derive the notion of 'chain', or whether the notion 'chain' is derivable from Surface Structure, with the result that the notion Deep Structure might itself go the way of the passive transformation. That is, in lieu of the transformational account it might be equally possible to generate such chains directly, i.e. without involving movement at all, thereby rendering Deep Structure epiphenomenal: reconstructible if desired, but strictly unnecessary. The issue is still open. It is not however, something that one can answer just by looking at a couple of passive sentences in English or any other language! None the less the answer is empirical: it will involve constructing a long series of arguments, each of which is supported by data subjected to a particular analysis and given a particular interpretation. Complexity and the distance of the data from the theory are not equivalent to removing the claims from the domain of fact.

In contrast, consider the historical development of Christian views on the divinity of Christ at the time of the Arian heresy (I take an example from the fourth century as this is probably sufficiently remote not to cause offence, though little has

changed). The dispute lasted for several centuries, was characterized by vicious skulduggery from a cast including 'George of
Cappadocia, a dubious character, who had been a pork-
contractor', by semantic distinctions of unparalleled subtlety
involving contrasts among *inter alia* homoousians and homoious-
ians, and by a total lack of any empirical base. Success depended
on rhetoric and force of arms. It is true that such social
considerations have been influential in furthering transformational
generative grammar against its rivals, and it is true that
Chomsky's 'awesome' rhetorical power has helped, but at bottom
the difference is one between dogma and rationality. Modern
linguistics has been characterized by the fervour typical of
religious discussion; it has, sadly, been marked by vitriol
reminiscent of the Byzantine heresies; it has, more positively,
provided guiding frameworks of ideas which give some insight
into the nature of the human mind, as religion may give some
insight into the human soul: but linguistic theory is ultimately
responsible for a range of predictions about empirical data which,
however indirectly, make it falsifiable. Not so religion. Indeed, to
the extent that linguistics is a continuation of the Galilean
intellectual tradition, it is, in Magee's words, part of 'the great
flowering of European drama, poetry, science, mathematics,
philosophy, music [which] began with the emancipation of these
activities from the Church'.

After returning from MIT to give some lectures in London, I
was once introduced by Randolph Quirk as coming 'hot foot from
St Noam'. The inspiration and charisma were accurate, but it is a
rare saint who has a theory, let alone one that changes.

Notes

p. 198   A typical example of the accusation that linguists subscribe to
dogma is provided by Hagège (1976).
p. 198   Popper (1976) draws parallels between scientific theories and
religious myths: cf. especially pp. 58ff.
p. 198   The *odium theologorum* is the 'hatred of the theologians'.
p. 198   Melanchthon, 1497–1560, was a leading theologian, educator,
evangelist and scholar.

p. 199   The linguist R. M. W. Dixon achieved some notoriety in the 1960s as a result of Chomsky's (1966b) destruction of Dixon (1963).

p. 199   The best history of the early years of Generative Grammar, including the rise and fall of Generative Semantics, is Newmeyer (1980).

p. 199   Chomsky's *Syntactic Structures* was published in 1957.

p. 200   The Standard Theory of *Aspects of the Theory of Syntax* refers to Chomsky (1965) and Katz and Postal (1964).

p. 200   For more details of the form of transformations, cf. the Appendix.

p. 201   On falsifiability, cf. Popper (1963), and essay 11 'Lellow Lollies'.

p. 202   Constraints on the power of transformations, leading to the so-called 'Lexicalist Hypothesis', were suggested in Chomsky (1970).

p. 203   For unbounded movement, cf. Chomsky (1977), and essay 17 'Useless Grammar'.

p. 203   The fullest exposition of Chomsky's theory without construction-specific rules is his (1981a).

p. 203   For parametric variation, cf. essay 6, 'The Oats have eaten the Horses' and references therein.

p. 204   For the notion of the deductive structure of a theory, with reference to Chomsky's work, cf. Moravcsik (1980).

p. 204   On sub-theories of grammar, and the notion 'chain', cf. Chomsky (1986).

p. 204   The dispute over the status of Deep Structure is illustrated in Brody (1987) and Chomsky (1987a).

p. 204   The details of the Arian heresy are taken from Previté-Orton (1960). The quotation is from p. 62.

p. 206   On the sociological determinants of the rise of Generative Grammar, see again Newmeyer (1980).

p. 206   The quotation from Magee is from his 1972: p. 35.

p. 206   MIT is the Massachusetts Institute of Technology, where Chomsky has worked since the mid-1950s.

19

A Seditious Chameleon

Life expectancy among linguists is generally high. Our worst occupational hazards tend to be mild irritants like being asked how many languages we speak (it all depends on how well you have to be able to speak them – knowing the Hungarian for 'haystack' won't get me very far in Budapest) or, more seriously, failing to convince the bureaucracy that our (sub-)discipline is as important as weapons technology, and therefore seeing it wither away as our colleagues and best students succumb to the blandishments of yuppiedom.

Living in straitened financial circumstances is not exhilarating. In the Third World I have been to conferences where participants were unable to provide a hand-out for their talks because there was no paper available; and I have failed to attend conferences because they were cancelled owing to lack of food supplies: very few academics are prepared to fast for the duration of even a minor colloquium.

But such vexations are trivial, and even the perils of doing field-work in a tropical jungle, with the attendant possibility of being molested by the local fauna, are minimal compared to the danger of being killed by a methane explosion in a coal-mine. Doing field-work among the Nupe of Nigeria I found poisonous spiders, scorpions and even a spitting cobra in my hut, but they were all as eager to escape from me as I was from them, before either of us could hurt the other; and even in the remoter parts of the Amazon or New Guinea only a very small percentage of visiting linguists are dispatched by the residents. According to my Nupe informants my greatest danger resided in the somewhat cavalier attitude I adopted towards chameleons. Local belief insisted that to hear a chameleon squeak was certain death (presumably sooner than otherwise), so when one invaded my hut, my equanimity was treated as yet another manifestation of English idiocy: as contemptible as my undisguised scepticism when told that stirring my soup with a chameleon's tail would render me immediately invisible. My continued and visible existence 25 years later seems to confirm that my perception of the danger was the appropriate one.

Not everywhere are the hazards of being a linguist so unhazardous. But the real dangers are always human, and nearly always come from humans of one's own tribe; either civil servants, secret police or religious fanatics.

Consider the case of N, a student from one of the less tolerant Islamic Republics, who returned home to teach linguistics with a PhD from London. Near the beginning of his first course of lectures he made the commonplace point that there are no primitive languages. Somewhat to the surprise of those who equate technological sophistication with general intellectual, and hence linguistic, ability, no language has any inherent structural advantage over any other. Anything you can express in your language, whatever it is, I can express in mine, and vice versa. It is important to be clear precisely what this means. Anyone who has studied a foreign language can cite endless examples like 'Schadenfreude' or 'sympathique' which have no exact equivalent in English, and most – perhaps all – languages have developed specialized vocabularies for the use of particular groups in the community when performing specific tasks. It is *not* claimed that all languages will have the same set of specialized vocabularies or, more generally, that every word in one language will have an exact equivalent in the next. English, spoken more widely than any other human language, has technical vocabularies for, say, molecular biology or the philosophy of psychology, which do not occur in Nupe, rendering the task of translating 'radioactive isotopes' or 'informational encapsulation' rather daunting. Equally, however, Nupe has expressions for distinguishing different phases of yam hoeing, for instance, which are expressible only periphrastically in English; and even the vocabulary of most of our own specialized sciences is replete with words borrowed not only from Classical Greek and Latin, but also from more exotic locations. Freud's seminal book *Totem and Taboo* contains in its title, words from the American Indian language Ojibwa and the Polynesian language Tonga, precisely because German and English had no appropriate equivalents.

The claim of non-primitivity is a claim about the grammatical resources of languages. All languages permit the construction of sentences of arbitrary length; all languages allow the formation of questions, negatives and imperatives; the deployment of metaphor and irony; all languages are equally efficient vehicles for avowals of love, threats of violence or conjectures about the moon. Despite romantic claims about French or Italian being the language of love, no language is really at a disadvantage when it comes to courtship and marriage. Least of all is there any language whose vocabulary is limited to a few hundred words or grunts – racist Victorian explorers to the contrary notwithstanding.

From this refutation of the claimed existence of primitive languages it is but a short step to the claim that all languages are equal: a claim that most linguists accept despite the obvious differences in the relative complexity of such sub-parts of the grammar as morphology (Classical Greek had a complex morphology, Classical Chinese had virtually no morphology), because complexity in one part of the system seems always to be offset by simplicity elsewhere, and all languages present a comparable degree of difficulty to the children acquiring them – essentially none.

N duly made the claim, almost in passing: to be instantly vilified and threatened with exposure as an enemy of the Islamic Revolution. Arabic is the language of the Qur'an; the Qur'an is the 'true word of God' as revealed to Muhammad at Mecca and Medina, and to suggest that any other language could be the equal of Arabic is sacrilege. Indeed, for a long time it was an offence to translate the Qur'an into any other language or, within Arabic, to emulate its style. Sacrilege is not something one indulges in lightly in these parts of the Middle East, and N was careful to avoid the issue in subsequent discussions. The alternative to this expediency was at best to lose his job, at worst his life.

I have been shouted at in England for saying in a lecture 'Anyone should be able to convince himself that . . .' because the use of the reflexive 'himself' was deemed to be sexist; but the penalty for arguing the point was an interesting if intermittently acrimonious sociolinguistic discussion, and not threats to my future. Not being a devout Muslim himself, N saw little merit in the claim for the superiority of (Qur'anic) Arabic, but he acted like David Abramovich Chwolson, a Jewish professor under the tsars, who converted to Greek Orthodoxy. When asked if he acted out of conviction or expedience, he replied '. . . entirely out of conviction – the conviction that it is better to be professor in the Imperial Academy in St Petersburg than a teacher in a *cheder* in Vilna'.

N's position was and is invidious, but he is still free and he still has his job. Another linguist from my department, Jack Mapanje, has not been so fortunate. Jack is a good example of Jakobson's version of Terence's aphorism '*Homo sum, humani nil a me alienum puto*': 'I am a linguist, nothing to do with language is alien to me'. Jack is a linguist in all senses of the word: he is a polyglot who grew up speaking Chiyao and Chichewa in his native Malawi; he is a linguist in the academic sense of having a PhD in linguistics (he wrote a perceptive thesis on phenomena of tense and aspect in his two native languages and English); and he is above all a poet – Malawi's most distinguished poet – whose best-known book, published while he was a student in London, is called *Of Chameleons and Gods*.

Both by his poetry and, in linguistics, by his work, his energy and his enthusiasm, Jack has brought prestige and international acclaim to Malawi. He was instrumental in setting up the Linguistic Association of SADCC countries, a union consisting of Angola, Botswana, Lesotho, Malawi, Mozambique, Swaziland, Tanzania, Zambia and Zimbabwe, and became its first chairman at the inaugural meeting he organized in Zomba with representatives from a dozen countries in 1984. He has travelled extensively around the world raising money for further conferences, adjudicating at Commonwealth poetry competitions, and even lecturing on linguistics. He would seem to be the kind of person any state would be anxious to advertise, especially a state such as Malawi, whose Life President (Hastings Banda) purports to be a staunch defender of Western cultural values. Yet in October 1987 Jack was detained in Malawi and his book was banned. Over a year later there are rumours that he had been charged with sedition, but there is no certain news.

Much of Jack's poetry is interpretable as politically critical. He

talks equally poignantly about the creation myths of the Chichewa
and the horrors of war; about 'skeletal Kampuchea children' and
'naive termites'; about prostitutes and propaganda. Any human
surveying the world we live in should get angry; no poet could be
blind to what is going on and a few have the courage not to
remain dumb about it. It is sad that the mindless authoritarian-
ism which has overtaken Malawi, a country where it is now a
treasonable offence to ask how old the Head of State is, should
result in the incarceration of someone who should be the country's
most eminent intellectual ambassador. It is sad, but depressingly
frequent, for reasons which have little to do with poetry. Writing
about Osip Mandelstam, another persecuted poet, murdered by
Stalin's myrmidons, Joseph Brodsky wrote:

A poet gets into trouble because of his linguistic, and, by implication, his
psychological superiority, rather than because of his politics. A song is a
form of linguistic disobedience, and its sound casts a doubt on a lot more
than a concrete political system: it questions the entire existential order.
And the number of its adversaries grows proportionally.

Quite. A few months before his detention Jack sent me the
following poem, recollecting his time in the Linguistics Department of University College London in Gordon Square.

>   April wishes for Gordon Square (a letter)
>
>   Dear Neil, as the toxic lizards of home crowd
>   In on us today, I recall those barriers in
>   Linguistics Gordon Square is so good at knocking
>   Down. You know how little I cared about those
>   Concrete gates that suspected me mugger on High
>   Street Barnet or framed in those hypocritical
>   Digs of Balham whether I sang about Wimbledon
>   Strawberries & cream or not. And knowing what
>   We know about dawns and bonfires, I believe I
>   Was not meant to map out Africa's dawn from
>   The dark alleys of London & I make no apology
>   For being a late visionary. It was kind I was
>   Spared the Victorian euphoria of bowler hats,
>   Flywhisks and image-fracturing London blitzes
>   That my fusty ancestors forever drill down our
>   Throats & flaked by those smoking tongues of

Brixton and Wood Green, it would have been dis-
honest to have pretended otherwise. So, here's
The season's peace for the crowd at the Square.

And dear Harun-Al Rashid, as the scorpions
Of Zomba gather at our keyholes to hear what
They have sewn, the kola nuts you offered me
Now sharpen. Jolting in that rusty, chattering
Citroen from the steel benches of Gordon Square
To the mouldy walls of York, I forgot to ask
Where you got kola nuts to break in the heart
Of London & the gates of York? And today, I
Discovered those photographs you forced on me
Boasting the York linguistics conference (with
Me sampling *Stones* and floating to inscrutable
Punk & you salaaming Mecca by the hour & steering
My 'rough' ways, you said). I hope you understand
Though: on my edge of Africa, without Opec oil
Or golden stools to show off about, kola nuts
Were merely symbolic fetters, bitter, crumbly
Not like spearmint gum & photographs cold
But as the Shepherds Bush offal we shared &
The *Daily Mirror* cones we ate our chips from
Come back today, I thought you might like to
Look at these bristly negatives, with love?

It is clear that if you identify with a scorpion of Zomba you
might take offence at the opening of the second stanza. Given an
appropriate context, almost anything can be offensive, and if the
cap fits . . . Fortunately, it is still (almost) inconceivable that one
could be imprisoned for sedition in this country for writing a
poem. I say 'almost' because of the unnerving recent example of
'*The love that dares to speak its name*', where the law of criminal
blasphemy was invoked (after centuries of desuetude) in order to
suppress a poem. Our life expectancy, as poets or linguists, is still
reasonably good. We should however, remain on our guard. The
chilling perspective on academic freedom provided by the
examples of N and Jack Mapanje should remind us that it takes
very little time to regress from a period of liberty to one where
freedom of speech is given only lip service. In the West,
suppression is usually more subtle (though the case of *Spycatcher*
indicates that the rapier is being replaced by the club) and

restricted to overtly subversive literature: one thinks of Chomsky and Herman's *Political Economy of Human Rights*, suppressed in the USA for some years. Even here there is virtually no threat to the liberty of the individuals as opposed to their ideas – as yet.

In Malawi, as here, the chameleon is renowned for its camouflage; among the Nupe its attributes are more sinister. For Shelley it was an ethereal creature that shouldn't be tempted by wealth or power, but most importantly it was – like the poet – free. If Jack and others in his position are to be free, we must fight any form of censorship, for all censorship portends despotism.

Notes

p. 209   The most eloquent statement of linguistic equality comes from Sapir (1921: p. 219): 'When it comes to linguistic form, Plato walks with the Macedonian swineherd, Confucius with the head-hunting savage of Assam.'

p. 211   The story about Chwolson is from Rosten (1971: p. 133).

p. 211   Terence's aphorism means: 'I am a man; I count nothing human indifferent to me.'

p. 212   The quotation from Brodsky is from his essay 'The Child of Civilization', in his (1987: p. 136).

p. 212   The poem by Jack Mapanje has not been published before, except in the University College London *Bulletin*, vol. 7, no. 6, p. 4 (November 1987). I am deeply appreciative of Jack's generosity in sending me this poem. I hope that publicizing his current fate will help to keep him from a worse one. An account of the Linguistics Association of SADCC countries appears in an earlier issue of the same publication: vol. 6, no. 6 (January 1985).

p. 213   '*The love that dares to speak its name*' is a poem by James Kirkup that was published in 1977 by *Gay News*. Mrs M. Whitehouse brought a successful private prosecution for blasphemy against *Gay News*, the first since 1922.

p. 214   Details of the attempted suppression of Chomsky and Herman's book are given in the prefatory note to the 1979 edition.

p. 214   The poem by Shelley is '*An Exhortation*', written in 1819.

Appendix

That we have different kinds of linguistic knowledge and that it needs to be explicitly formalized is reasonably uncontentious. *How* this formalization should be effected is a matter of considerable disagreement, as any data can be described in an indefinitely large number of different ways, and even within any one theory the modes of description are continually changing as new insights are achieved and old models overthrown. For syntax, what follows is a simplified, somewhat modified, but relatively uncontroversial overview of the system developed by Chomsky and his associates over the past 35 years. It bears most resemblance to the so-called 'Standard Theory' of Chomsky's *Aspects of the Theory of Syntax*, but a number of changes have been incorporated in silence. For phonology, I have included more traditional work, as the body of research before the Chomskyan Revolution was substantially larger in this area than in syntax.

Syntax

The notion 'sentence' is taken as given, and to characterize sentence structure we start off with Phrase Structure (or PS) rules. Phrase Structure rules (also known as Constituent Structure rules) are of the form given in (1) and are said to generate sentences – hence the name Generative Grammar:

1a S   → NP VP
1b NP → (Det) (adj) N
1c VP → V (NP) (PP)
1d PP → P NP

S is an abbreviation for Sentence, NP for Noun Phrase, VP for Verb Phrase, PP for Prepositional Phrase, Det for Determiner, Adj for Adjective, N for Noun, V for Verb and P for Preposition. The arrow means 'consists of' and the parentheses '()' indicate optionality, so the first rule can be taken as saying that 'A sentence may consist of a Noun Phrase followed by a Verb Phrase'. This of course is useful only if you know what a Noun Phrase and a Verb Phrase are, so the next two rules spell that out: 'A Noun Phrase consists of a Noun optionally preceded by a Determiner or an Adjective or both', and 'A Verb Phrase consists of a Verb optionally followed by a Noun Phrase or a Prepositional Phrase or both'. The fourth rule does the same thing for Prepositional Phrase.

Provided we also have a lexicon of the sort described in the Introduction and simplistically illustrated in (2):

2   N   *includes* koala, lecture, rabbi, Miranda, idea, Hugo
    V   "   be, eat, say, kiss, generate, sigh, think
    Adj   "   pretty, Maltese, furry, red, oblong
    Det   "   the, a, some, which
    P   "   in, at, to, by, with, from

this embryonic grammar will generate a large number of sentences, usually represented in the form of a *tree* as illustrated in (3):

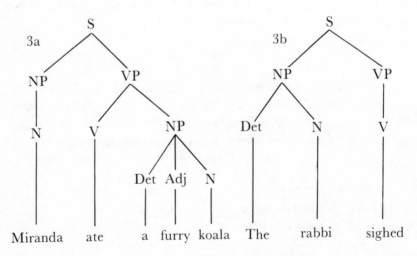

It is not an accident that, in rules and structures of the kind illustrated, Verb Phrases always contain Verbs, Noun Phrases contain Nouns, Adjective Phrases contain Adjectives, and so on. The lexical categories Verb, Noun and Adjective are said to be the *heads* of their respective phrasal categories, and it is customary to express the obvious generalization by using XP to subsume all of VP, NP, PP, etc. and X to subsume all of V, N, P etc. This enables us to write a general rule schema: 'XP → ... X ...', saying that any phrasal category will have a lexical head of the same type.

A sentence is *grammatical* (by definition) if it is generated by the grammar, and *ungrammatical* if it is not. A major part of linguistic analysis consists of ensuring that the rules you write jointly generate only *acceptable* sentences and fail to generate *unacceptable* ones. 'Acceptability' refers to the judgements of the native speaker of the kind I appealed to in the Introduction in assuming that sentences like those in (4) were unacceptable (and should therefore not be generated by the grammar if it has been correctly constructed), whereas examples like those in (5) should all be generated.

4a   *Demolished the greenhouse the hurricane.
4b   *Never I have seen such a gale.
5a   The hurricane demolished the greenhouse.
5b   I have never seen such a gale.
5c   Never have I seen such a gale.

The fragment of a grammar in (1) and (2) generates not only the examples diagrammed in (3) and repeated in (6), but also those in (7):

6a   Miranda ate a furry koala.
6b   The rabbi sighed.
7a   The Maltese Miranda is red koala.
7b   Some lecture generated.

(7a) is unlikely to be used very often, but is perfectly grammatical (you just need to imagine a cannibalistic situation in which various people called Miranda from sundry different countries are served up disguised as different kinds of coloured animal flesh!);

(7b) is ungrammatical and entails that the grammar will have to be modified to prevent it being generated. In this case, verbs have to be *sub-categorized* into those which are 'transitive', that is, require an object, like 'generate'; those which are 'intransitive', that is, do not require an object, like 'glitter'; those which require both an object and a Prepositional Phrase such as 'in the garage', like 'put', and so on.

One of the central concepts in syntax is that of *constituent*: any item or sequence of items that can be traced exhaustively to a single 'node' in a tree. A node is any point in a tree from which a 'branch' (i.e. a line) emanates. Every lexical item is a constituent and in (3a) 'a furry koala' is a constituent (of the type NP) and 'ate a furry koala' is a constituent (of the type VP), but neither 'ate a' nor 'Miranda ate' nor 'furry koala' are constituents.

Instead of using trees, grammarians often use brackets, either labelled as in (8a) or unlabelled as in (8b), to represent syntactic structure. (8a) contains exactly the same information as (3a); (8b) contains the same information as (3a) minus the node labels:

8a   [$_S$[$_{NP}$[$_N$ Miranda]] [$_{VP}$[$_V$ ate] [$_{NP}$[$_{Det}$ a] [$_{Adj}$ furry] [$_N$ koala]]]]

8b   [[[Miranda]] [[ate] [[a] [furry] [koala]]]]

If only part of the sentence is relevant to the discussion, say the VP, just that part is bracketed off, as in (9):

9   Miranda [ate a furry koala]

The mini-grammar given in (1) and (2) is obviously inadequate to generate all the sentences of English, but I will limit myself to two quite different kinds of addition to it. First, the number of sentences the grammar can generate is finite, but we can construct sentences of indefinite length. We can enable our grammar to accommodate this ability by making it *recursive*. According to (1c), Verb Phrases consist of a Verb optionally followed by a Noun Phrase, a Prepositional Phrase or both. A further possibility is for the Verb to be followed by another 'complement' Sentence, as in (10):

10   Hugo said [$_S$ Miranda ate a furry koala]

The grammar will generate this sentence if we add to the rules in
(1) a further rule (11):

11   VP → V S

which will allow an infinite number of other possibilities such as
(12):

12   The rabbi thought [s Hugo said [s Miranda ate a furry
      koala]]

By the simple addition of (11), itself just one of a number of
recursive rules, the grammar is able to reflect one aspect of our
creativity. In fact (11) is just a special case of a more general rule.
We saw above that X and XP can be used as cover terms for
different categories, so we might expect that not only verbs could
be followed by S, and indeed any of the major lexical categories
may be subcategorized for a sentential complement, as illustrated
in (13):

13a   Fred *believes* [that gerbils are infectious]
13b   The *claim* [that gerbils are infectious] is insane
13c   I am *certain* [that gerbils are infectious]
13d   The claim is implausible *in* [that gerbils are infectious]

where a verb, a noun, an adjective and a preposition are each
followed by the same sentential complement. This could be
captured formally by changing (11) to (14):

14   XP → X S

and even that formulation can be generalized to include other
types of complement phrase.

The second addition is of a different rule type, the *transformation* –
hence the name *Transformational Grammar*. Although the grammar
we have developed can now generate an infinite number of
sentences, to generate *all* the sentences of the language using only
Phrase Structure rules would leave certain regularities and
generalizations unexpressed.

Consider a slightly different version of (10) given in (15):

15 A furry koala, Hugo said Miranda ate.

This sentence is not generated by the Phrase Structure rules already given, and although it would be possible to add a new one which did generate it, for instance, (16):

16 S → NP NP VP

the result would be undesirable. First, such a rule, in conjunction with the others, would 'overgenerate' in that it also allows the generation of unacceptable sequences such as (17):

17 The koala the rabbi ate the food.

Secondly, such a rule would fail to account for the fact that even though it is in initial position in (15) the constituent 'a furry koala' is still the direct object of the verb 'eat', just as it is in (10), and thirdly, it doesn't account for the *relatedness* of (10) and (15): a relatedness reflected in their synonymy.

All these problems are solved simultaneously by postulating a new kind of rule – a *transformation* – which, instead of specifying the structure of single constituents as Phrase Structure rules do, relates one whole tree structure to another. The tree structure for (10) is given in (18a) and the related structure for (15) into which it is converted is given in (18b):

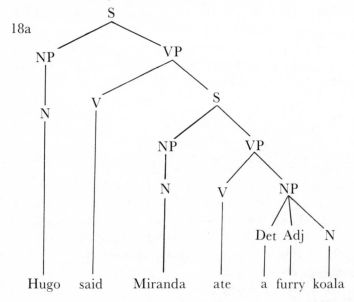

18b

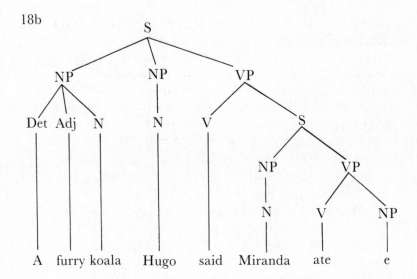

The transformation has *moved* the NP constituent 'a furry koala' from the end of the sentence to the beginning, leaving behind an *empty category* indicated by 'e'. The rule formalizes the relatedness of the two sentences – more accurately of the sentence types of which (10) and (15) are tokens; it obviates the need for any rule like (16); and it avoids the problem of 'overgeneration' that (16) brought with it.

Sentences related transformationally are comparable to isomeric compounds which have the same molecular formula but different structural formulae and different reactive properties. Like the pair of structures in (18), dimethyl ether and ethanol, represented in (19), have a common set of parts and share some substructure, but have a different superficial appearance and different uses.

$$
\begin{array}{cc}
\text{H} & \text{H} \\
| & | \\
19a \quad \text{H} - \text{C} - \text{O} - \text{C} - \text{H} \\
| & | \\
\text{H} & \text{H} \\
\text{Dimethyl ether}
\end{array}
\qquad
\begin{array}{cc}
\text{H} & \text{H} \\
| & | \\
19b \quad \text{H} - \text{C} - \text{C} - \text{O} - \text{H} \\
| & | \\
\text{H} & \text{H} \\
\text{Ethanol}
\end{array}
$$

All grammatical theories allow for different *levels of representation* capturing syntactic, semantic and phonological generalizations.

Transformational Grammar makes the additional, controversial, claim that it is desirable to postulate *two* levels of representation within the syntax: the *Deep Structure* – the set of trees generated by the Phrase Structure rules, which provides the input to the transformational rules, and the *Surface Structure* – the set of trees produced by the operation of the transformations. All sentences are analysed at both levels of representation, though in cases where no transformation is applied, the Deep Structure and Surface Structure are identical. The role of transformations, whether they are necessary, desirable, pernicious or irrelevant, is a matter of ongoing debate.

Within Generative Grammar, the syntax is accorded 'priority', in that rules from the other components have access to syntactic information, but the rules of the syntax are unable to use phonological or semantic information. As a result, the grammar is usually represented as having the form in (20):

20

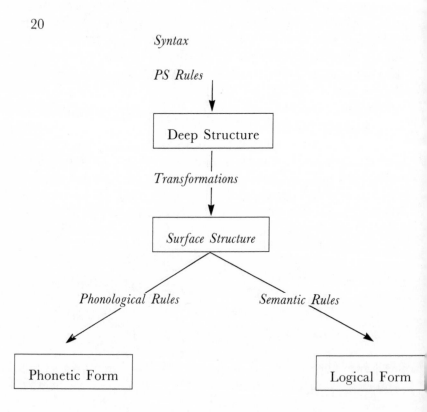

where *italics* indicate systems of rules, roman indicates levels of representation, and the arrows show the logical ordering among components.

Phonology

As can be seen from (20), the phonology and the semantics are treated as 'interpetative' in that the rules of these components operate on structures generated by the syntax. In the case of the phonology, the rules specify the pronunciation of sentences which have already been given a syntactic analysis. Not all differences in pronunciation need to be represented: no two utterances of the same word are physically identical, but most of the variation is insignificant because it doesn't serve to distinguish between different words or sentences. 'Pig' is 'pig' whether growled in a bass or squeaked in falsetto.

The essence of phonology is contrast. Whereas the two different pronunciations of 'pig' didn't serve to differentiate the words uttered, a change in any of the three *segments* 'p', 'i' or 'g' could serve to identify a different word: for instance, '*big*', '*pug*' or '*pit*'. In the first instance, the phonology of a language must specify all those sound differences which can subserve differences of lexical identity: the *phonemic* differences.

In English 'p' and 'b' are pronounced differently and constitute separate *phonemes* because the contrast between them can keep apart different lexical items. Phonemes are represented by putting symbols, or sequences of symbols, in oblique strokes, so 'pig' is represented /pig/. The two 'l's in 'little' are also pronounced differently, but the contrast between them cannot distinguish different words, and is said to be 'sub-phonemic' or *phonetic*. Phonetic sequences are represented by putting symbols in square brackets, so 'little' is represented as /litəl/ phonemically and as [litəɬ] phonetically. Phonetic differences may be phonemic in one language and not in another. The contrast between [p] and [b] is phonemic in English but not in Finnish; the contrast between [p] and [pʰ] is not phonemic in English but it is in Hindi. Even though [p] and [pʰ] are not contrastive in English, both sounds do occur. When initial, /p/ in English is usually 'aspirated' (pronounced with an audible puff of air, as can be seen by pronouncing 'pin' in front of a match flame), so the phonemic sequence /pin/ is pronounced as the phonetic sequence [pʰin]. When /p/ occurs after /s/, it is usually unaspirated so that the phonemic sequence /spin/ is pronounced as the phonetic sequence [spin] – with no effect on flames. Sounds which occur in 'complementary distribution' – in consistently different environments like [p] and [pʰ] in English – are called *allophones* of the same phoneme.

English has 44 different phonemes: 24 consonants and 20 vowels and diphthongs, but the English alphabet only has 26 letters, so many phonemes are represented in ordinary writing by sequences of letters, and some contrasts are not represented at all. For instance 'th' represents one phoneme at the beginning of 'this' and a different one at the beginning of 'thistle', so phonologists use two different symbols for them. The problem is even more severe when it is necessary to represent sub-phonemic differences of the kind seen in 'little', so phoneticians standardly use the alphabet of the International Phonetic Association (IPA) to represent phonetic and phonemic sequences. Using the transcription of the IPA, the consonants of English are normally tabulated as in (21):

21	p		t	tʃ	k		*p*in, *t*in, *ch*in, *k*in
	b		d	dʒ	g		*b*in, *d*in, *g*in, be*g*in
	f	θ	s	ʃ		h	*f*in, *th*ine, *s*in, *sh*in, *h*int
	v	ð	z	ʒ			*v*ine, *th*ine, ru*s*e, rou*g*e
	m		n			ŋ	ra*m*, ra*n*, ra*ng*
	w		r	l	j		*w*hat, *r*ot, *l*ot, *y*acht

Rather than being arranged alphabetically the phonemes in (21) are arranged by *place* and *manner* of articulation. The first column, /p, b, f, v, m, w/, are all *labials*, in which the main organ of articulation is the lips; /θ, ð/ are both *dentals*, articulated with the tongue touching or between the teeth; /t, d, s, z, n, l, r/ are all *alveolars*, articulated with the tongue touching the alveolar ridge; /tʃ, dʒ, ʃ, ʒ/ are all *palato-alveolars*, with the tongue making contact with the roof of the mouth between the alveolar ridge and the hard palate; /j/ is a *palatal*, with the tongue making contact with the hard palate; /k, g, ŋ/ are all *velars*, with the back of the tongue touching the soft palate (the velum); and /h/ is a *glottal*, in which air escapes through the glottis and creates some friction throughout the vocal tract. The columns are not perfectly aligned in order to reflect the fact that while /p/ and /f/, for instance, are both 'labial', /p/ is 'bilabial' (articulated with the lips touching each other) and /f/ is 'labio-dental' (articulated with the lower lip touching the upper teeth).

The rows correspond to the manner of articulation. The first two rows are *stops*, in which the passage of air through the mouth is briefly but completely blocked. The third and fourth rows are *fricatives*, in which the articulation causes audible friction, but does not make a complete closure. The difference between the first and third rows on the one hand and the second and fourth rows on the other, is that the former are *voiceless* and the latter *voiced*. The difference can be heard most easily by putting your fingers in your ears and saying first /s/ and then /z/. With /z/ there should be an audible buzzing as the vocal cords vibrate to cause the voicing. The fifth row consists of *nasals*, sounds in which the air escapes through the nose rather than the mouth, and the bottom row consists of *sonorants*, sounds produced with so-called spontaneous vocal cord vibration.

This tabular arrangement according to the properties of the groups of sounds involved is a convenient way of showing phonetic similarity, but it is not strictly speaking part of phoneme theory. By abstracting a universal set of such properties, the *distinctive features*, which are necessary and sufficient for the description of the phonologies of all natural languages, generative phonology formalizes the notion of phonetic similarity and simultaneously lays the foundation for the statement of phonological rules. Although the distinctive features are given articulatory, auditory or acoustic definitions, they are (like all constructs of a competence grammar) neutral as between perception and production, and are taken to be psychologically real in the sense of the discussion in the Introduction.

The 'voiced/voiceless' contrast which distinguishes the phonemes in the first two pairs of rows in (21) is attributed to the distinctive feature [voiced] which can be either positively or negatively specified as [+voiced] or [−voiced]. (By convention, distinctive features are placed in square brackets, whether they are being used to describe traditional phonemic contrasts or to give a narrow phonetic representation.) Similarly, /m, n, ŋ/ are all

characterized as [+nasal]; the fricatives are [+continuant], and
so on. The distinctions among the different places of articulation
are less obviously amenable to the kind of 'binary' feature analysis
used so far. Intuitively, it seems as if we have a continuum
stretching from the front of the mouth (the lips) to the back (the
glottis), but when one looks at the rules of the phonology it turns
out that certain pairs of consonants pattern together more
frequently than others. For example, /p/ and /k/ often form a
natural class to the exclusion of /t/ and /tʃ/, leading to the
conclusion that the continuum should be divided in such a way as
to reflect this. The standard analysis is then one which divides
speech sounds into those which are articulated with the front of
the tongue: /t, tʃ, n, l . . ./ and labelled [+coronal] as opposed to
those which are not so articulated: /p, k, h . . ./ and labelled
[−coronal]. Similarly sounds articulated in the front of the mouth
are designated [+anterior], those articulated in the back of the
mouth [−anterior]. This gives us the ability to characterize four
places of articulation with two distinctive features as shown in
(22):

22   [+coronal, +anterior] – alveolars, dentals, etc.
     [+coronal, −anterior] – palato-alveolars, retroflexes, etc.
     [−coronal, +anterior] – labials, labio-dentals, etc.
     [−coronal, −anterior] – velars, glottals, etc.

Phonological rules are expressed in terms of changes to classes of
segments defind by particular combinations of distinctive features.
For example, the fact that vowels are somewhat nasalized before a
nasal consonant would be represented by the rule in (23):

23   V → [+nasal] / —— [+nasal]

That is, vowels (V) receive the feature [+nasal] in the
environment before another segment with the feature [+nasal].
The arrow here means 'acquires the feature'; the oblique stroke
introduces the environment in which the rule operates, and the
dash shows whether the segment affected by the rule occurs before
or after the segment constituting that environment.

   In phonology as in syntax, much effort is being devoted to
eliminating idiosyncratic rules in favour of general principles.

This is often effected by moving away from the rigidly linear sequence of segments illustrated in (23) and factoring out statements to do with pitch, stress, nasality, and so on, and stating them independently. Such analyses are referred to as 'non-linear' or 'multi-dimensional'. One example is given in essay 11, 'Lellow Lollies'.

Notes

p. 215   Radford (1988) provides an extended introduction to the argumentation and formalization of generative syntax in the same spirit as this book. Horrocks (1987) is an excellent overview contrasting different theories and their attendant formalisms. Each of the theories discussed is 'generative' in the sense of being explicitly formalized. There has been some unilluminating polemic recently on the question whether 'generate' in the mathematical sense is appropriately applied to a theory which concentrates on capturing universal principles rather than describing sentences. For some comments, cf. Chomsky (ms: n.1).

p. 217   For X-bar syntax, i.e. the kind of syntax incorporating variables over categories, see Chomsky (1970). The clearest introduction is again Radford (1988).

p. 217   The possibility of making (7b) acceptable by quoting it as part of a linguistics course is excluded: such metalinguistic usage would give every sequence of noises the same status as every other one.

p. 219   It should be noted that some versions of generative grammar, in particular 'Generalized Phrase Structure Grammar', exploit alternative kinds of phrase structure rule instead of using transformations. The standard reference to this work is Gazdar et al. (1985). For interesting comparative discussion, cf. Horrocks (1987).

p. 220   The formalization of transformations is largely irrelevant to the issues of this book, so I have ignored them. There are considerable problems in deciding what the appropriate 'derived constituent structure' for an example such as (15) should be. The tree in (18b) is not uncontroversial. For discussion, cf. the references cited above.

p. 224   The table in (21) is the same as that in essay 9, 'Y', which reproduces some of the exegesis given here.

p. 226   A brief but competent overview of current phonological theory is given in Basbøll (1988).

Glossary

I have attempted to include in this Glossary all those terms which might be unfamiliar to the lay reader, or which, despite their familiarity, might have been used in an unfamiliar way. A glossary partly overlapping in coverage with this one can be found in Smith and Wilson (1979). The best dictionary of linguistic terminology is Crystal (1985). I have drawn on both the earlier glossary and Crystal's *Dictionary* freely and frequently. For semi-technical and traditional linguistic vocabulary Collins' *Dictionary* is outstanding.

acceptable: An utterance is acceptable to a native-speaker if it is readily comprehensible and relevant. Acceptable utterances generally, but not invariably, correspond to grammatical sentences. Acceptability is a matter of the theory of performance whereas grammaticality is a matter of competence.

accommodation: The process whereby speakers modify their speech so that it approximates more or less closely to that of their interlocutors.

acquisitional adequacy: An alternative term for 'explanatory adequacy' (qv), emphasizing the importance for a theory of being able to account for the possibility of first-language acquisition.

adequacy: level of success achieved by a grammar or theory. See: observational adequacy, descriptive adequacy and explanatory adequacy.

agreement: Two forms are said to agree if they are both marked for the same grammatical feature. In French, articles and adjectives must agree in gender with the noun they modify, so that we have '*une bonne table*' (a good table) but '*un bon pupitre*' (a good desk), where *table* is feminine and *pupitre* is masculine.

alethic: A term borrowed from modal logic to distinguish the kind of truth characteristic of the proposition involved: e.g. the use of the modal verb 'must' in 'The president has been assassinated so he must be dead', indicates an alethic, i.e. necessary, truth. It contrasts with epistemic and deontic.

allophone: The allophones of a phoneme are the various different pronunciations of that phoneme as determined by its position in the word. For instance, vowels in English have relatively long allophones before voiced consonants, and relatively short allophones before voiceless consonants, so that the phoneme /a/ is pronounced with a longer allophone in 'bad' than in 'bat'.

alpha (α): A variable over constituents. See 'Move-α'.

alveolar: A consonant articulated with the front of the tongue against the alveolar ridge (the tooth ridge): e.g. /t/ and /n/ in English.

ambiguity: A word or sentence which has more than one linguistically determined meaning is ambiguous: e.g. the word 'kiwi' can refer to either a flightless bird or a fruit; the sentence 'She left me angry' can mean either that she made me angry or that she was in a temper when she departed.

ambiposition: A discontinuous form which is similar to a preposition but whose parts occur one on each side of a constituent: e.g. *for . . . 's sake.*

anaphor: A type of Noun Phrase which has no independent reference but must be related to ('bound by') some antecedent from which it derives its reference. Reflexive and reciprocal pronouns are anaphoric in the sentences: 'Margaret admires *herself*' and 'Margaret and Dennis admire *each other*'.

anterior: A distinctive feature which characterizes sounds whose point of articulation is further forward in the mouth than that of English /tʃ/ ('ch'): e.g. /t/, /f/.

argument: Noun Phrases such as 'Fred' and 'the soup' in 'Fred slurped the soup' are semantic arguments of 'slurp'. Sub-categorized (qv) Noun Phrases are arguments, but expletives like 'it' and 'there' are not arguments. Within current Government–Binding theory an argument is a Noun Phrase that requires a thematic role.

aspect: A grammatical category pertaining to the duration or type of temporal activity encoded by the verb. Traditional aspectual contrasts are those between the simple and the progressive, as in 'Mavis ate a lobster' and 'Mavis was eating a lobster'; the completed (or 'perfective') and the incompleted (or 'imperfective'), as in 'I (have) read the book' and 'I was reading the book', and so on. Aspect is a non-deictic category, whereas tense is a deictic category.

aspiration: The articulation of a speech sound, usually a stop such as 't' or 'p', with sufficient force to make friction from the escaping air audible. In English, the stops /p/, /t/, and /k/ are aspirated and so pronounced [p^h], [t^h] and [k^h].

assmilation: A phonological process whereby a segment adopts the point or manner of articulation of another segment (usually) adjacent to it. In informal speech in English, alveolars such as /t/, /d/ and /n/ assimilate to the point of articulation of an immediately following consonant, so that 'good boy' may be pronounced [gub boi].

Autosegmental Phonology: A phonological theory in which statements about pitch, stress and some other phonetic features are made *auto*nomously of statements about the segmental structure of sentences. It is motivated by the fact, for instance, that in many tone languages, pitch changes may signal differences of grammatical structure independently of the sequence of consonants and vowels involved.

autosegmental tier: A level of representation in Autosegmental Phonology at which statements of a particular kind are made. Tonal regularities are stated on one tier, segmental regularities, such as the possible sequences of consonants and vowels, are stated on an independent tier.

auxiliary verb: A sub-class of verbs with some atypical syntactic or morphological properties. In English, regular verbs, such as 'like', form questions with 'do' ('Do hedgehogs like treacle?') and cannot precede the subject ('*Like hedgehogs treacle?'), whereas auxiliary verbs such as 'can/could' have the opposite properties ('Could hedgehogs like treacle?', '*Do hedgehogs can/could like treacle?').

background implication: In Relevance Theory, an implication in the focal scale (qv) of an utterance which has contextual effects indirectly by making available some relevant context which will itself have contextual effects. See also foreground implication.

bilabial: Speech sounds articulated by bringing the two lips together: e.g. /p, b, m/ in English.

binding: That module of Government–Binding Theory which deals with the relation between Noun Phrases and their linguistic antecedents, if any. In 'Esme surprised herself', the reflexive 'herself' is *bound* by the Noun Phrase 'Esme', with which it is coreferential; in 'Esme surprised her', the pronoun 'her' can *not* be bound by the Noun Phrase 'Esme', and the two Noun Phrases cannot be coreferential.

bound: A constituent is bound if it is coindexed with an *argument* (qv) which c-commands it (roughly, that occurs higher in the tree). A constituent which is not bound is 'free'. See also Binding.

bounding: That module of Government–Binding Theory which deals with locality conditions on rules or representations. The main condition of bounding theory is 'subjacency' which stops a transformation from moving a constituent 'too far'. Thus, in a sentence like 'A rise in the price of oil was announced', the phrase 'in the price of oil' may be moved to the right to give 'A rise was announced [in the price of oil]'; but the phrase 'of oil' cannot be moved to give '*A rise in the price was announced [of oil]'.

brackets: A formal device for showing hierarchical constituent structure of the kind equivalently represented by a tree. Thus the following two representations of 'The Wombles live in Wimbledon' contain exactly the same information:

$[_S[_{NP}[_{Det}\text{The}][_N \text{ Wombles}]][_{VP}[_V\text{live}][_{PP}[_P\text{in}]$
$[_{NP}[_N\text{Wimbledon}]]]]]$

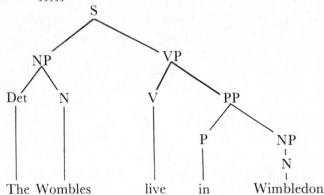

Case: A grammatical property of Noun Phrases differentiating subjects, objects and so on, by means of the morphological difference between nominative, accusative and so on. In English, morphological differences are characteristic only of pronouns, as in the contrast between 'I' and 'me' or 'he' and 'him' in 'I saw him' and 'He saw me'. In Government–Binding Theory, Case is one module of the theory and refers to an abstract syntactic feature (which may or may not have morphological effects) devised to account for a wide range of contrasts including that between: 'I would like [John to be the winner]' and '*[John to be the winner] is unlikely' (cf. '[For John to be the winner] is unlikely').

Case filter: The requirement that every (non-empty) Noun Phrase must be assigned abstract Case. The Case filter accounts for the contrasting examples in the immediately preceding entry: 'like' and 'for' assign case to 'John' in the first and last examples, but nothing assigns case to 'John' in the second example, so it is ungrammatical.

centre-embedding: If one constituent is embedded (qv) inside another so that material from this latter constituent occurs both to left and right of the former, it is said to be centre-embedded. In a sentence like 'John said nothing yesterday', we can replace 'nothing' by the sentence 'Bill thought something funny today', giving 'John said [Bill thought something funny today] yesterday'. This centre-embedding can be continued (with devastating results for comprehensibility) by replacing 'something funny' with the further sentence 'Harry would go tomorrow', yielding: 'John said [Bill thought [Harry would go tomorrow] today] yesterday'. If the sentences are embedded, but not centre-embedded, the result is comprehensible even if not stylistically felicitous: 'John said yesterday (that) Bill thought today (that) Harry would go tomorrow'.

chain: In Government–Binding Theory, a chain provides a history of the movement from Deep Structure to Surface Structure of some constituent, in the form of a listing of the positions it has occupied. In the passive sentence 'Ben was hypnotized e by Carl', the Noun Phrase 'Ben' has been moved by transformation from the position marked by 'e' to its position at the beginning of the sentence. The sequence <Ben, e> then constitutes a chain.

click: A speech sound, typical of the Khoisan languages of Southern Africa, which involves making a velar closure (which causes a partial vacuum when the back of the tongue is lowered), and abruptly releasing a closure further forward in the mouth. In English, clicks are used only for expressing disapproval (tut, tut) or encouraging horses.

cluster: A sequence of consonants without intervening vowels. 'Smith' begins with the phonemic cluster /sm/ and ends with the orthographic cluster 'th'.

code-mixing: The use of elements from two or more languages in a single utterance. Code-mixing (and code-switching – qv) are common in bilingual communities, such as Canada, Imperial Russia, and perhaps most of the world. A good example of a sentence exhibiting code-mixing is *'Tous les hommes de génie sont des drunkards et des gamblers qui boivent like fish'* from Dostoevski's *The Devils.*

code-switching: The use of different languages (or different styles of the same language) depending on the situation in which one is speaking. For instance, many people in England speak Punjabi at home and English at school.

cohesion: Those properties of a text or utterance which relate sentences (or other sequences) to each other. It includes the use of anaphoric pronouns, connectives such as 'however', the choice of lexical items, and so on. All are illustrated by the italicized items in: 'Thelonious loved jazz. *However, the great man* didn't realize *it* was addictive.'

co-indexing: A device to indicate coreference or referential dependence. It is usually indicated by subscripts on the appropriate items, as in 'Johnson$_i$ believed he$_j$ was a harmless drudge', where the subscript 'i' and 'j' may be specified as being the same or different, according as 'Johnson' and 'he' are to be taken as referring to the same person or not.

competence: Knowledge of language. That part of our knowledge, including phonology, syntax, morphology and semantics, which is exclusively linguistic. Our competence is partly learned and partly innate.

complement: A constituent, typically a Noun Phrase or a clause, for which a verb is sub-categorized. The verb 'persuade' in English selects both a Noun Phrase complement and a clausal complement in examples like 'The princess persuaded [her husband] [that he should emigrate].'

complementary distribution: Two sounds are in complementary distribution if they consistently occur in specific and different environments; thus, the allophones of a phoneme are in complementary distribution. For instance, the phoneme /p/ has two allophones: [p] which occurs after /s/ (as in 'spit') and [pʰ] which occurs initially (as in 'pit').

component: Our knowledge of language can be divided into different kinds: e.g. syntactic, phonological, and so on. The parts of the grammar which deal with those types of knowledge are referred to as components or modules.

consistency: The phenomenon whereby it is possible to predict some property of the syntax of a language on the basis of some other property. For instance, languages which have postpositions usually have the verb final in the sentence, whereas languages which have prepositions usually have the verb initial or medial in the sentence. Languages of these kinds are said to be 'consistent'.

consonant harmony: A phonological process, typical of first-language acquisition, in which the consonants of a word are all pronounced with the same consonant or with consonants from the same class. For example, the pronunciation of 'dog' as [gog], or 'duck' as [gʌk] where the alveolar /d/ has harmonized to the final velar /g/ or /k/.

constituent: Any sequence of elements which forms a syntactic unit is a constituent. (Technically: any sequence which can be traced exhaustively to a single node in a tree.)

constraint: Any limitation placed on the operation of a grammatical rule. The principle of 'subjacency' (qv) constrains transformations so that they cannot move constituents too far.

context: The set of premises you assume or construct in interpreting an utterance.

contextual effects: When an utterance is interpreted in some context it can have contextual effects, either (1) by strengthening some assumption you already hold, or (2) by contradicting some assumption you already hold, or (3) by allowing the deduction of some proposition that you could not have deduced on the basis of the utterance alone or the context alone.

conversational implicature: An implication of an utterance that one has to infer in order to make that utterance relevant. The response 'I don't like blood sports' to the question 'Are you coming to the debate?' conversationally implicates that the debate has some of the properties of blood sports and that the speaker is therefore not going to go.

co-ordination: Two or more constituents of equivalent syntactic status linked by 'conjunctions' such as 'and' or 'or'. In 'Kasparov won the championship *and* his opponent burst into tears', the clauses are coordinated (or 'conjoined') by the conjunction *and.*

co-reference: Noun Phrases which designate (refer to) the same individual are said to be co-referential. In 'Belinda admired herself in the mirror, but the vain creature didn't notice her double chin', 'Belinda' and 'herself' are necessarily co-referential, and may or may not be coreferential with 'the vain creature'. Co-reference is standardly indicated by coindexation (qv).

coronal: A distinctive feature characterizing consonants articulated with the tip or front of the tongue: e.g. /t, d, s, l,/ in English.

Deep Structure: In Transformational Generative Grammar, Deep Structure is defined as that level of representation which is the output of the Phrase Structure Rules and Lexicon, and the input to the transformational component.

default: A choice adopted when no explicit alternative is imposed by rule. The default interpretation of the 'past' tense ending *–ed* on English verbs such as *loved* is that it refers to past time: e.g. 'She loved me'. This default reading may be overruled by the presence of other elements such as *if*: thus in 'If she loved me, I would be deliriously happy', the time referred to is the present.

definite description: A Noun Phrase such as 'the man with two left feet' which refers to a particular individual by means of a construction including the definite article ('the') or equivalent. It is in contrast with proper nouns such as 'Fred' or 'Taras Bulba', and indefinite Noun Phrases like 'a wallaby'.

deixis: Deictic expressions are those such as the personal pronouns ('I/you') and expressions of time ('now/then') or place ('here/there') whose referents are only identifiable if one knows who the participants in a conversation are, or when and where they are speaking. For instance, 'It is cold in here now' will be construed differently on different occasions of utterance. Deictic terms are largely coextensive with the 'indexical expressions' of philosophy.

dental: A consonant articulated with the tip of the tongue in contact with the teeth. In English /θ/ is dental, and in French /t, d, n/ are dental, whereas their English counterparts are alveolar (qv).

deontic: Relating to obligation and permission. The modal auxiliary 'must' is used deontically in 'You must be home by midnight'. It contrasts with alethic and epistemic.

derived constituent structure: When a transformation applies to a tree is converts it into a different tree with a partially different structure known as the derived constituent structure.

descriptive adequacy: The level of success achieved by a grammar which not only accounts for the observed data of a language (see observational adequacy) but does so in psychologically plausible terms by also accounting for the intuitions of the native speaker.

dialect: A variety of a language characteristic of a particular geographical region or social class. The 'standard' language is one dialect among many.

directionality: The claim that the syntactic component of a grammar has priority over the other components in the sense that phonological and semantic rules may refer to syntactic information, but syntactic rules are unable to refer to phonological or semantic facts. Also known as the principle of autonomous syntax.

discontinuous structure: Any constituent whose parts may be separated by other material. In English, phrasal verbs such as 'pick up' may be continuous as in 'Pick up the alligator' or discontinuous as in 'Pick the alligator up'. Discontinuous constituents are typically the result of the application of a transformation.

discourse topic: A syntactic constituent whose referent is what a text or discourse is deemed to be about. It is typically encapsulated in a title or caption.

distinctive feature: A set of universal, putatively innate, phonological properties by reference to which it is possible to describe the speech sounds of all possible human languages. Examples are [voiced], [coronal], [nasal].

dysphasia: Impairment of language caused by brain damage.

echo question: A question which seeks information about a mis-heard or incredible part of a preceding utterance by repeating everything except that part: 'You saw *what* in the woodshed?'

ellipsis: The omission of part of a sentence which can be supplied on the basis of grammatical or contextual information. The bracketed part of 'I tried to get Bernard to import a batch of tortoises but he refused (to import a batch of tortoises)' would normally be ellipsed.

embedded: When a sentence has another sentence as one of its constituents, this second sentence is said to be 'embedded' inside the first. For instance, the sentence 'My cat looks like a cauliflower' is embedded as a constituent of the sentence 'Annabel thinks [my cat looks like a cauliflower]'.

empty category: A grammatical element which is syntactically present but has no phonetic realization. The subject of the embedded sentence in 'I want [e to go there]' or 'It is illegal [e to go there]' is an empty pronominal category represented by 'e'.

encyclopaedia: The mental repository of our non-linguistic know-ledge, typically accessed via particular lexical items. For instance, hearing the word 'bear' will (subconsciously) trigger not only the linguistic information that it is a noun, is pronounced [beə], and denotes a kind of animal; but also the encyclopaedic information that bears are furry, friendly, found in Mongolia, hibernate, are spelt 'b-e-a-r', etc. Encyclopaedic knowledge typically differs from person to person, whereas linguistic knowledge is typically the same.

epistemic: Relating to knowledge or belief. The modal auxiliary 'must' is used epistemically in 'That must be the postman at the door'. It contrasts with alethic and deontic.

explanatory adequacy: The level of success achieved by a theory which provides an explanation of how one can acquire one's first language, or how a choice can be made among competing descriptively adequate (qv) grammars on the basis of universal considerations.

expletive: A grammatical element such as 'it' in 'It is obvious that frogs are taking over' or 'there' in 'There appears to be a kangaroo in the bath' which, despite its syntactic position, is not an argument (qv) and has no semantic content.

finite: A clause which is overtly marked for the contrast between e.g. past and present tense is finite. 'Esme loves me' and 'Esme loved me' are both finite, whereas the embedded clause in 'I want [Esme to love me]' is non-finite.

focal scale: In Relevance Theory, the focal scale is a set of ordered implications (whose ordering is determined by stress place- ment) which guide the hearer in interpreting an utterance. On hearing an utterance like 'Bruce molested the *wombat*', the hearer will successively access the hypotheses that: 'Bruce did something', 'Bruce molested something' and 'Bruce molested the wombat', each of which entails the immediately preceding one, and which jointly constitute the focal scale of the utterance.

focus: One of the surface structure constituents which receives the main stress of an utterance. The focus of 'Alison fried my *oyster*' could be any of the constituents 'oyster', 'my oyster', 'fried my oyster' and the whole sentence.

foreground implication: In Relevance Theory, an implication in the focal scale of an utterance which has contextual effects which make it relevant in its own right.

free: A Noun Phrase is free if it is not bound (qv). Pronouns, such as 'him', must be free in their governing category (qv). In 'Don thinks [Jack resembles him]', 'him' must be free in the bracketed clause, hence it can not be coreferential with 'Jack', but it may be bound outside that clause and so could be coreferential with 'Don'.

fricative: A speech sound articulated with audible friction but without complete closure: e.g. /s, f, θ/in English.

functionalism: The view that grammatical phenomena can be explained on the basis of their pragmatic or communicative function.

generate: A set of rules whose output is a particular language (or set of sentences) is said to generate that language.

Generative Grammar: A grammar which uses a formal set (or set of sets) of rules and principles to characterize the sentences or other constituents of a language.

Generative Phonology: The kind of phonology found in a Generative Grammar. Typically the rules of the phonology are interpretive (cf. directionality) and not generative in the sense of the rules of the syntax.

Generative Semantics: A linguistic theory of the 1960s and early 1970s whose proponents gave priority to semantic representations rather than syntactic representations, which they derived from the former.

glottal stop: A speech sound in which there is an audible release of a closure in the glottis (larynx). In Cockney and other varieties of English it is typically used between vowels where the standard language has a /t/: as in 'wa'er' [wɔːʔə] for 'water'.

governed: A lexical category, such as a Verb or Preposition, governs its complement Noun Phrase. In 'I saw Fred in the pub', 'saw' governs 'Fred', and 'in' governs 'the pub'.

governing category: The domain, either a clause (S) or a Noun Phrase, within which particular grammatical relations obtain. In English, a reflexive such as 'himself' must be bound (qv) within its governing category, but a pronoun such as 'him' must be free within its governing category.

Government: One of the central notions in Government–Binding Theory, pertaining to the relation between a head of a construction and those categories dependent on it.

grammatical: The grammar of a language consists of a set of rules which generate the sentences of that language. Any sentence generated by those rules is, by definition, grammatical, and any sentence not generated is ungrammatical. Grammaticality is only one of the determinants of acceptability (qv).

harmony: (1) See consonant harmony; (2) An alternative term for consistency (qv).

head: The most important, and usually obligatory, constituent of a phrase. Noun is the head of the Noun Phrase, Verb is the Head of the Verb Phrase, and so on. The notion of head is central to X-bar theory and to the theory of Government.

Head-first/Head-last: A parameter of Universal Grammar according to which the head of a phrase will precede (Head-first) or follow (Head-last) its complement.

imperative: The sentence structure standardly used to give orders: e.g. 'Don't be silly', 'Show me the way to go home'.

imperfective: A term from the grammatical theory of aspect (qv) referring to events which are in some way viewed as incomplete, ongoing or unfinished.

implicature: Any assumption which is communicated, but not explicitly communicated. The utterance 'Ivan already has too many books' has as one possible implicature the assumption that I should not buy him the book he is asking for. See also conversational implicature.

indirect question: A question which is embedded as the complement of a verb: e.g. 'Guess [who's coming to dinner]'.

informant: A native speaker of a language from whom one gets information in the form of intuitions of well-formedness, ambiguity, etc. about that language. Linguists usually use themselves as informants for their native language.

intonation: Variation in pitch which has the sentence rather than the word as its domain. Intonation is indicated to a limited extent by punctuation, as in the contrast between 'He's won' and 'He's won?'

intransitive: A verb which cannot occur with a direct object is called 'intransitive': e.g. 'The silver *sparkled*' but '*The butler *sparkled* the silver'. Cf. sub-categorization.

labelled bracket: A linear representation of a tree structure. See bracket.

labial: A speech sound in which the lips constitute the main point of articulation: eg. /p, b, m, f, v/ in English.

labio-dental: A speech sound articulated by bringing together the upper teeth and the lower lip: e.g. /f, v/ in English.

labio-velar: A unitary speech sound in which there is simultaneous closure at the lips and the soft palate. Such sounds do not occur in English, but are typical of certain West African languages: e.g. /kp, gb/ in Ewe or Nupe.

lateral: A distinctive feature used to characterize sounds pronounced with a passage of air along the side of the tongue: e.g. /l/ in English.

level of representation: Our linguistic knowledge is of various different kinds: phonological, syntactic, and so on. Each of the components of the grammar dealing with these different kinds of knowledge defines a level of representation. Transformational grammar is unusual in claiming that there are at least two levels of representation within the syntax: Deep Structure and Surface Structure (qv). Technically, a level of representation is defined as the output of a set of rules which have formal properties in common.

lexicon: The mental dictionary containing information about all the words in our language. The lexicon consists of 'lexical entries' specifying the phonological, morphological, syntactic, semantic and encyclopaedic properties of each word in our vocabulary.

local domain: The part of a structure within which some grammatical process has to take place. See governing category.

locality: The phenomenon whereby certain grammatical processes are limited to operating within certain specified domains. See bounding and governing category.

logical form: A level of representation in the grammar which serves as an interface between Surface Structure and the Language of Thought, and contains all the contribution of syntax to meaning.

modal verb: A sub-class of auxiliary verb (qv) whose usual function is to specify concepts such as possibility and necessity: e.g. 'may, must, shall'. See also mood.

module: A component of the grammar or a sub-part of such a component with proprietary rules or categories: e.g. Binding theory, Theta theory.

mood: A grammatical category expressing semantic differences pertaining to certainty, possibility, doubt, necessity, etc. See alethic, deontic and epistemic.

morpheme: The minimal syntactic unit. Words consist of morphemes, so 'countesses' consists of the three morphemes {count}, {–ess} and {–es}, of which the first happens also to be a word, but the latter two can occur only in conjunction with such a word.

morphology: The study of the internal structure of words in terms of morphemes (qv).

motherese: A form of language used when talking to or about young children, involving the use of forms such as 'bunny', 'doggie', and putative simplifications to the grammar. Baby-talk.

Move-Alpha (Move-α): A general principle in Government–Binding Theory which reduces all movement rules (transformations) to the single statement 'Move anything anywhere'. 'Alpha' is a variable over syntactic categories: it may refer to

Noun Phrases, Prepositional Phrases, Verbs, and so on. The resulting problem of overgeneration (qv) is solved by placing constraints, universal or language-particular, on the movement.

nasal: A distinctive feature characterizing sounds pronounced with passage of air through the nose as well as or instead of through the mouth: e.g. /m, n/ in English.

natural class: Any class of phonemes which can be more economically specified (in terms of distinctive features) than any subset of that class. For instance, the class of nasals, /m, n, ŋ/ in English can be characterized by means of the single distinctive feature specification [+nasal], whereas to characterize say /n/ alone would necessitate the less economical specification [+nasal, +coronal].

neutralization: The phenomenon whereby a contrast is lost in some environment. For example, the voicing contrast between /p/ and /b/ in English (as in 'pin' and 'bin') is neutralized after /s/: the orthographic 'p' in 'spin' has some of the features of the /p/ in 'pin' and some of the features of the /b/ in 'bin'.

node: Any point in a tree from which a branch (i.e. a line) emanates.

Non-linear Phonology: Any theory of phonology (for instance, Autosegmental, Metrical or Dependency) which treats some phenomena – e.g. pitch and stress – independently of its treatment of the linear sequence of consonant and vowels.

Noun Phrase: A syntactic constituent consisting of an obligatory head Noun and optional modifiers such as articles, adjectives and complements: e.g. 'crocodiles', 'those yellow shoes', 'boxes with pigs in'. Pronouns (qv) are also a type of Noun Phrase.

Object: A constituent of a sentence, usually a Noun Phrase, which is traditionally associated with the goal or patient (direct object) or beneficiary (indirect object) of the action or state described by the verb. For example, in 'Harry gave his girlfriend a mango', 'a mango' is the direct object and 'his girlfriend' is the indirect object.

observational adequacy: The level of success attained by a grammar which represents the data in some appropriate notation.

open: A vowel pronounced with the tongue in the lowest possible position: e.g. /a/ in English 'hat'.

orderliness: A pragmatic principle, due to Grice, which enjoins one to 'be orderly': for instance, by making the sequential order of one's clauses directly reflect the ordering in time of the events they describe. e.g. 'Blackwood wasn't paying attention so he revoked' is more orderly than 'Blackwood revoked because he wasn't paying attention'.

overgeneralization: When children acquiring their first language extend beyond its domain in the adult language a rule they have learned, they are said to overgeneralize. For example, the addition of regular endings to irregular verbs, giving 'come/comed' instead of 'come/came'.

overgeneration: A grammar which maximizes the generality of the rules and principles it contains, e.g. by reducing all movement processes to the single statement 'Move-α', over-generates in the sense that it characterizes as well-formed or grammatical, sentences which are unacceptable to the native speaker. The solution to the problem is to *constrain* the rules of the grammar by means of universal principles: in the present case, for instance, by subjacency. (qv).

palatal: A consonant articulated with the front of the tongue close to or in contact with the hard palate: e.g. /j/ representing the first sound in English 'yes'.

palato-alveolar: A consonant articulated with the front of the tongue raised towards the hard palate and the tip or blade of the tongue in contact with the alveolar ridge: e.g. /ʃ/ ('sh') in English 'ship'.

parameter: Principles of Universal Grammar have *parameters* which define the limits within which the rules of the grammar one is learning are fixed by experience. For instance, word-order differences among languages are in large part a function of the Head-first/Head-last parameter (qv).

Parametric Variation: The variability in grammar allowed by universal principles. See parameter.

participle: A non-finite form of the verb used adjectivally or in the formation of so-called compound tenses: e.g. 'A *crying* baby' or 'He had been *crying*'.

particle: A word such as 'up', 'down' or 'over' which combines with a verb to form a separate lexical item: e.g. 'look up' in 'He looked up the address'. Particles differ from prepositions in being separable from their associated verb: e.g. 'He looked the address up' contrasts with the impossible '*He looked the girl at' (cf. 'He looked at the girl').

passive: A type of sentence in which the goal or patient is typically the subject, and the verb is morphologically marked: e.g. 'James was bitten by a small octopus' is the passive equivalent of the active 'A small octopus bit James'.

perfective: A term from the grammatical theory of aspect (qv) referring to events which are viewed as completed or as a whole.

performance: The use of language in speaking and understanding utterances is known as linguistic performance. Linguistic competence (qv), or knowledge of language, is only one factor in performance, which also involves our physical and mental state. The core concept in a theory of performance is Relevance (qv).

pharyngal: Speech sounds pronounced with a constriction in the pharynx. They do not occur phonemically in English, but are common in Arabic and related languages.

phoneme: Those sounds which can signal a possible difference of lexical meaning between items in a language are phonemes. In English, /s/ and /z/ are phonemically distinct (i.e. difference phonemes) because of the contrast between e.g. 'sip' and 'zip'. The same phoneme may be pronounced slightly differently in different positions in the word: e.g. the ls at the beginning and end of 'lull', but such allophonic differences never signal lexical differences (in English), and hence are not phonemic. Cf. allophone.

phonemic representation: See phoneme. A representation of pronunciation which includes only phonemically contrastive information, without fine phonetic or allophonic detail.

phonetic form: In Generative Grammar, the output of the rules of the phonological component. See phonetic representation.

phonetic representation: A representation which includes all rule-governed properties of pronunciation, whether phonemic or allophonic.

phonology: The module of a grammar that deals with the sound structure of a language and its relation to the syntax. The study of the sound systems of possible languages.

Phrase Structure Rule: A rule which explicitly specifies the syntactic structure of a sentence or smaller phrase by 're-writing' one category as a sequence of other constituent categories or words. The statement that 'a Noun Phrase consists of an obligatory Noun optionally preceded by a Determiner and optionally followed by a complement Sentence' (as in 'the claim that ducks are mammals') could be formalized by the Phrase Structure Rule: NP → (Det) N (S).

plosive: A speech sound articulated with an abruptly released closure: e.g. /b, d, g/ in English.

postposing: The movement of a constituent, typically an agentive Noun Phrase, to the end of the sentence. In early versions of transformational grammar, the Noun Phrase 'the tank' in the passive sentence 'Marvin was depressed by the tank' was postposed from initial subject position to final position.

postposition: The equivalent of a preposition but occurring after rather than before the Noun Phrase it governs: e.g. 'ago' in 'a week ago'.

pragmatics: The theory of utterance interpretation and the use of language more generally. Pragmatics is a major part of the field of linguistic performance (qv). See also Relevance.

Prepositional Phrase: A syntactic constituent consisting of an obligatory head Preposition and a following Noun Phrase: e.g. 'with a hammer'.

presupposition: The presuppositions of a sentence are the conditions that must obtain for it to be either true or false. For example, both 'The King of France is bald' and 'The King of France is not bald' presuppose that there is a king of France and assert that he either is or is not bald. If there is no king of France, there is a presupposition failure and the utterance is correspondingly hard to interpret.

Principle of Relevance: In Relevance Theory, the principle that by uttering a sentence the speaker is offering a guarantee that his utterance is worth the hearer's attention.

Projection Principle: In Government–Binding Theory, the principle that sub-categorized (qv) lexical information must be represented at every syntactic level. For example, the lexical entry for the verb 'hit' in English, specifies that it must have two arguments, a subject and an object, as in 'Marx hit Engels'. Where there appears to be only one Noun Phrase, as in 'Engels was hit', the Projection Principle ensures that the understood argument is explicitly represented, in this case by the empty category (qv) 'e', giving the structure 'Engels was hit e'.

pronoun – pronominal: A syntactic class of words whose members are usually referentially dependent on a Noun Phrase: e.g. 'it' replaces 'the fried egg' in 'The fried egg was burnt, but I still ate it'. In Government–Binding Theory, 'pronominals' include both overt and empty pronouns. See Binding and empty category.

Proposition: The semantic content of a sentence or utterance. Corresponding actives and passives, such as 'Simon mugged the beadle' and 'The beadle was mugged by Simon', have the same propositional content but have different stylistic effects.

pseudo-passive: A sentence type in which the prepositional object following an intransitive verb undergoes movement of the same kind as does the object of a transitive verb: e.g. '*The bed* has been slept in'.

quantifier: Any element such as 'all', 'some', 'each' or the numerals which specify the quantity of the rest of the Noun Phrase containing them.

recursion: Any set of Phrase Structure Rules (qv) which reintroduces on the right-hand side of an arrow a category symbol which already appears on the left hand side of some rule is 'recursive': e.g. the rule NP → NP PP. A grammar which contains recursive rules has a potentially infinite output.

reflexive: A pronoun marked by '–self' or '–selves' which is coreferential with some antecedent NP: e.g. 'herself' in 'The lady is deceiving herself'. See Binding.

relative clause: A clause which is part of a Noun Phrase and of which it modifies the head: e.g. 'who stole my harp' in '[The man who stole my harp] is a fiend'.

Relevance: An utterance is relevant if it has contextual effects (qv) in some context. Other things being equal, the greater the contextual effects and the smaller the processing effort involved, the greater the relevance.

reversible passive: A passive sentence in which either Noun Phrase could be placed in subject position and plausibly construed as the agent: e.g. 'The hunter was frightened by the tiger' is reversible, because 'The tiger was frightened by the hunter' is equally natural, whereas 'The hunter was shot by the tiger' is relatively implausible *vis-à-vis* (the non-reversible) 'The tiger was shot by the hunter'.

schema: A formalism abbreviating a number of rules into a single statement: e.g. XP → X Comp subsumes VP → V Comp, NP → N Comp, etc.

schwa: The name for the neutral vowel [ə] heard in English at the beginning of words such as 'above', 'apart', 'assemble'.

semantics: The study of meaning, in particular, the linguistically determined meaning of a sentence or phrase.

sentence: The fundamental unit of grammar, taken to be a theoretical primitive. The sentence belongs to the study of competence (qv), the corresponding performance notion being the *utterance,* and the corresponding logical notion being the *proposition.*

sonorant: A distinctive feature which characterizes sounds made with a vocal cord position such that 'spontaneous' voicing is possible: e.g. in English, the vowels and /w, r, m, l/ etc.

standard language: A dialect with an army and a navy.

stative: A class of verb (contrasted with 'dynamic' verbs) which describe states of affairs rather than actions: e.g. 'know', 'own' in English. Syntactically, stative verbs are subject to a number of restrictions, such as the inability to occur in the progressive: e.g. '*He is knowing English'.

stop: A speech sound whose articulation involves a complete closure in the vocal tract: e.g. /p, t, k/ in English.

strident: A distinctive feature characterizing consonants whose articulation involves more acoustic noise than non-strident sounds: e.g. /s, z, tʃ, dʒ/ in English.

string: Any consecutive sequence of syntactic elements.

structure-dependent: All syntactic rules in all languages operate on structures rather than on unstructured strings of words. For example, to form a question in English one moves the auxiliary to the left of the subject Noun Phrase, deriving e.g. 'Is the asparagus ready?' from 'The asparagus is ready'. It is not possible for any human language to have a rule which moves the auxiliary to the left of 'the next three words', or which permutes the second and fourth words in a sentence, or which makes verbs the third word.

sub-categorization: A syntactic category, such as Verb, is sub-categorized in terms of the categories it can co-occur with. For instance, a transitive (qv) verb, such as 'polish', must be followed by a direct object Noun Phrase; an intransitive (qv) verb, such as 'sparkle', cannot be so followed; a di-transitive verb such as 'give', requires two objects, and so on.

subjacency: A locality constraint which restricts the operation of transformational rules. See 'bounding'.

subject: That Noun Phrase, usually associated with the agent of the action described in the sentence, which determines such morphological processes as subject-verb agreement: e.g. 'the kipper(s)' in 'The kipper tastes awful' and 'The kippers taste awful'. In generative grammar, it is customary to distinguish the Deep Structure (or 'logical') subject from the Surface Structure subject, since in some sentence types, e.g. passive, these may be different. Thus, in 'The kippers were stolen by a passing traffic warden', the Deep Structure subject is 'a passing traffic warden', but the Surface Structure subject (the Deep Structure object) is 'the kippers', which determines the form of the verb 'were'.

subordinate clause: A clause embedded (qv) as a constituent of another clause: e.g. 'because she kissed me' in 'I fainted because she kissed me'. It contrasts with co-ordination (qv).

sub-theory: An alternative term for module (qv).

suprasegmental: A phonological effect which extends over more than one segment: e.g. pitch and stress phenomena. The apparent independence of such effects is a major motivation for the theory of Autosegmental Phonology (qv).

Surface Structure: In early Transformational Generative Grammar, Surface Structure was defined as that level of representation which is the output of the Transformational rules. In recent versions of generative grammar, Surface Structure is usually referred to as S-Structure: that level which is both the output of Move-α (qv) and the input to the rules of the phonological component and the Logical Form component.

syncope: A phonological process whereby a sound or syllable is omitted from the middle of a word: e.g. the informal pronunciation of 'library' as [laibri:].

tense: A grammatical category pertaining semantically to (deictic) distinctions of time (past, present and future), and morphologically to distinctions both of time and of aspect, mood and various other categories.

Thematic Theory (Theta Theory): That module of Government–Binding Theory which deals with the semantic roles associated with the arguments of a verb. For example, 'scream' requires an 'agent', 'fall over' requires a 'theme' (or 'patient'), 'kiss' requires an 'agent' and a 'patient', etc.

tone language: Any language such as Ewe, Nupe or Chinese in which pitch variation serves to differentiate lexical items: e.g. in Nupe, *wá* on a high tone means 'to want', *wa* on a mid tone means 'to lay an egg', and *wà* on a low tone means 'to be weak'.

topic and comment: A pragmatic distinction between what a sentence is about (the topic) and the statement made about it (the comment).

topicalization: A syntactic process whereby a constituent is moved to the front of the sentence: e.g. 'A mongoose I'd really love to see', derived from 'I'd really love to see a mongoose'.

trace: An empty category (qv) marking the place from which a constituent has been moved by a transformation. Cf. the Projection Principle.

transformation: A grammatical rule which converts one tree into another. The set of transformations in a grammar convert Deep Structures into Surface Structures. In Goverment–Binding Theory all transformations have been reduced to the single, maximally general statement 'Move–α' (qv).

transitive: A verb which requires a direct object is called transitive: e.g. 'Thoth *stroked* the ibis' but '*Thoth *stroked*'. Cf. subcategorization.

tree: A diagrammatic representation of the constituent structure of a sentence. See brackets.

truth conditions: Those conditions which must obtain in the real world in order for a sentence to report a true state of affairs.

typology: The study of the ways in which languages may differ from each other. See Parametric Variation.

unacceptable: An utterance is unacceptable to a native speaker if it is either incomprehensible or irrelevant or both. (Un)grammaticality is only one determinant of (un)acceptability. See acceptable.

unbounded movement: The removal of a constituent to a position indefinitely far from its Deep Structure origin (in apparent violation of subjacency): e.g. In 'Kipling thought the natives believed the mongoose would kill the cobra', the Noun Phrase 'the cobra' may be questioned to produce the sentence: 'Which cobra did Kipling think the natives believed the mongoose would kill?'

ungrammatical: A sentence is ungrammatical with respect to a grammar if it is not generated by the rules of that grammar. Ungrammatical sentences are prefixed with an asterisk (*) as in '*Maggie is implausible to change her mind.'

universal: Linguistic theory has to provide for the description of all possible human languages. The set of categories, features, principles and rules thus provided constitute the universal vocabulary of the theory. Some categories, such as Noun and Verb, occur in every grammar, and are termed 'absolute' universals, whereas others, such as article, are used only in the description of some languages and are called 'relative' universals. 'Implicational' universals are those which, while not being characteristic of any individual language, are true of the set of languages as a whole. Thus for any language, Verb-initial word-order is said to imply the presence of prepositions rather than postpositions.

Use-theory of meaning: A semantic theory (more accurately a kind of embryonic pragmatic theory), due to Austin and Searle (building on work by Wittgenstein), which attempted to reduce the meaning of words and sentences to their possible uses.

utterance: A string of words produced on a particular occasion. It is the performance correlate of the competence notion of sentence (qv).

velar: A consonant articulated with contact between the back of the tongue and the velum (soft palate): e.g. /k, g/ in English.

Verb Phrase: A syntactic constituent consisting of an obligatory head Verb and any of various optional complements, such as Noun Phrases, Prepositional Phrases, and so on.

voice: A distinctive feature which characterizes sounds articulated with concomitant vocal cord vibration: e.g. the vowels and /b, d, g, m, n, w, l/ in English.

vowel harmony: A situation in which all the vowels of a word are pronounced with some feature in common (e.g. all are front or all are rounded), or a process whereby such similarity is brought about by phonological rule. It is typical of early first-language acquisition and also of the adult phonologies of languages such as Turkish.

Whorf hypothesis: The hypothesis, due to Benjamin Lee Whorf and Edward Sapir, that the structure of our native language determines our conceptual categorization of the world.

WH question: A question including a *wh*-word (which, what, when, where, why, how, etc.) which requires an answer providing specific information, so that an answer with 'yes' or 'no' is always inappropriate. For example: 'What would you like?' is appropriately answered by 'A toothpick', but not by 'Yes please'.

X-bar Theory: That module of Government–Binding Theory which deals with the properties of Phrase Structure. The central principle of X-bar theory is that every phrase XP, where X may be replaced by V(erb), N(oun), P(reposition) or A(djective), contains a category of the same type X as its head: i.e. Verb Phrases have Verbs as their head, Noun Phrases have Nouns as their heads, and so on. The order of this head with respect to any possible complements is determined by the Head-first/Head-last parameter (qv).

Bibliography

Ansre, G. (1961): *The Tonal Structure of Ewe. Hartford Studies in Linguistics 1*. Hartford, Conn.

Austin, J. (1962): *How to do Things with Words*. Oxford: Clarendon Press.

Bach, E. (1970): Problominalization. *Linguistic Inquiry*, 1: pp. 121–2.

Basbøll, H. (1988): Phonological Theory. In F. Newmeyer (ed.), *Linguistics: The Cambridge Survey*, Cambridge: Cambridge University Press: vol. 1, pp. 192–215.

Belloc, H. (1899): *A Moral Alphabet*. London: Edward Arnold.

Berghe, P. L. van der (1983): Human Inbreeding Avoidance: Culture in Nature. *Behavioral and Brain Sciences*, 6: pp. 91–123.

Berko, J. and Brown, R. (1960): Psycholinguistic Research Methods. In P. Mussen (ed.), *Handbook of Research Methods in Child Development*, New York: Wiley: pp. 517–57.

Bever, T. (1976): The Influence of Speech Performance on Linguistic Structure. In T. Bever, J. Katz and T. Langendoen (eds), *An Integrated Theory of Linguistic Abilities*, Hassocks: Harvester Press: pp. 65–88.

Bierce, A. (1911/1958): *The Devil's Dictionary*. New York: Dover.

Bishop, D. V. M. (1977): *Comprehension of Grammar in Normal and Abnormal Development*. University of Oxford: D.Phil Thesis.

—— (1982): *TROG: Test for Reception of Grammar*. Abingdon: Thomas Leach (on behalf of the Medical Research Council).

Blank, M., Gessner, M. and Esposito, A. (1978): Language Without Communication: a case study. *Journal of Child Language*, 6: pp. 329–52.

Blass, R. (1985): Cohesion, Coherence and Relevance. MS: University College London.

Bloom, L., Tackeff, J. and Lahey, M. (1984): Learning *to* in complement constructions. *Journal of Child Language*, 11: pp. 391–406.

Braine, M. (1976): Review of N. V. Smith's *The Acquisition of Phonology*. *Language* 52: pp. 489–98.

Bresnan, J. (ed.) (1982): *The Mental Representation of Grammatical Relations*.

Cambridge, Mass.: MIT Press.

Brodsky, J. (1987): *Less than One: Selected Essays*. Harmondsworth: Penguin.

Brody, M. (1987): Review discussion on Chomsky's *Knowledge of Language*. *Mind and Language*, 2: pp. 165–77.

Brown, G. and Yule, G. (1983): *Discourse Analysis*. Cambridge: Cambridge University Press.

Burgess, A. (1986): New light on Language. In A. Burgess, *But do Blondes prefer Gentlemen?*, New York: McGraw-Hill: pp. 186–9. (First appeared in *The Observer* in 1979.)

Burkhardt, F. and Smith, S. (eds) (1986): *The Correspondence of Charles Darwin*, vol. 2, 1837–1843. Cambridge: Cambridge University Press.

Bynon, J. (1977): The Derivational Processes Relating Berber Nursery Words to their Counterparts in Normal Inter-adult Speech. In C. Snow and C. Ferguson (eds), *Talking to Children*, Cambridge: Cambridge University Press: pp. 255–69.

Calvino, I. (1982): *Cosmicomics*. London: Abacus.

Calvino, I. (1986): *Mr Palomar*. London: Picador.

Carden, G. (1986): Blocked Forward Co-reference: theoretical Implications of the Acquisition Data. In B. Lust (ed.), *Studies in the Acquisition of Anaphora. vol. 1: Defining the Constraints*, Reidel, Dordrecht.

Carston, R. (1987): Review of D. Premack *Gavagai!*. *Mind and Language*, 2: pp. 333–49.

—— (1988): Language and Cognition. In F. Newmeyer (ed.), *Linguistics: The Cambridge Survey*, Cambridge: Cambridge University Press: vol. 3, pp. 38–68.

Chalmers, A. F. (1982): *What is this thing called Science?* Milton Keynes: Open University Press.

Chomsky, N. (1955): *The Logical Structure of Linguistic Theory*. Unpublished MS. Published (with a new introduction) as Chomsky (1975a).

—— (1957): *Syntactic Structures*. The Hague: Mouton.

—— (1961): Some Methodological Remarks on Generative Grammar. *Word*, 17: pp. 219–39.

—— (1963): Formal Properties of Grammars. In R. Luce, R. Bush and E. Galanter (eds), *Handbook of Mathematical Psychology*, New York: Wiley: vol. 2, pp. 323–418.

—— (1964a): The Logical Basis of Linguistic Theory. In *Proceedings of the Ninth International Congress of Linguists*, ed. H. Lunt, The Hague: Mouton: pp. 914–78. (Revised as Chomsky (1964b).)

—— (1964b): *Current Issues in Linguistic Theory*. The Hague: Mouton.

—— (1965): *Aspects of the Theory of Syntax*. Cambridge, Mass.: MIT Press.

—— (1966a): *Cartesian Lingusitics*. New York: Harper & Row.

—— (1966b): *Topics in the Theory of Generative Grammar*. The Hague: Mouton.

—— (1967): The Formal Nature of Language. In E. Lenneberg, *Biological Foundations of Language*, New York: Wiley: pp. 397–442.

—— (1970): Remarks on Nominalization. In R. Jacobs and P. Rosenbaum (eds), *Readings in English Transformational Grammar*, Waltham, Mass.: Ginn & Co: pp. 184–221.

—— (1972): *Language and Mind*. New York: Harcourt Brace Jovanovich. (Enlarged edn.)

—— (1973): Conditions on Transformations. In S. Anderson and P. Kiparsky (eds), *A Festschrift for Morris Halle*, New York: Holt, Rinehart & Winston: pp. 232–86.

—— (1975a): *The Logical Structure of Linguistic Theory*. New York: Plenum.

—— (1975b): Questions of Form and Interpretation. *Linguistic Analysis*, 1: pp. 75–109.

—— (1975c): *Reflections on Language*. New York: Pantheon.

—— (1977): 'On *Wh*-Movement'. In P. Culicover, T. Wasow and A. Akmajian (eds), *Formal Syntax*, New York: Academic Press: pp. 71–132.

—— (1980a): *Rules and Representations*. Oxford: Basil Blackwell.

—— (1980b): On Binding. *Linguistic Inquiry*, 11: pp. 1–46.

—— (1980c): Discussion of Putnam's Comments. In M. Piattelli-Palmarini (ed.), *Language and Learning: The Debate between Jean Piaget and Noam Chomsky*, Cambridge, Mass.: Harvard University Press: pp. 310–24.

—— (1981a): *Lectures on Government and Binding*. Dordrecht: Foris.

—— (1981b): Knowledge of Language: Its Elements and Origins. *Philosophical Transactions of the Royal Society London*, B 295: pp. 223–34.

—— (1981c): Principles and Parameters in Syntactic Theory. In N. Hornstein and D. Lightfoot (eds), *Explanation in Linguistics*, London: Longman: pp. 32–75.

—— (1982): *The Generative Enterprise: A Discussion with Riny Huybregts and Henk van Riemsdijk*. Dordrecht: Foris.

—— (1986): *Knowledge of Language: Its Nature, Origin and Use*. New York: Praeger.

—— (1987a): Reply (to reviews of *Knowledge of Language* by M. Brody and A. George). *Mind and Language*, 2: pp. 178–97.

—— (1987b): Transformational Grammar: Past, Present and Future. In *Generative Grammar: Its Basis, Development and Prospects*. Special Issue, *Studies in English Linguistics and Literature*, Kyoto University of Foreign Studies: pp. 33–80.

—— (1987c): *Language in a Psycholinguistic Setting*. Special Issue of *Sophia Linguistica: Working Papers in Linguistics*, 22, Tokyo: Sophia University.

—— (1988a) *Language and Problems of Knowledge: The Managua Lectures.* Cambridge, Mass.: MIT Press.

—— (1988b): *The Culture of Terrorism.* London: Pluto Press.

—— (Ms) Some Notes on Economy of Derivation and Representation. MIT mimeo.

Chomsky, N. and Halle, M. (1968): *The Sound Pattern of English,* New York: Harper & Row.

Chomsky, N. and Herman, E. (1979): *The Political Economy of Human Rights,* 2 vols. London: Spokesman.

Christaller, J. G. (1875): *A Grammar of the Asante and Fante Language called Twi.* Basel.

Clark, H. H. and Clark, E. V. (1977): *Psychology and Language: An Introduction to Psycholinguistics.* New York: Harcourt Brace Jovanovich.

Cohen, I. B. (1980) *The Newtonian Revolution.* Cambridge: Cambridge University Press.

Collins Dictionary of the English Language (1986): 2nd edn. London: Collins.

Comrie, B. (1976): *Aspect.* Cambridge: Cambridge University Press.

—— (1981a) *Language Universals and Linguistic Typology.* Oxford: Basil Blackwell.

—— (1981b): *The Languages of the Soviet Union.* Cambridge: Cambridge University Press.

—— (1983): On the Validity of Typological Studies: A Reply to Smith. *Australian Journal of Linguistics,* 3: pp. 93–6.

Cross, T. (1977): 'Mothers' Speech Adjustments: The Contribution of Selected Child Listener Variables. In C. Snow and C. Ferguson (eds), *Talking to Children,* Cambridge: Cambridge University Press: pp. 151–88.

Crystal, D. (1985): *A Dictionary of Linguistics and Phonetics.* Oxford: Basil Blackwell.

Curtiss, S. (1988): Abnormal Language Acquisition and Grammar: Evidence for the Modularity of Language. In L. Hyman and C. Li (eds), *Language, Speech and Mind: Studies in Honour of Victoria A. Fromkin.* London: Routledge & Kegan Paul: pp. 81–102.

D'Agostino, F. (1986): *Chomsky's System of Ideas.* Oxford: Clarendon Press.

Delany, S. R. (1967): *Babel-17.* London: Gollancz.

Derbyshire, D. (1977): Word Order Universals and the Existence of OVS Languages, *Linguistic Inquiry,* 8: pp. 590–8.

Derbyshire, D (1985): *Hixkaryana and Linguistic Typology.* Arlington, Texas: Summer Institute of Linguistics.

Derbyshire, D. and Pullum, G. (1981): Object-Initial Languages. *International Journal of American Linguistics,* 47: pp. 192–214.

Dixon, R. M. W. (1963): *Linguistic Science and Logic.* The Hague: Mouton.

Dodd, B. and Campbell, R. (eds) (1987): *Hearing by Eye: The Psychology of Lip-reading.* Hillsdale, N.J.: Lawrence Erlbaum Associates.

Dodd, B. and Hermelin, B. (1977): Phonological Coding by the Prelinguistically Deaf. *Perception & Psychophysics,* 21: pp. 413–17.

Downes, W. (1977): The Imperative and Pragmatics. *Journal of Linguistics,* 13: pp. 77–97.

Dryer, M. S (1988): Object–Verb Order and Adjective–Noun Order: Dispelling a Myth. *Lingua,* 74: pp. 185–217.

Ducrot, O. and Todorov, T. (1981): *Encyclopaedic Dictionary of the Sciences of Language.* Oxford: Basil Blackwell.

Edmondson, J. A. and Plank, F. (1978): Great Expectations: An Intensive Self-Analysis. *Linguistics & Philosophy,* 2: pp. 373–413.

Elgin, S. H. (1984): *Native Tongue.* New York: DAW Books.

Encyclopaedia Britannica (1975): 15th edn, 30 vols. Chicago.

Evans, G. (1982): *The Varieties of Reference.* Oxford: Oxford University Press.

Ferguson, C. (1977): Baby-Talk as a Simplified Register. In C. Snow and C. Ferguson (eds), *Talking to Children,* Cambridge: Cambridge University Press: pp. 209–35.

Fernald, A. (1984): The Perceptual and Affective Salience of Mothers' Speech to Infants. In L. Feagans, C. Garvey and R. Golinkoff (eds), *The Origins and Growth of Communication,* Norwood, N.J.: Ablex Publishing Co.: pp. 5–29.

Feyerabend, P. K. (1975): *Against Method: Outline of an Anarchistic Theory of Knowledge.* London: New Left Books.

Field, H. (1973) Theory Change and the Indeterminacy of Reference. *Journal of Philosophy,* 70: pp. 462–81.

Fodor, J. A. (1975): *The Language of Thought.* New York: Crowell.

—— (1983): *The Modularity of Mind.* Cambridge, Mass.: MIT Press.

Foley, W. and van Valin, R. (1984): *Functional Syntax and Universal Grammar.* Cambridge: Cambridge University Press.

Franklyn, J. (1985): *A Dictionary of Rhyming Slang.* London: Routledge & Kegan Paul.

Frazier, L. (1988): Grammar and Language Processing. In F. Newmeyer (ed.), *Linguistics: The Cambridge Survey,* Cambridge: Cambridge University Press: vol. 2, pp.15–34.

Fromkin, V. A. (1973): *Speech Errors as Linguistic Evidence.* The Hague: Mouton.

—— (1988): Grammatical Aspects of Speech Errors. In F. Newmeyer (ed.) *Linguistics: The Cambridge Survey.* Cambridge: Cambridge University Press: vol. 2, pp. 117–38.

Gale, R. M. (ed.) (1968): *The Philosophy of Time.* Sussex: Harvester Press.

Gallager, R. G. (1975): Information Theory. *Encyclopaedia Britannica:*

vol. 9, pp. 574–80.

Gazdar, G., Klein, E., Pullum, G. and Sag, I. (1985): *Generalized Phrase Structure Grammar*. Oxford: Basil Blackwell.

Gimson, A. C. (1962): *An Introduction to the Pronunciation of English*. London: Edward Arnold.

Giora, R. (1985): A Text-based Analysis of Non-narrative Texts. *Theoretical Linguistics*, 12: pp. 115–35.

Givón, T. (1979): *On Understanding Grammar*. New York: Academic Press.

Gleitman, L. (1981): Maturational Determinants of Language Growth. *Cognition*, 10: pp. 103–14.

Gleitman, L. and Wanner, E. (1982): The State of the State of the Art. In E. Wanner and L. Gleitman (eds), *Language Acquisition: The State of the Art*, Cambridge: Cambridge University Press: pp. 3–48.

Golding, W. (1955): *The Inheritors*. London: Faber.

Goldman-Eisler, F. (1958): Speech Production and the Predictability of Words in Context. *Quarterly Journal of Experimental Psychology*, 10: pp. 96–106.

Goldsmith, J. (1979) *Autosegmental Phonology*. New York: Garland.

Gould, S. J. (1980): *Ever Since Darwin*. Harmondsworth: Penguin.

—— (1983): *The Mismeasure of Man*. Harmondsworth: Penguin.

—— (1984): *Hen's Teeth and Horse's Toes*. Harmondsworth: Penguin.

Greenberg, J. (1963): Some Universals of Grammar with Particular Reference to the Order of Meaningful Elements. In J. Greenberg (ed.), *Universals of Language*, Cambridge, Mass.: MIT Press: pp. 73–113.

Gregory, R. L. (1973): The Confounded Eye. In R. L. Gregory and E. H. Gombrich (eds), *Illusion in Nature and Art*. London: Duckworth: pp. 49–95.

Grice, H. P. (1975): Logic and Conversation. In P. Cole and J. Morgan (eds), *Syntax and Semantics 3: Speech Acts*, New York: Academic Press: pp. 41–58.

Hagège, C. (1986): *La grammaire générative: réflexions critiques*. Paris: Presses Universitaires de France.

Halle, M. (1970): Is Kabardian a Vowel-less Language? *Foundations of Language*, 6: pp. 95–103.

Halliday, M. A. K. (1967–68): Notes on Transitivity and Theme in English. *Journal of Linguistics*, 3: pp. 37–81, 199–244; 4: pp. 179–215.

—— (1975): *Learning how to Mean*. London: Edward Arnold.

Hampton, C. (1970) *The Philanthropist*. London: Faber & Faber.

Harris, M. and Coltheart, M. (1986): *Language Processing in Children and Adults*. London: Routledge & Kegan Paul.

Hawkins, J. (1980): On Implicational and Distributional Universals of Word Order. *Journal of Linguistics*, 16: pp. 193–235.

—— (ed.) (1988a): *Papers in Universal Grammar: Generative and Typological Approaches*. Special Issue, *Lingua*, 74.

—— (ed.) (1988b): *Explaining Language Universals*. Oxford: Basil Blackwell.

Hawkins, J. and Gilligan, G. (1988): Prefixing and Suffixing Universals in Relation to Basic Word Order. *Lingua*. 74: pp. 219–59.

Hawkins, P. (1984): *Introducing Phonology*. London: Hutchinson.

Haywood, J. and H. Nahmad (1962): *A New Arabic Grammar*. London: Lund, Humphries.

Heinze, E. E. (1977): *Die Übersetzung der sexuellen Anspielungen Shakespeares ins deutsche vom 18. bis 20. Jahrhundert*. Ph.D. Dissertation for the University of Tennessee, Knoxville.

Hill, J. H. (1988): Language, Culture and World View. In F. Newmeyer (ed.) *Linguistics: The Cambridge Survey*. Cambridge: Cambridge University Press: vol. 4, pp. 14–36.

Hofstadter, D. (1980): *Gödel, Escher, Bach: an Eternal Golden Braid*. New York: Vintage Books.

Horn, L. (1988): Pragmatic Theory. In F. Newmeyer (ed.), *Linguistics: The Cambridge Survey*, Cambridge: Cambridge University Press: vol. 1, pp. 113–45.

Hornstein, N. (1977): Towards a Theory of Tense. *Linguistic Inquiry*, 8: pp. 521–57.

Hornstein, N. and Lightfoot, D. (1981): *Explanation in Linguistics: The Logical Problem of Language Acquisition*. London: Longman.

Horrocks, G. (1987): *Generative Grammar*. London: Longman.

Hudson, R. A. (1972): Evidence for Ungrammaticality. *Linguistic Inquiry*, 3: p. 227.

—— (1980): *Sociolinguistics*. Cambridge: Cambridge University Press.

—— (1981): Some Issues on Which Linguists can Agree. *Journal of Linguistics*, 17: pp. 333–44.

—— (1984): *Word Grammar*. Oxford: Basil Blackwell.

Hughes, T. (1967): *Wodwo*. London: Faber.

Hulst, H. van der and Smith, N. S. H. (eds) (1982): *The Structure of Phonological Representations*, 2 vols. Dordrecht: Foris.

—— (eds) (1985): *Advances in Non-linear Phonology*. Dordrecht: Foris.

Huxley, T. H. (1894): Biogenesis and Abiogenesis. *Collected Essays*, vol. 8.

Innes, G. (1962): *A Mende Grammar*. London: Macmillan.

Irwin, J. V. and Wong, S. P. (eds) (1982): *Phonological Development in Children: 18 to 72 Months*. Carbondale: Southern Illinois University Press.

Jackendoff, R. (1972): *Semantic Interpretation in Generative Grammar*. Cambridge, Mass.: MIT Press.

Jakobson, R., Fant, G. and Halle, M. (1951): *Preliminaries to Speech*

Analysis. Cambridge, Mass.: MIT Press.

Joos, M. (ed.) (1957): *Readings in Linguistics*. Chicago: University of Chicago Press.

Karmiloff-Smith, A. (forthcoming) Beyond Modularity: A Developmental Perspective on Human Consciousness.

Katz, J. J. (1981):*Language and other Abstract Objects*. Oxford: Basil Blackwell.

Katz, J. J. and Postal, P. M. (1964): *An Integrated Theory of Linguistic Descriptions*. Cambridge, Mass.: MIT Press.

Keenan, E. (1976): Remarkable Subjects in Malagasy. In C. Li (ed.), *Subject and Topic*, New York: Academic Press: pp. 247–301.

—— (1978): The Syntax of Subject-Final Languages. In W. Lehmann (ed.), *Syntactic Typology*, Austin: University of Texas Press: pp. 247–301.

Keenan, E. and Comrie, B. (1977): Noun Phrase Accessibility and Universal Grammar. *Linguistic Inquiry*, 8: pp. 63–99.

Keenan, E.O. and Schieffelin, B. (1976): Topic as a Discourse notion. In C. Li (ed.), *Subject and Topic*, New York: Academic Press: pp. 335–384.

Kempson, R. (1988): Grammar and Conversational Principles. In F. Newmeyer (ed.) *Linguistics: The Cambridge Survey*, Cambridge: Cambridge University Press: vol. 2, pp. 139–63.

Kempson, R. and Cormack, A. (1979): Ambiguity and Quantification. *Linguistics & Philosophy*, 4: pp. 259–309.

King, H. (1970) On Blocking the Rules for Contraction in English. *Linguistic Inquiry, 1: pp. 134–6.*

Klima, E. (1975): Sound and its Absence in the Linguistic Symbol. In J. F. Kavanagh and J. E. Cutting (eds), *The Role of Speech in Language*. Cambridge Mass.: MIT Press: pp. 249–70.

Köhler, O. R. A. et al. (1975): African Languages. *Encyclopaedia Britannica*: vol. 1, pp. 218–32.

Koster, J. (1987): *Domains and Dynasties*. Dordrecht: Foris.

Kuipers, A. H. (1960): *Phoneme and Morpheme in Kabardian*. The Hague: Mouton.

Kuno, S. (1973): *The Structure of the Japanese Language*. Cambridge, Mass.: MIT Press.

Labov, W. (1972): *Sociolinguistic Patterns*. Oxford: Basil Blackwell.

Ladusaw, W. (1988): Semantic Theory. In F. Newmeyer (ed.) *Linguistics: The Cambridge Survey*, Cambridge: Cambridge University Press: vol. 1, pp. 89–112.

Lakatos, I. (1970): Falsification and the Methodology of Scientific Research Programmes. In I. Lakatos and A. Musgrave (eds), *Criticism and the Growth of Knowledge*, Cambridge: Cambridge University Press: pp. 91–195.

Lakoff, G. (1968): Pronouns and Reference. Indiana University Linguistics Club. Reprinted in J. McCawley (ed.) (1978) *Syntax and Semantics: Notes from the Linguistics Underground*. New York: Academic Press: vol. 7, p. 275–335.

Lambton, A. K. S. (1974): *Persian Grammar*. Cambridge: Cambridge University Press.

Landau, B. and Gleitman, L. (1985): *Language and Experience: Evidence from the Blind Child*. Cambridge, Mass.: Harvard University Press.

Lees, R. B. (1957): Review of Noam Chomsky's *Syntactic Structures*. *Language*, 33: pp. 375–408.

Lees, R. B. and Klima, E. (1963): Rules for English Pronominalization. *Language*, 39: pp. 17–28.

Lehmann, W. (ed.) (1978): *Syntactic Typology*. Austin: University of Texas Press.

Lem, S. (1968, English translation 1983): *His Master's Voice*.

Li, C. (ed.), (1976): *Subject and Topic*. New York: Academic Press.

Li, C. and Thompson, S. (1976): Subject and Topic: A New Typology of Language. In C. Li (ed.), *Subject and Topic*, New York: Academic Press: pp. 457–89.

Lodge, D. (1984): *Small World*. Harmondsworth: Penguin.

Lukes, S. and Galnoor, I. (1987): *No Laughing Matter: A Collection of Political Jokes*. London: Penguin.

Lyons, J. (1977): *Semantics*. 2 vols. Cambridge: Cambridge University Press.

MacKay, D. G. (1973): Spoonerisms: The Structure of Errors in the Serial Order of Speech. In V. Fromkin (ed.), *Speech Errors as Linguistic Evidence*, The Hague: Mouton: pp. 164–94.

Macken, M. (1980): The Child's Lexical Representation: The *Puzzle-Puddle-Pickle* Evidence. *Journal of Linguistics*, 16: pp. 1–17.

Magee, B. (1972): *Aspects of Wagner*. London: Panther (Granada).

Mapanje, J. (1981): *Of Chameleons and Gods*. London: Heinemann.

May, R. (1985): *Logical Form*. Cambridge, Mass.: MIT Press.

McGregor, R. S. (1972): *Outline of Hindi Grammar*. Oxford: Clarendon Press.

Miller, G. and Chomsky, N. (1963): Finitary Models of Language Users. In R. Luce, R. Bush and E. Galanter (eds), *Handbook of Mathematical Psychology*, New York: Wiley: vol. 2: pp. 419–91.

Monod, J. (1970): *Chance and Necessity*. Glasgow: Collins.

Moravcsik, J. M. (1980): Chomsky's Radical Break with Modern Traditions. *Behavioral and Brain Sciences*, 3: pp. 28–9.

Morgan, E. (1984): The Aquatic Hypothesis. *New Scientist*, 102: pp. 11–13.

Newham, R. (1971): *About Chinese*. Harmondsworth: Penguin.

Newmeyer, F. J. (1980): *Linguistic Theory in America*. New York: Academic Press.

Newport, E. L., Gleitman, H. and Gleitman, L. (1977): Mother, I'd Rather Do it Myself: Some Effects and Non-effects of Maternal Speech Style. In C. Snow and C. Ferguson (eds), *Talking to Children*, Cambridge: Cambridge University Press: pp. 109–49.

Nunberg, G. (1978): *The Pragmatics of Reference*. Indiana University Linguistics Club.

Osgood, C. E. and Tanz, C. (1977): Will The Real Direct Object in Bitransitive Sentences Please Stand Up? In A. Juilland (ed.) *Linguistic Studies Offered to Joseph Greenberg*, Saratoga, Cal.: Anma Libri: vol. 3: pp. 537–90.

Oxford English Dictionary (1971): Oxford: Oxford University Press.

Pais, A. (1982): *'Subtle is the Lord': The Science and the Life of Albert Einstein*. Oxford: Oxford University Press.

Palmer, F. R. (1984): *Grammar*. Harmondsworth: Penguin.

—— (1986): *Mood and Modality*. Cambridge: Cambridge University Press.

Partridge, E. (1955): *Shakespeare's Bawdy*. London: Routledge & Kegan Paul.

Piattelli-Palmarini, M. (ed.) (1980): *Language and Learning: The Debate between Jean Piaget and Noam Chomsky*. Cambridge, Mass.: Harvard University Press.

Pinker, S. (forthcoming) *Learnability and Cognition: The Acquisition of Argument Structure*.

Popper, K. (1963): *Conjectures and Refutations: The Growth of Scientific Knowledge*. London: Routledge & Kegan Paul.

—— (1976): *Unended Quest*. Glasgow: Fontana/Collins.

Premack, D. (1986): *Gavagai! or the Future History of the Animal Language Controversy*. Cambridge, Mass.: MIT Press.

Previté-Orton, C. W. (1960): *The Shorter Cambridge Medieval History*. 2 vols. London: Cambridge University Press.

Prince, E. (1988) Discourse Analysis: A Part of the Study of Linguistic Competence. In F. Newmeyer (ed.) *Linguistics: The Cambridge Survey*, Cambridge: Cambridge University Press: vol. 2, pp. 164–82.

Pullum, G. K. (1977): Word-Order Universals and Grammatical Relations. in P. Cole and J. Sadock (eds), *Syntax and Semantics: Grammatical Relations*, New York: Academic Press: vol. 8, pp. 249–77.

Pullum, G. K. and Gazdar, G. (1982): Natural Languages and Context-Free Languages. *Linguistics & Philosophy*, 4:, pp. 471–504.

Putnam, H. (1980): What is Innate and Why: Comments on the Debate. In M. Piattelli-Palmarini (ed.), *Language and Learning: The Debate between Jean Piaget and Noam Chomsky*, Cambridge, Mass.: Harvard

University Press: p. 287–309.

Radford, A. (1988): *Transformational Grammar: A First Course*. Cambridge: Cambridge University Press.

Redfern, W. (1984): *Puns*. Oxford: Basil Blackwell.

Reichenbach, H. (1947): *Elements of Symbolic Logic*. New York: Free Press.

Reinhart, T. (1981): Pragmatics and Linguistics: An Analysis of Sentence Topics. *Philosophica*, 27: pp. 53–94.

—— (1983): *Anaphora and Semantic Interpretation*. London: Croom Helm.

Rizzi, L. (1982): Violations of the *wh*-Island Constraint in Italian and the Subjacency Condition. In L. Rizzi, *Issues in Italian Syntax*, Dordrecht: Foris: pp. 49–76. (First published (1980) in *Journal of Italian Linguistics* 5: pp. 157–95.)

Roeper, T. and Williams, E. (eds) (1987): *Parameter Setting*. Dordrecht: Reidel.

Rohrer, C. (ed.) (1980): *Time, Tense and Quantifiers*. Tübingen: Max Niemeyer Verlag.

Rosten, L. (1971): *The Joys of Yiddish*. Harmondsworth: Penguin.

Rouveret, A. and Vergnaud, J. -R. (1980): Specifying Reference to the Subject: French Causatives and Conditions on Representations. *Linguistic Inquiry*, 11: pp. 97–202.

Ruhlen, M. (1976): *A Guide to the Languages of the World*. Stanford: Stanford University.

Russell, B. (1905): On Denoting. *Mind*, 14: 479–93.

Sapir, E. (1921): *Language*. New York: Harcourt, Brace & World.

Schieffelin, B. (1979): Getting it Together: An Ethnographic Approach to the Study of the Development of Communicative Competence. In E. Ochs and B. Schieffelin (eds), *Developmental Pragmatics*, New York, N.Y.: Academic Press: pp. 73–108.

Searle, J. (1969): *Speech Acts*. Cambridge: Cambridge University Press.

Sebastian, E. (1983): *Constraints in Hiligaynon Syntax*. Unpublished University of London M.A. Dissertation.

Shaw, G. B. (1941): Preface to R. A. Wilson's *The Miraculous Birth of Language*. London: British Publishers' Guild.

—— (1962): *Androcles and the Lion*. Harmondsworth: Penguin.

Silvertsein, M. (1976): Hierarchy of Features and Ergativity. In R. M. W. Dixon (ed.) *Grammatical Categories in Australian Languages*, New Jersey: Humanities Press: pp. 112–71.

Slobin, D. (1978): Universal and Particular in the Acquisition of Language. Paper presented for the workshop on language acquisition: state of the art. University of Pennsylvania, May 1978.

Smith, A. (1988): Language Acquisition: Learnability, Maturation, and the Fixing of Parameters. *Cognitive Neuropsychology*, 5: pp. 235–65.

Smith, C. S. (1978): The Syntax and Interpretation of Temporal

Expressions in English. *Linguistics & Philosophy* 2: pp. 43–99.

Smith, N. V. (1967a): *An Outline Grammar of Nupe*. London: SOAS.

—— (1967b): The Phonology of Nupe. *Journal of African Languages*, 6: pp. 153–69.

—— (1968): Tone in Ewe. *Massachusetts Institute of Technology Research Laboratory of Electronics, Quarterly Progress Report*, 88: pp. 290–304. Reprinted in E. Fudge (ed.) (1973), *Readings in Phonology*, Harmondsworth: Penguin: pp. 354–69.

—— (1971): Puggles and Lellow Lollies. *The Listener*, 2227: pp. 759–60.

—— (1973): *The Acquisition of Phonology*. London: Cambridge University Press.

—— (1975): Universal Tendencies in the Child's Acquisition of Phonology. In N. O'Connor (ed.), *Language, cognitive deficits and retardation*, IRMMH Study Group 7. Butterworth: pp. 47–65.

—— (1978): Lexical Representation and the Acquisition of Phonology. In B. Kachru (ed.), *Linguistics in the Seventies: Directions and Prospects*, Special Issue, *Studies in the Linguistic Sciences*, 8: pp. 259–73.

—— (1980): Review of W. Lehmann (ed.), *Syntactic Typology*. *Journal of Linguistics*, 16: pp. 150–64.

—— (1981a): Consistency, Markedness and Language Change: On the Notion 'Consistent Language'. *Journal of Linguistics*, 17: pp. 39–54.

—— (1981b): Grammaticality, Time and Tense. *Philosophical Transactions of the Royal Society, London*, B 295: pp. 253–65.

—— (ed.) (1982a): *Mutual Knowledge*. London: Academic Press.

—— (1982b): Review of B. Comrie's *Language Universals and Linguistic Typology*. *Australian Journal of Linguistics*, 2: pp. 255–61.

—— (1983a): *Speculative Linguistics*. An inaugural lecture delivered at University College London. Published by the College.

—— (1983b): On interpreting conditionals. *Australian Journal of Linguistics*, 3: pp. 1–23.

—— (1983c): A Rejoinder to Comrie. *Australian Journal of Linguistics*,. 3: pp. 97–8.

—— (1983d): Review of J. V. Irwin and S. P. Wong (eds), *Phonological Development in Children: 18 to 72 Months*. *Linguistics*, 21: pp. 751–2.

—— (1987a): Universals and Typology. In S. Modgil and C. Modgil (eds), *Noam Chomsky: Consensus and Controversy*, Sussex: The Falmer Press: pp. 57–66.

—— (1987b): Reply to Kilby. In S. Modgil and C. Modgil (eds), *Noam Chomsky: Consensus and Controversy*, Sussex: The Falmer Press: pp. 77–8.

—— (1988): Principles, Parameters and Pragmatics. *Journal of Linguistics* 24: pp. 189–201.

Smith, N. V. and Smith, A. (1988): A Relevance-Theoretic Account of Conditionals. In L. Hyman and C. Li (eds), *Language, Speech and Mind:*

Studies in Honour of Victoria A. Fromkin, London: Routledge & Kegan Paul: pp. 322–52.

Smith, N. V. and Wilson, D. (1979): *Modern Linguistics: The Results of Chomsky's Revolution*. Harmondsworth: Penguin.

Snow, C. and Ferguson, C. (eds) (1977): *Talking to Children*. Cambridge: Cambridge University Press.

Spencer, A. (1986): Towards a Theory of Phonological Development. *Lingua*, 68: pp. 3–38.

Sperber, D. (1985): Apparently Irrational Beliefs. In D. Sperber, *On Anthropological Knowledge*, Cambridge: Cambridge University Press: pp. 35–63.

Sperber, D. and Wilson, D. (1986a): *Relevance: Communication and Cognition*. Oxford: Basil Blackwell.

—— (1986b): Loose Talk. *Proceedings of the Aristotelian Society*, new series, vol. 86: pp. 153–71.

—— (1987): Précis of *Relevance: Communication and Cognition*. *Behavioral and Brain Sciences*, 10: pp. 697–754.

Sridhar, S. N. (1988): *Cognition and Sentence Production*. New York: Springer Verlag.

—— (Forthcoming) *Kannada*.

Sridhar, S. N. and Sridhar, K. (1980): The Syntax and Psycholinguistics of Bilingual Code-Mixing. *Canadian Journal of Psychology*, 34: pp. 407–16.

Sutton, C. (1988): The Secret Life of the Neutrino. *New Scientist*, 117: pp. 53–7.

Taglicht, J. (1984): *Message and Emphasis: On Focus and Scope in English*. London: Longman.

Thompson, D'A. W. (1942): *On Growth and Form*. 2 vols. Cambridge: Cambridge University Press.

Trudgill, P. (1986): *Dialects in Contact*. Oxford: Basil Blackwell.

Vance, J. (1974): *The Languages of Pao*. St Albans: Mayflower.

Vattuone, B. (1975): Notes on Genoese Syntax: Kernel VOS Strings and Theme-Rheme Structures. *Studi Italiani di Linguistica Teorica ed Applicata*, 4: pp. 335–78.

Verheijen, R. (1986): A PS Syntax for Emphatic Self Forms. *Linguistics*, 24: pp. 681–95.

Watson, I. (1975): *The Embedding*. London: Quartet Books.

Waugh, A. (1988): From Oxymoron to Boiled Egg, Review of N. Chomsky's *The Culture of Terrorism*. *The Independent*: London: 26 March 1988.

Wells, G. (1981): *Learning through Interaction: The Study of Language Development*. Cambridge: Cambridge University Press.

Wells, J. C. (1982): *Accents of English*. 3 vols. Cambridge: Cambridge

University Press.

Whorf, B. L. (1950) *Four Articles on Metalinguistics*. Washington.

Wilson, D. and Sperber, D. (1981): On Grice's Theory of Conversation. In P. Werth (ed.), *Conversation and Discourse*, London: Croom Helm: pp. 155–71.

Winograd, T. (1983): *Language as a Cognitive Process. Vol. I: Syntax*. Reading, Mass.: Addison-Wesley.

Wood, B. (1987) Who is the 'Real' *Homo habilis? Nature*, 327: pp. 187–8.

Wright, G. H. von (1951): *An Essay in Modal Logic*. Amsterdam: North Holland.

Yamada, J. (1988): The Independence of Language: Evidence from a Retarded Hyperlinguistic Individual. In L. Hyman and C. Li (eds), *Language, Speech and Mind: Studies in Honour of Victoria A. Fromkin*, London: Routledge & Kegan Paul: pp. 175–206.

Index

This index gives exhaustive references to all the subjects dealt with except those like 'English', which occur on virtually every page, and those like 'sentences', for which I have referred only to the definitional discussion in the Appendix. Items prefaced with an asterisk are defined in the Glossary.